IMAGES
of America

CLERMONT FAYETTE COUNTY IOWA

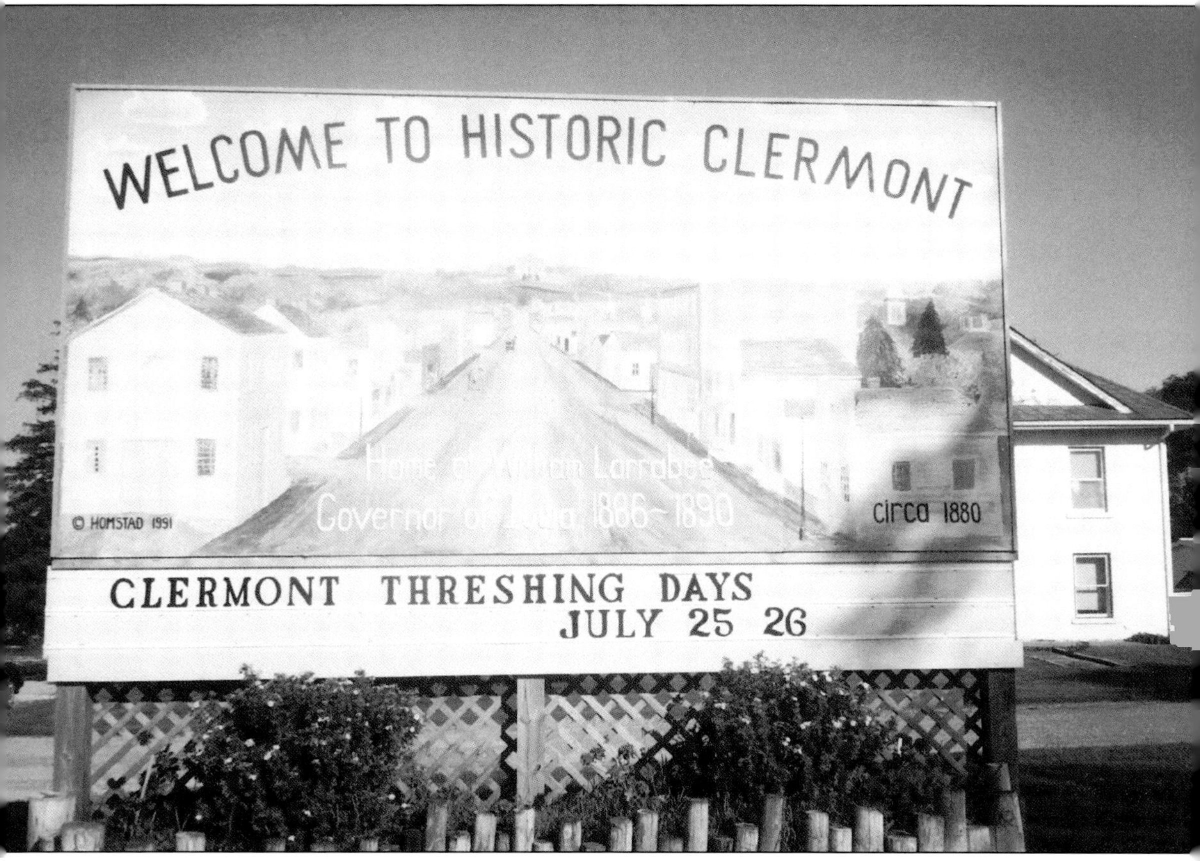
WELCOME TO HISTORIC CLERMONT
© HOMSTAD 1991
circa 1880
CLERMONT THRESHING DAYS
JULY 25 26

IMAGES
of America

CLERMONT FAYETTE COUNTY IOWA

Jane Jurgens

ARCADIA
PUBLISHING

Copyright © 1999 by Jane Jurgens
ISBN 978-0-7385-0148-2

Published by Arcadia Publishing
Charleston, South Carolina

Printed in the United States of America

Library of Congress Control Number: Applied for.

For all general information, please contact Arcadia Publishing:
Telephone 843-853-2070
Fax 843-853-0044
E-mail sales@arcadiapublishing.com
For customer service and orders:
Toll-Free 1-888-313-2665

Visit us on the Internet at www.arcadiapublishing.com

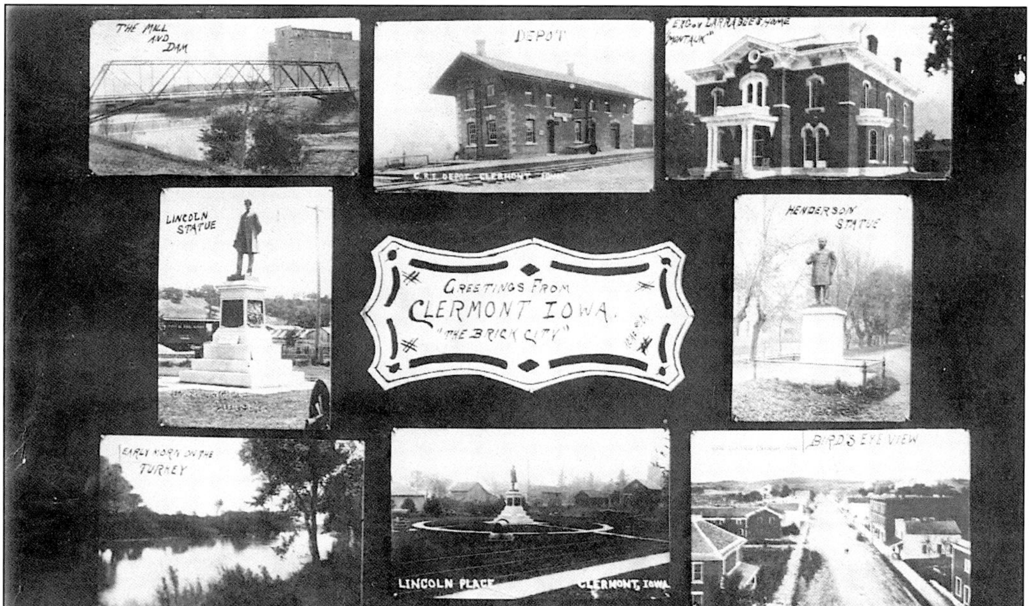

GREETINGS FROM CLERMONT, IOWA, "THE BRICK CITY."

Contents

ACKNOWLEDGMENTS

The photographs reproduced for this volume have been selected from my own and other private collections as well as from the collections of the State Historical Society of Iowa. I gratefully acknowledge the State Historical Society for permission to publish photographs from the collections in Iowa City and at the Montauk Historic Site. I want to especially thank the staff at Montauk Historic Site and the Clermont Historical Society for their assistance and support of the project. Finally, I wish to thank the people of Clermont who are always "on hand" with a story or a photograph. Special thanks to Nadine West, Vernon Oakland, Arlene Davisson, Linda Solheim, MaryAnn Gibson, Marti and Carol Swenson, and Jim Anderson, Ardis and Jack Dibble of Postville, with a special acknowledgment to the late Frances Cline and to my mother Anna Bigler Jurgens for their treasured memories and recollections. I also wish to thank the folks at the Brick City Mercantile for sending me the reproductions of many of these photographs. The following printed materials were of assistance in completing the introductory material for the chapters and for preparing some of the captions for the photographs: *Historic Clermont* (Clermont, 1967), *Historical and Architectural Survey of Selected Properties in Clermont, Iowa* (Cottage Grove, MN), *The History of Fayette County, Iowa* (Chicago, 1878), *Past and Present of Fayette County, Iowa* (Indianapolis, 1910), as well as the oral and written accounts left by the late Frances Cline. Reconstructing the history of a place is not an easy task. Although much of the history of Clermont has already been lost, must of its past is yet to be uncovered. Some of its stories will never be told while others still wait to be documented. Clermont is fortunate to have so many people taking such a great interest in the preservation of its history. I continue to participate in this task. Clermont remains vital and growing while retaining the charm of an earlier time. Many people have loved and continue to love this town and the beauty of the surrounding area. Those who have moved away return for frequent visits. Tourists and visitors who come to Clermont to tour the many historic sites often comment that "This is a pretty town."

As I complete this volume, my mother Anna Bigler Jurgens, former resident of Clermont, has recently passed her 90th birthday. The book is respectfully dedicated to her.

Introduction

I went on to Clermont P.M. about four miles. It is on this side of the Turkey River. A number of buildings. A sawmill, a carding mill and one or two stores. The Turkey is a very pretty stream about three rods wide. There is a bridge across it here and a dam, a good mill privilege. They tell me the river abounds in good mill privileges. They expect to have a flouring mill here in another season. Cold, cold, cold.

—Diaries of William Larrabee Sr., November 5, 1853

Clermont is located on the east and west banks of the Turkey River, in the county of Fayette, in the northeast corner of the state of Iowa. Proceeding down Highway 18, you come to Clermont, located in a beautiful, almost idyllic valley, surrounded by the green and gold (or white depending on the season!) of rich agricultural farmland. The towns that surround Clermont include Elgin, West Union (county seat), Wadena, Postville, and Fayette. Fayette County was one of the last counties in Iowa to be settled, as it was less accessible than other parts of the state. Clermont was one of many towns along the Turkey River that was dependent upon the river as a cheap means of transportation and as an almost inexhaustible source of hydropower. Clermont's history comprised agriculture, flour milling, lumberyards, sawmills, brickmaking, and small shopkeepers.

The earliest pioneer settlers to the area were an Andrew Moats and a man called Delaplaine, who built a cabin near the river in 1848. The town was platted by John Thompson in 1851 and recorded in 1855. The name of Norway was considered for a time, but the name of "Clermont" was finally decided upon. The Clermont of the very early 1850s consisted of only five log buildings facing the river on what was then Water Street, as well as a sawmill and a half-finished hotel. At this time, the first bridge had not been built across the Turkey. Nearly all the land surrounding the town was heavily timbered, especially on the south side of the river, and there was plenty of lumber to construct cabins and other structures. The building of the brick mill and cooper mill were major events in Clermont and increased the importance of the town as a trading center. The Irish, Germans, and Norwegians also began arriving in the valley in the mid-1850s. Attracted by the inexpensive and fertile land that was available, together with the new possibilities of what living in a river town could offer, they settled mostly in the environs of Clermont in separate districts or "neighborhoods."

The railroad came to Clermont in 1871, and with it came new industry and opportunities for expansion as the railway opened up new markets. A great variety of small businesses were thriving as Clermont continued to grow and prosper. During the railroad era, William Larrabee was instrumental in the growth of the town with his diverse business interests and political connections. By 1895, the *Clermont Herald* cited Clermont as "The Oldest and Most Substantial Town in Fayette County . . . No town of equal population can boast of being in better financial condition than Clermont." Clermont was indeed off to a good start.

There are countless stories, memories, and recollections that make up the history of Clermont and preserve its heart. Many generations have lived and worked in this town that has a unique history all its own. Many descendants of the pioneer and immigrant families still live in the environs of Clermont, and the town remains vital as new people and families move in. We hope to pass something on to future generations.

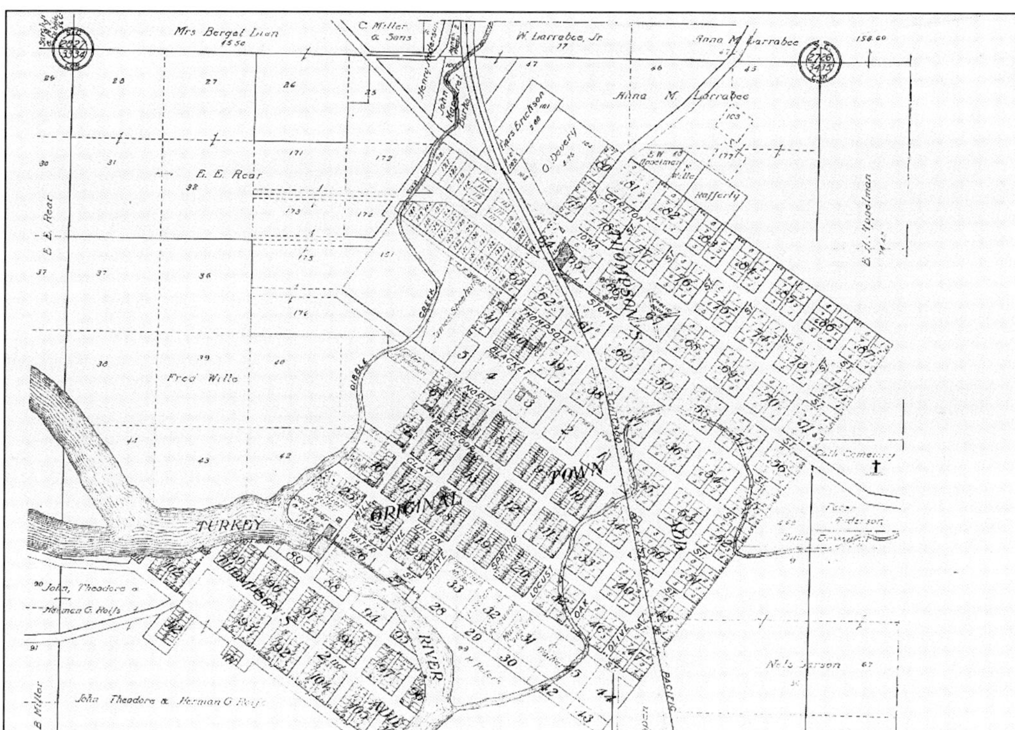

Early Plat Map of Clermont. The map as originally platted by Carlton & Thompson in 1851 clearly shows the adaptation of the traditional gridiron pattern of rectilinear streets and small lots to accommodate the Turkey River. The map shows the original Thompson addition to the town.

One

Clermont "Askew"

Something is wrong with the town of Clermont. The sun does not rise or set quite right on this lovely little Iowa town, and it can be quite disconcerting if you are new to the area. Imagine a town laid out in a rectangle with two opposite ends pulled tight and you will know what Clermont is all about. We can only guess at the lasting effect that this unique configuration may have had on the local population over the years. Everyone who lives (and most likely who has ever lived) in Clermont is aware of the "problem," and it has always been a source of amusement. You do not look north or south, you look northeast and southwest. You can imagine the confusion when properties are described. Homeowners cannot point to the north corner or the south corner but always to the northeast corner or the southwest side. Does this fact make Clermont special among the towns of Iowa? Does it make the people special? Maybe, but I think it is only generations of living, experiencing, and passing down that really make the town and its people special.

As you descend into Clermont proceeding northeast down Highway 18, several major landmarks of the town are clearly visible even at a distance. They greet the visitor now as they greeted many who came to Clermont in the past. They include the Larrabee mansion at the most distant northeast corner on the hill, the dome (once a spire) of the Catholic church, the Union Sunday School, and the Episcopal Church of the Saviour. The following photographs introduce you to Clermont. They provide early (and some more recent) views and glimpses of Highway 18, Main (now Mill) Street, and the bridges. Once you are firmly planted (and even buy a house) in Clermont, the town won't really seem "angled" at all.

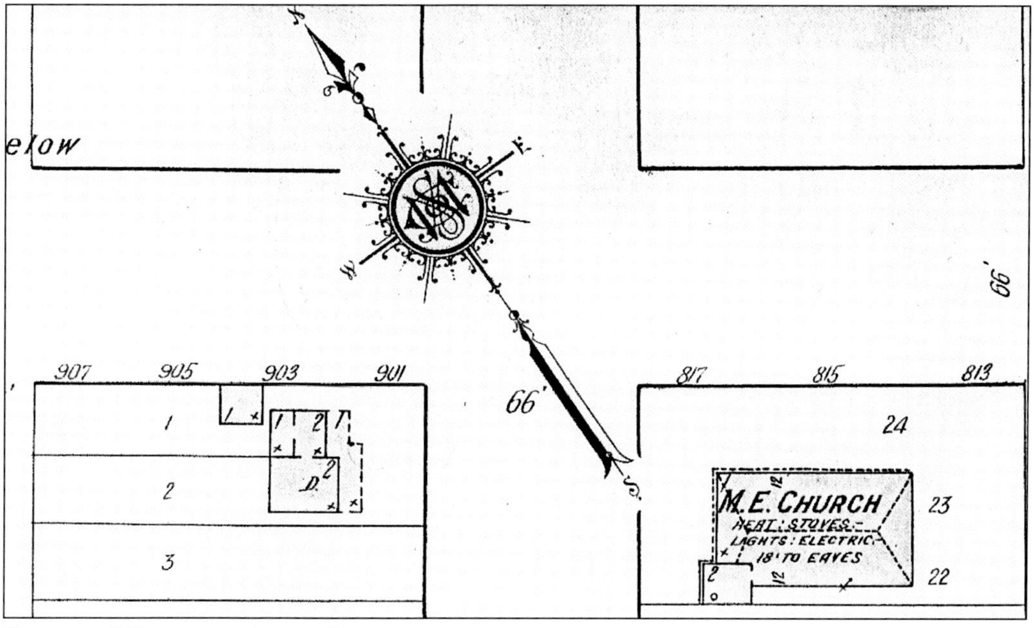

Compass "Clermont Askew."

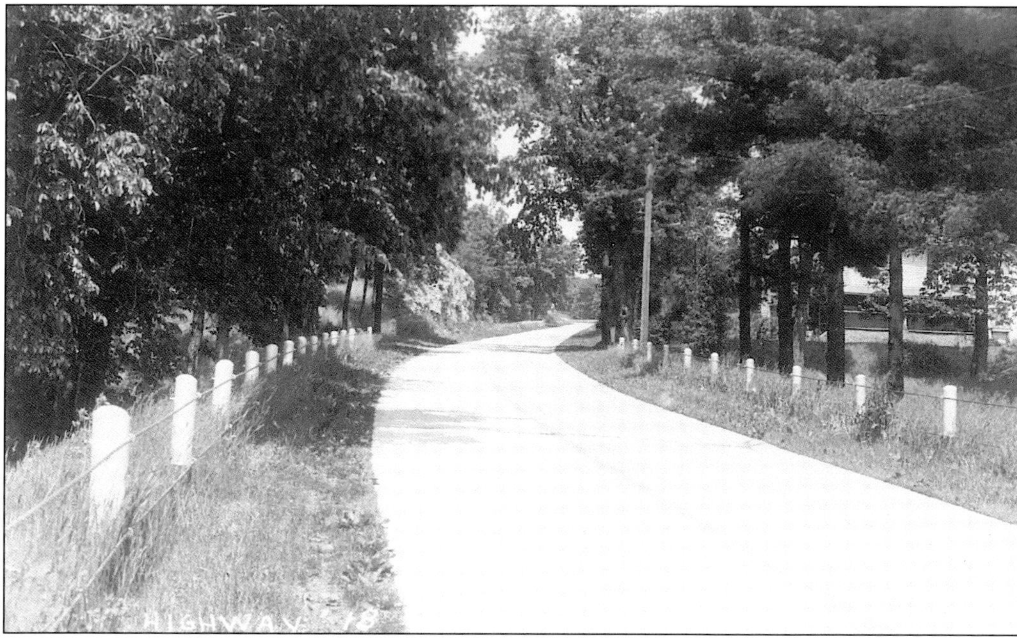

EARLY VIEW OF HIGHWAY 18.

CURRENT VIEW DOWN HIGHWAY 18 TO CLERMONT.

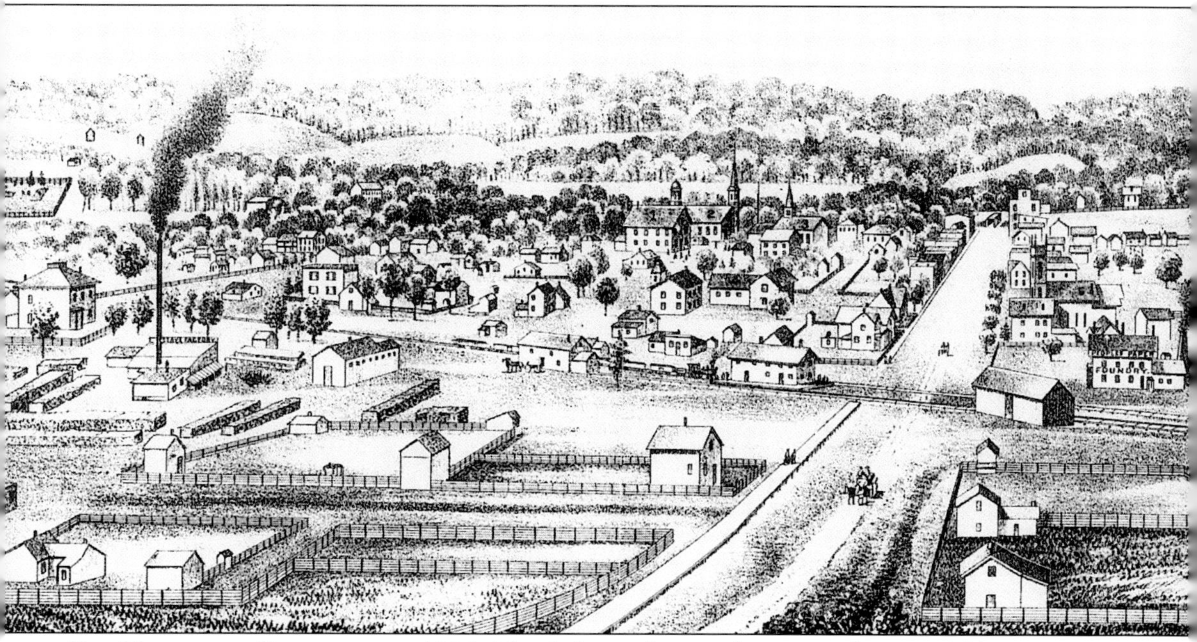

THE VILLAGE OF CLERMONT, C. 1875. This lithograph provides a rare glimpse of Clermont in 1875. Shown is the Old Public School (1), the Methodist church (2), the Presbyterian church (3), the Catholic church (4), and the Episcopal church (5).

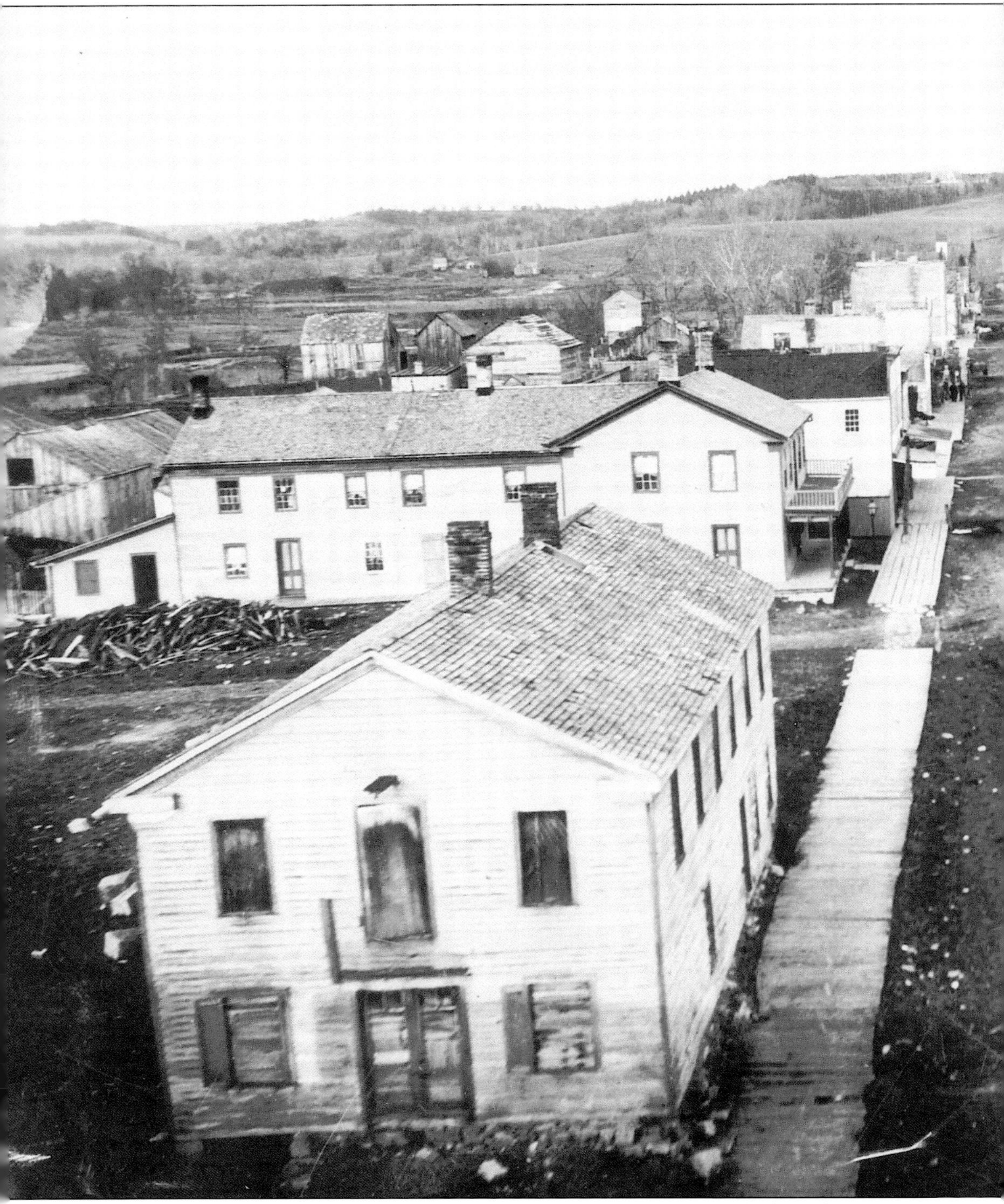

Clermont Business District, c. 1895. Roy McQueen, who worked at the newspaper in Clermont, took this remarkable photograph of Mill Street (main street). The view faces northeast towards Montauk. The steeples (left to right) of the Catholic church, the Union Sunday School, the old Public School, the Lutheran church, and the Commercial Hotel are

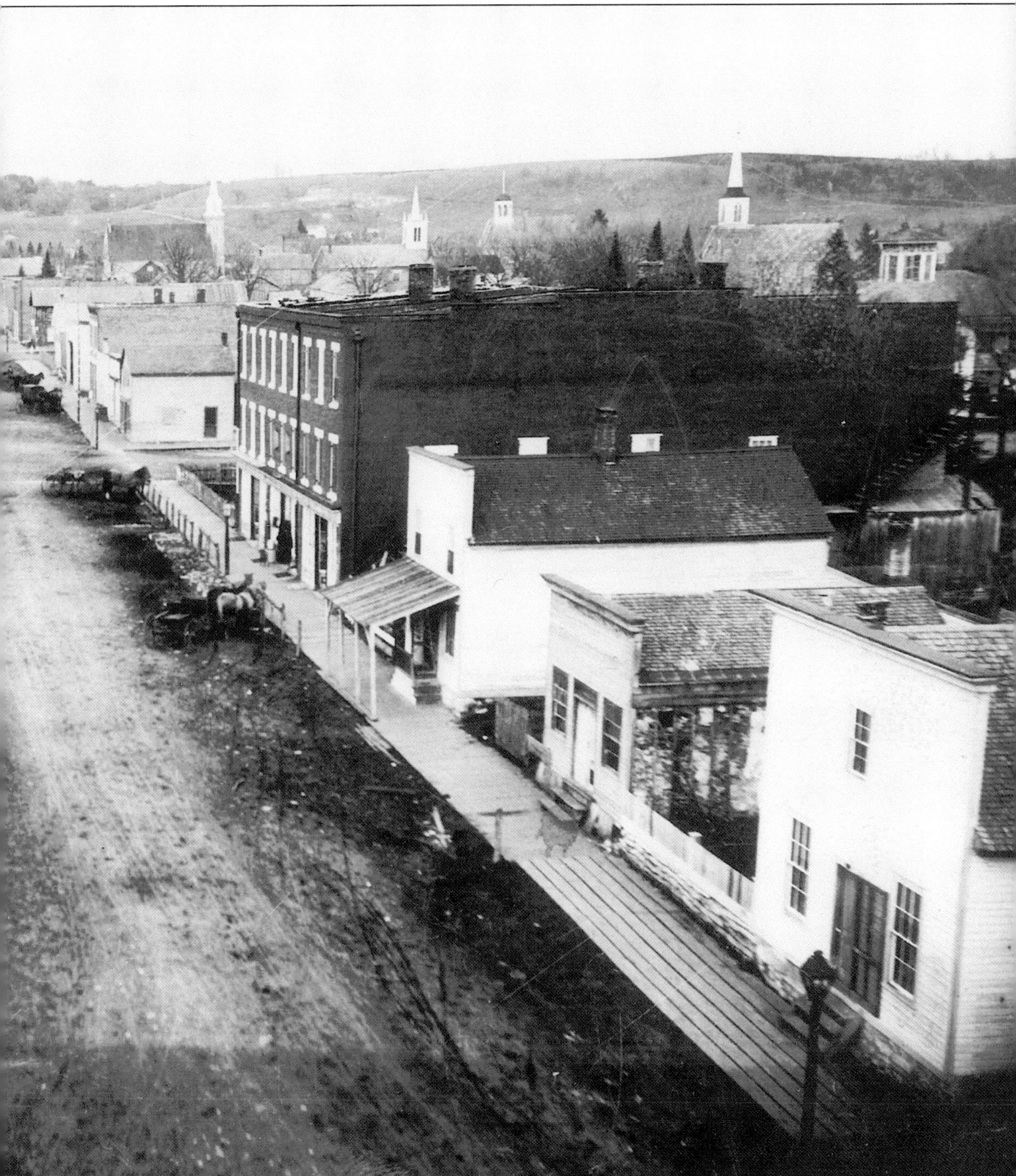

clearly seen. According to the late Frances Cline, one of the town historians, General Ulysses S. Grant stayed one night at the old Clermont Hotel or the "Browns Hotel" (second structure with balcony on left side of the street). Mr. McQueen no doubt took this photograph somewhere on top of the Mill.

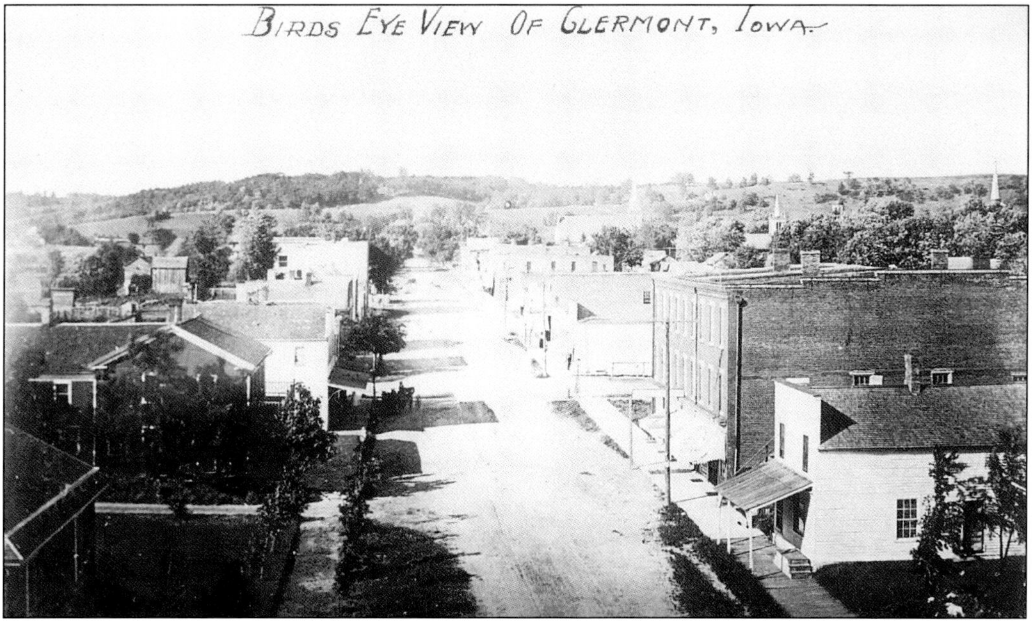

BIRD'S-EYE VIEW OF CLERMONT, C. 1880. Note the "awnings" on the buildings to the left that are not present on the photograph below, as well as the board sidewalks. This is probably an earlier view of the town.

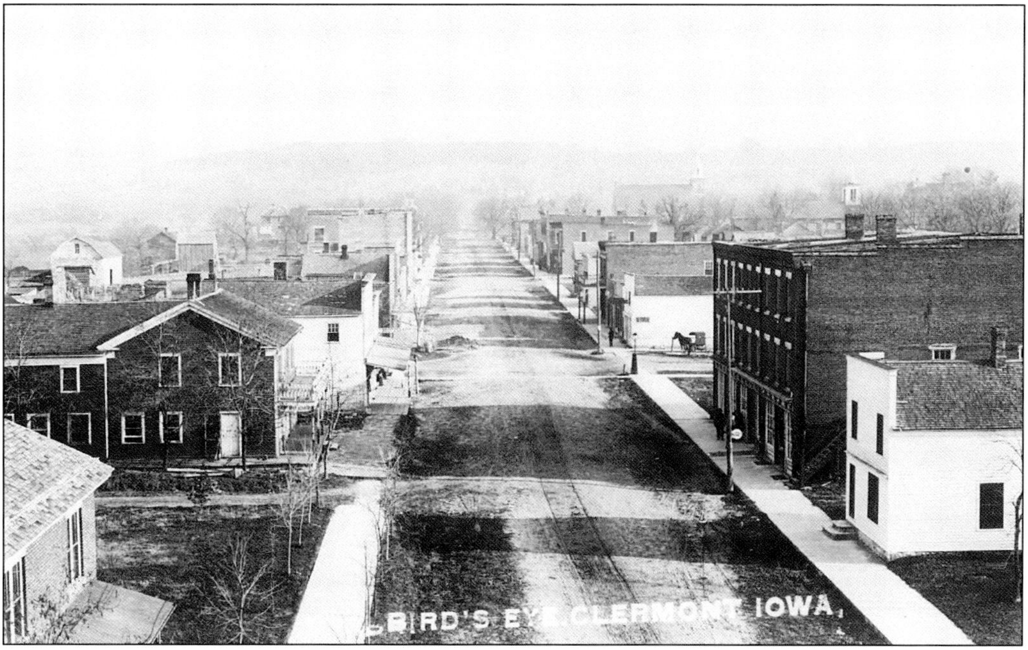

BIRD'S-EYE VIEW OF CLERMONT.

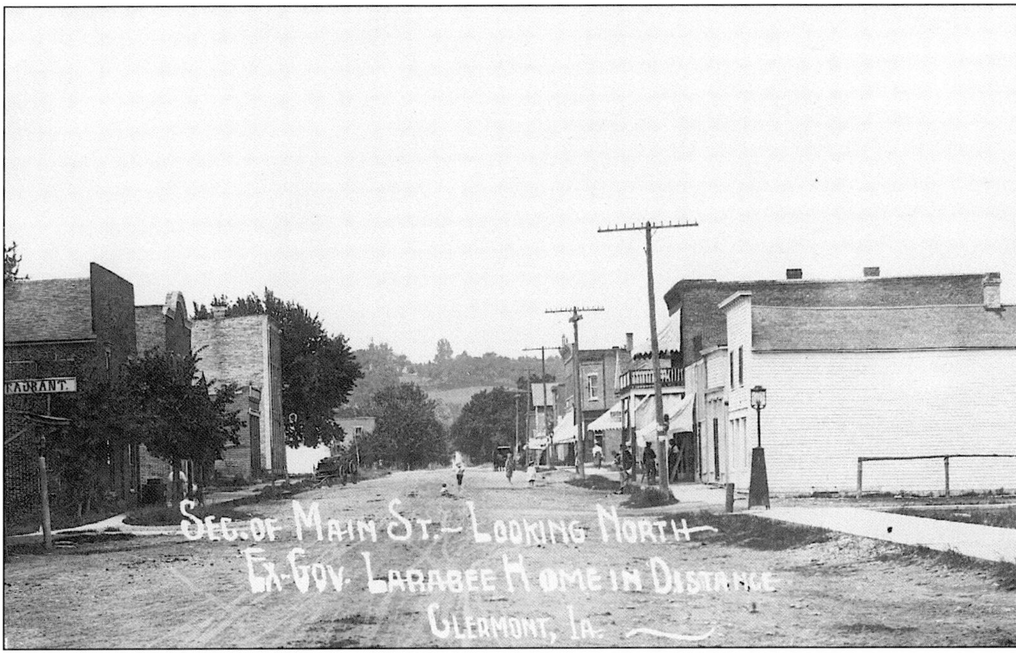

MAIN STREET IN CLERMONT, C. 1900?

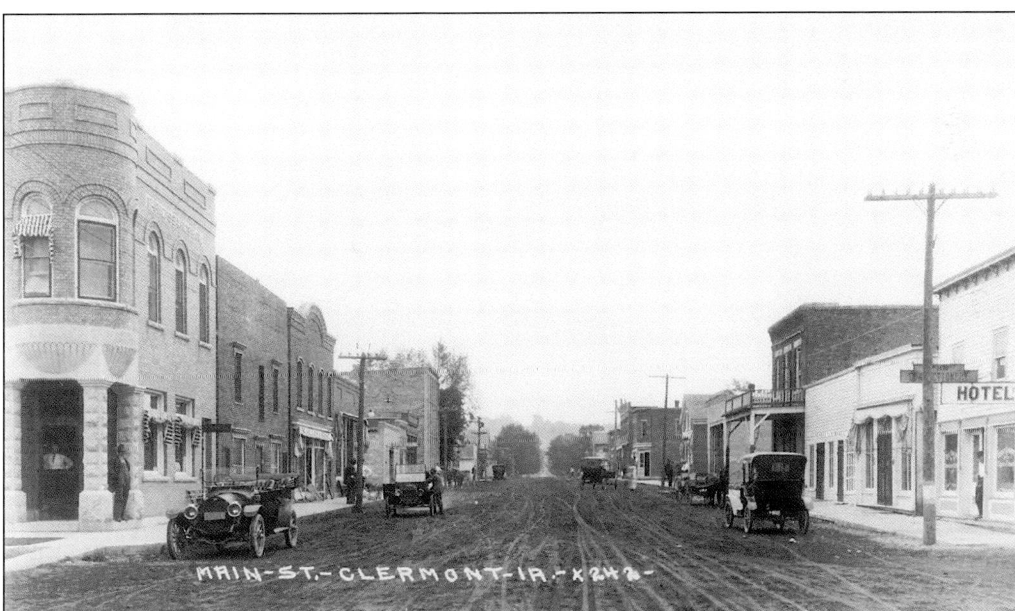

MAIN STREET IN CLERMONT, C. 1915. Note the Farmer's Savings Bank, left foreground.

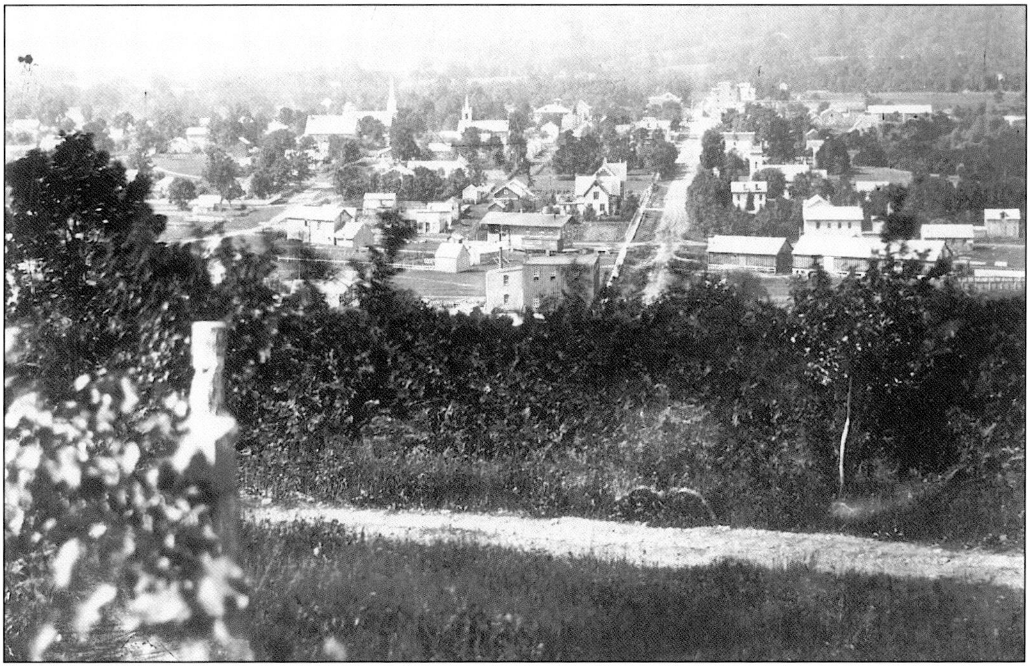

EARLY VIEW OF CLERMONT FROM MONTAUK, C.1890S. The white spire of the Catholic church can be seen as well as the Union Sunday School, which can barely be seen in the distance.

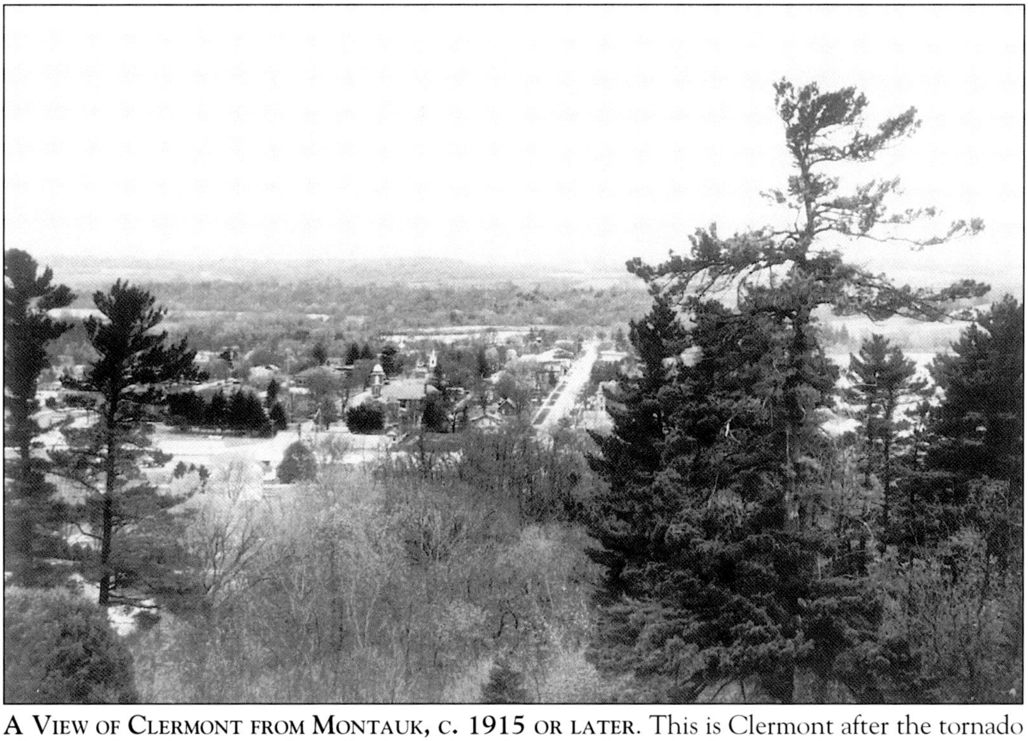

A VIEW OF CLERMONT FROM MONTAUK, C. 1915 OR LATER. This is Clermont after the tornado of 1913. The white spire of the Catholic church was replaced by the white dome.

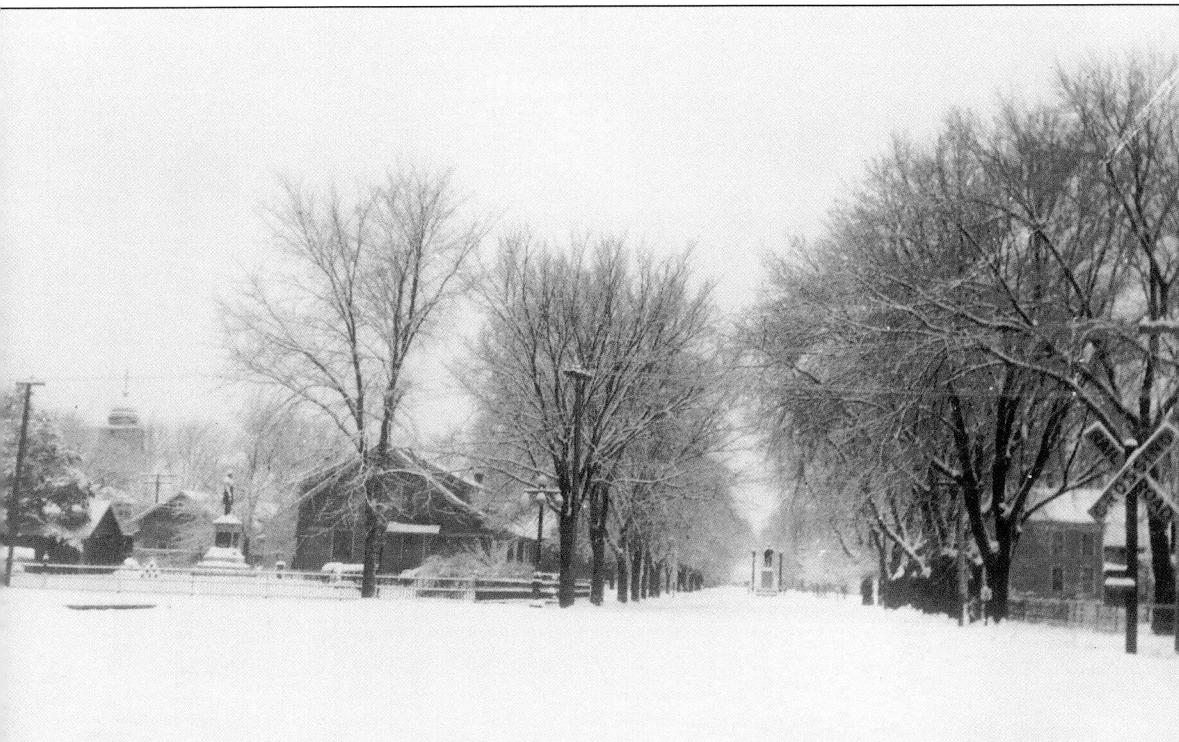

CLERMONT, C. 1912. This view of the town is looking west along Main Street. In this remarkable photograph, you can clearly see Lincoln Park with the statue of Lincoln and the cannon and cannon balls, as well as the statue of David Henderson standing in the center of the street.

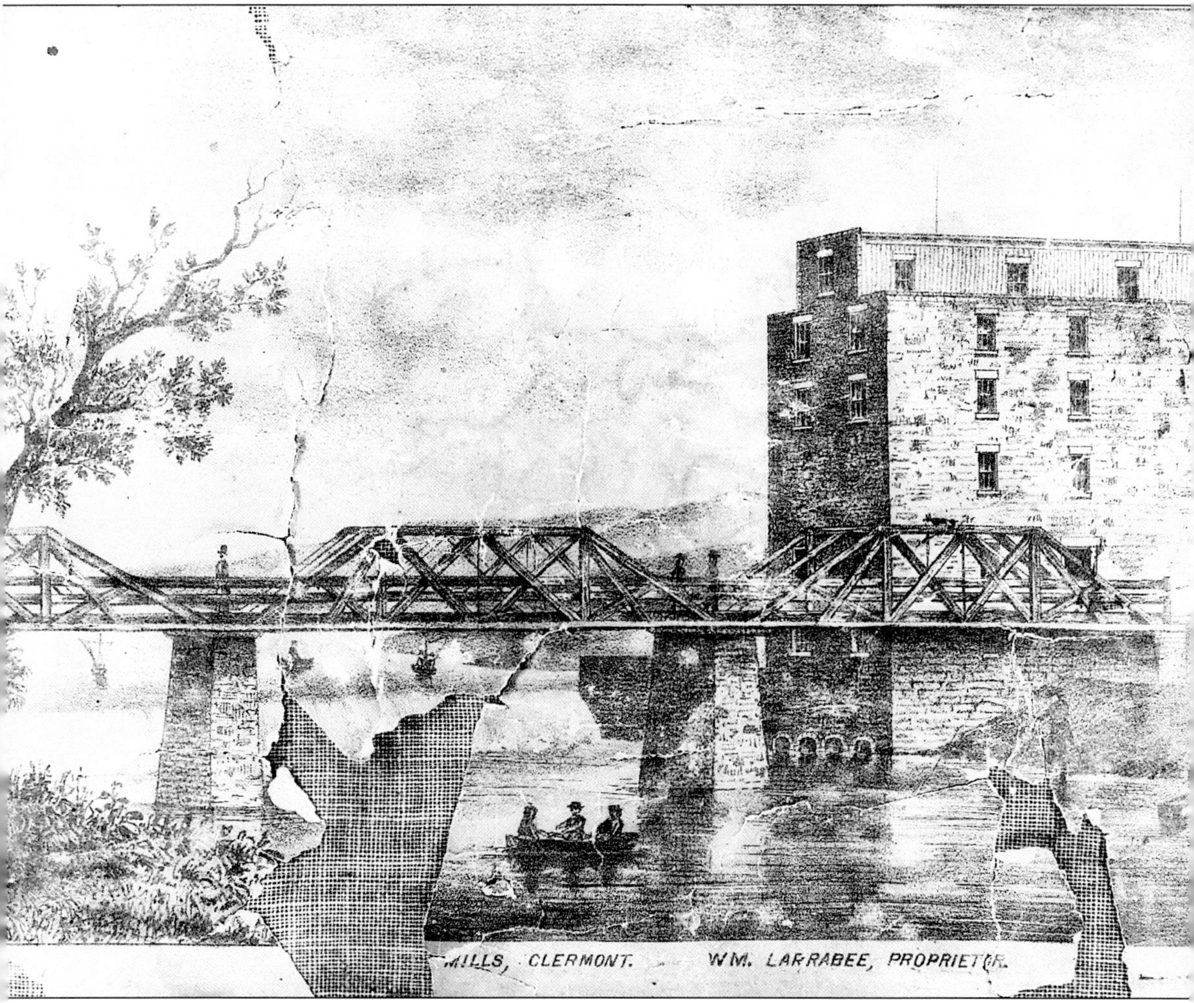

OCTOBER 1861. This is probably the first bridge constructed across the Turkey River directly leading into the town. The sketch also provides an early view of the Brick City Mills. At this time, William Larrabee is identified as the current operator of the mill.

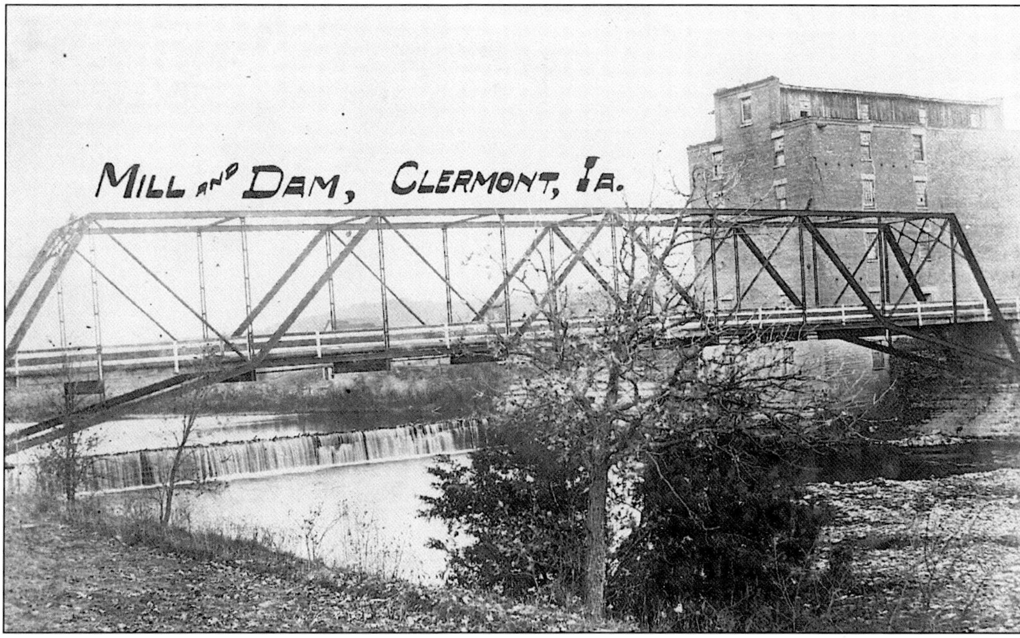

VIEW OF THE SECOND BRIDGE, C. 1908. This bridge leads directly into Clermont. The exact date of construction of this steel truss bridge is unknown, but it may have been built around 1895.

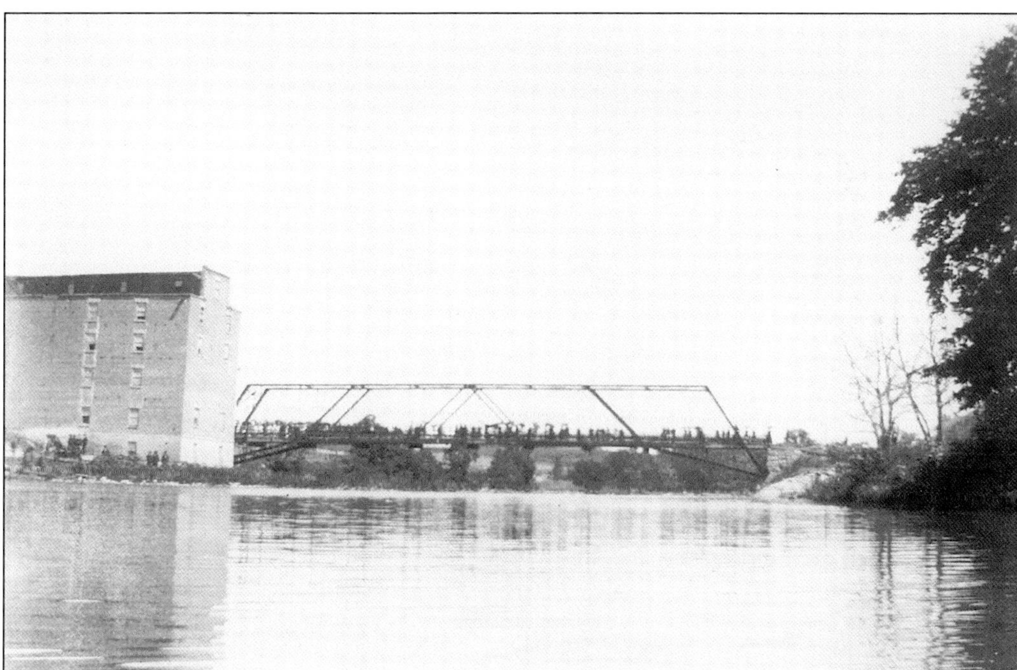

STEEL TRUSS BRIDGE. Here is a view of the mill on the left.

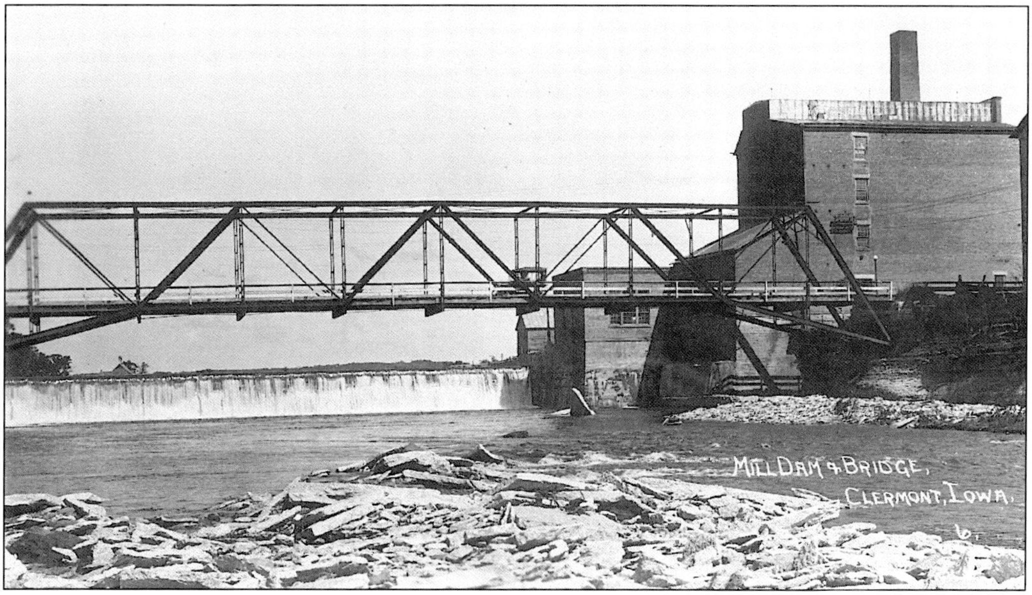

STEEL TRUSS BRIDGE. This 1918 or 1924 view has the the addition of the Power Plant.

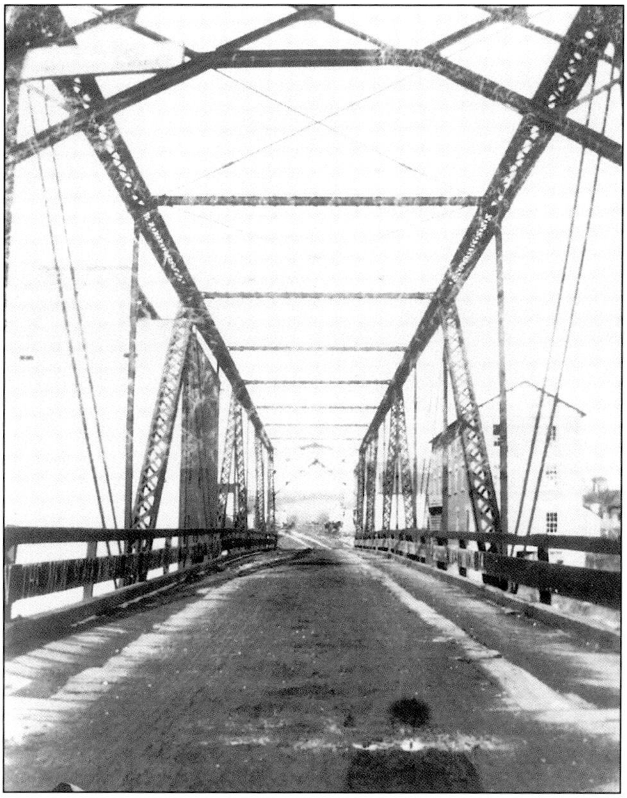

STEEL TRUSS BRIDGE, DETAIL. This is an early view of the bridge facing southwest. The mill is on the right.

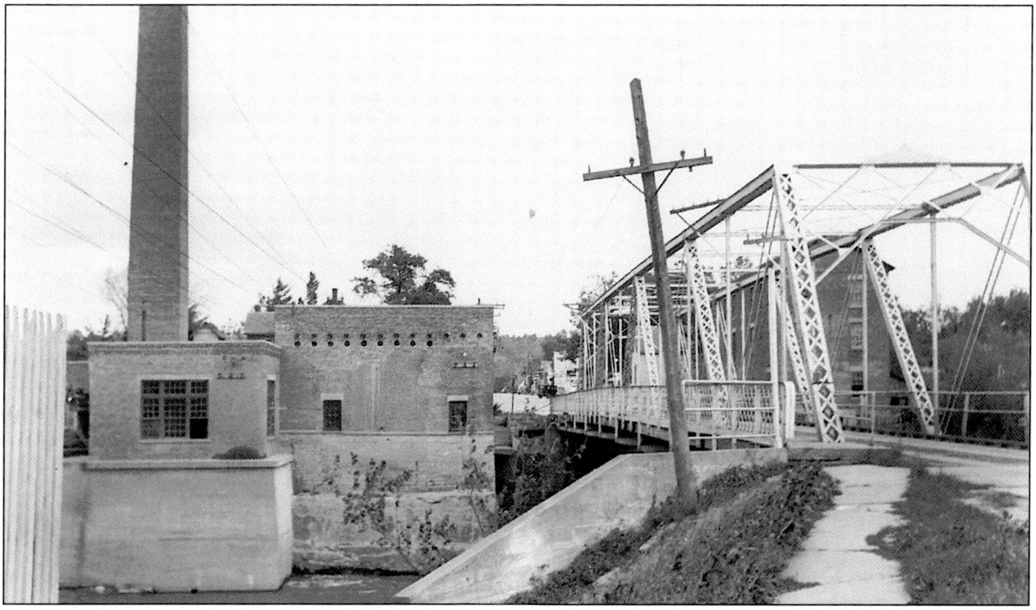

VIEW OF BRIDGE WITH POWER PLANT, C. 1924.

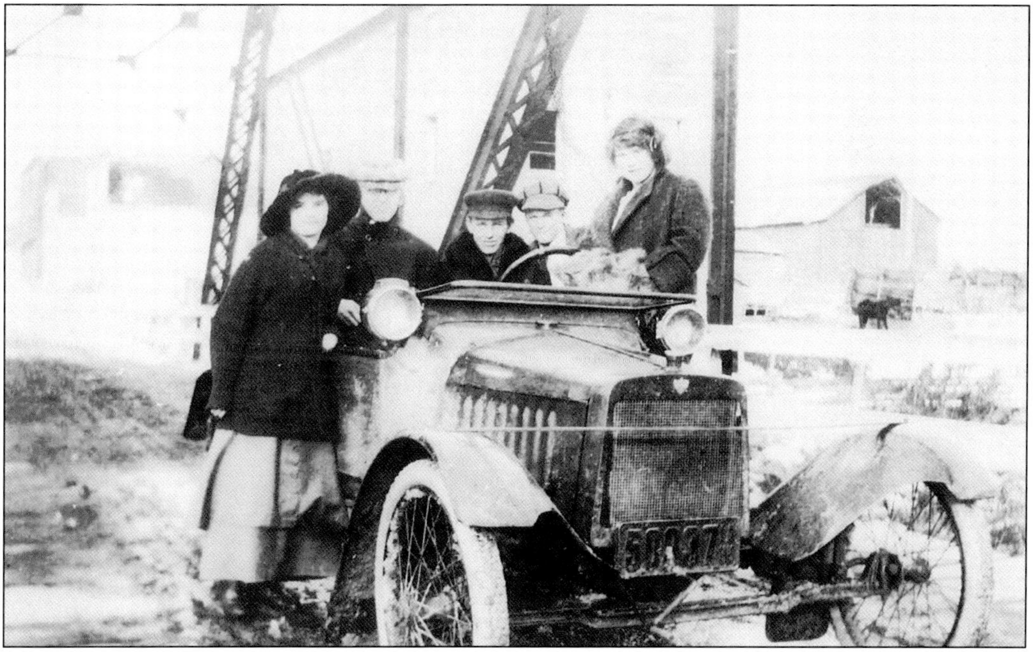

CLERMONT RESIDENTS ON THE STEEL TRUSS BRIDGE, C. 1915.

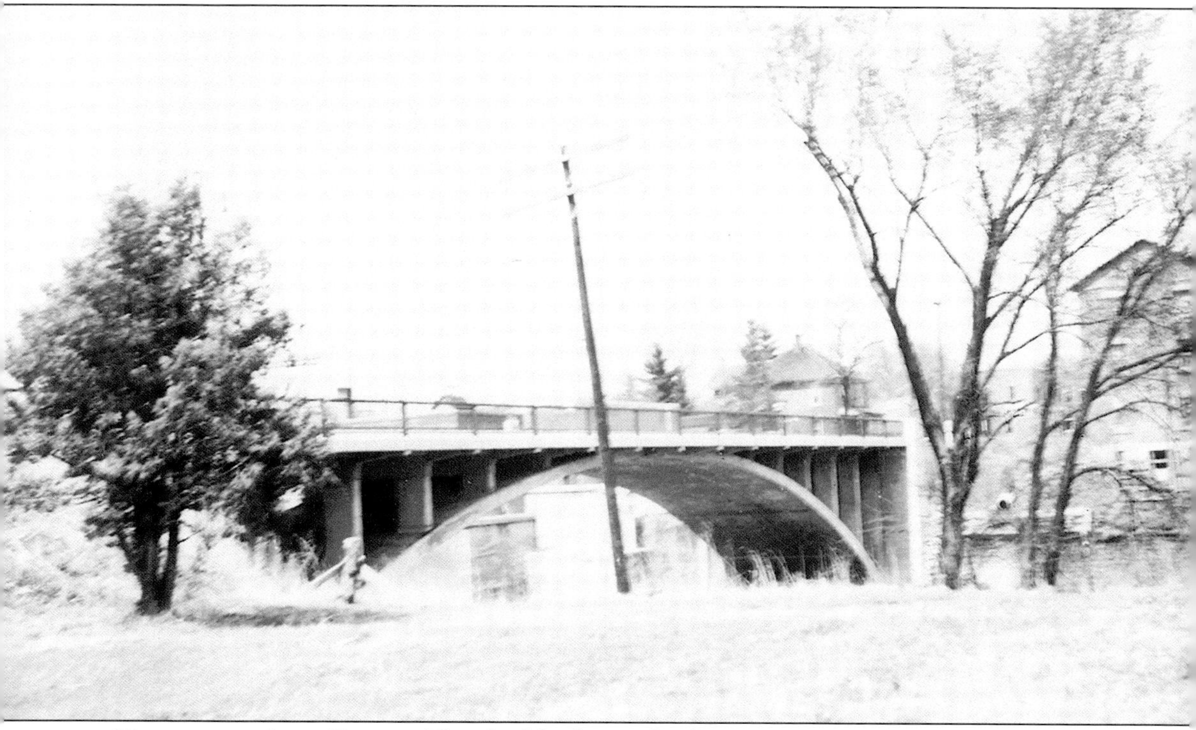

VIEW OF THE ARCH BRIDGE. The third bridge at this location was a concrete arch bridge built in 1942 with a span of 192 feet.

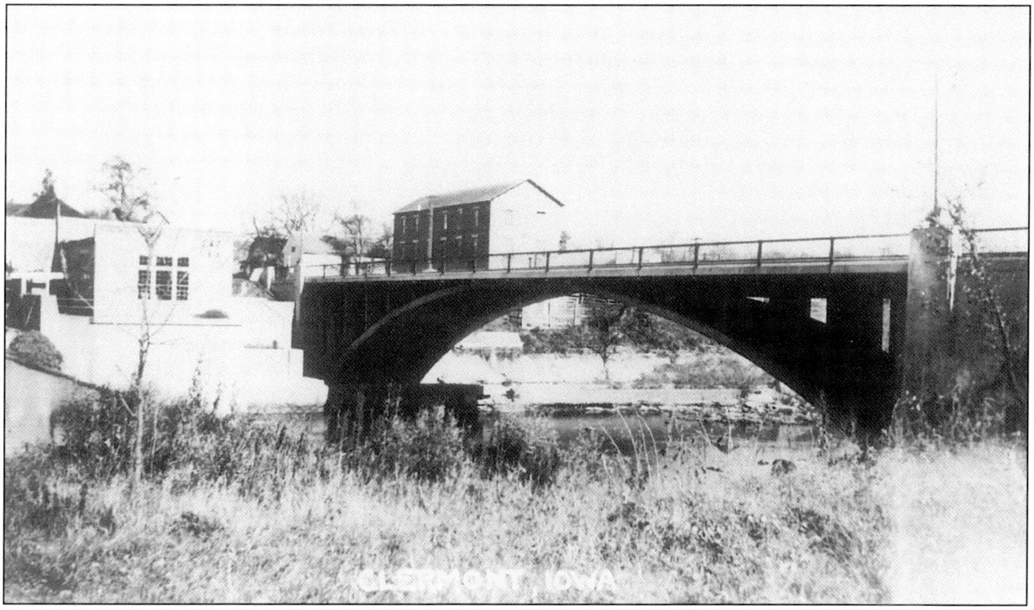

VIEW OF THE ARCH BRIDGE. The Power Plant is located on the left.

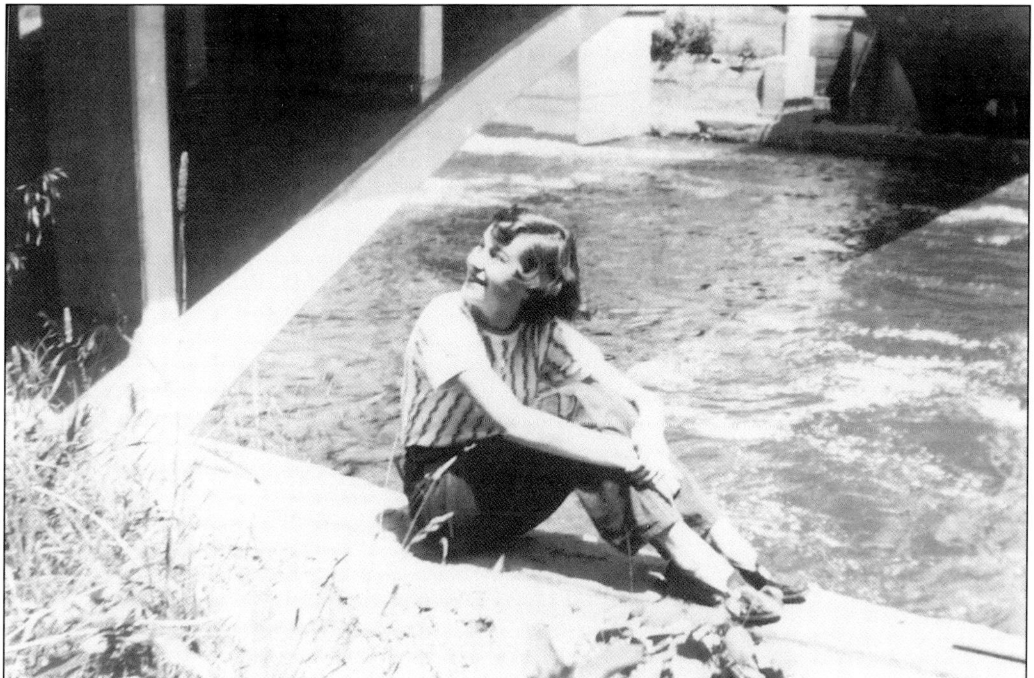

UNDER THE ARCH BRIDGE, C. 1951. The girl in the photograph is Judy Hogan (nee Jurgens), who often visited Clermont with her family.

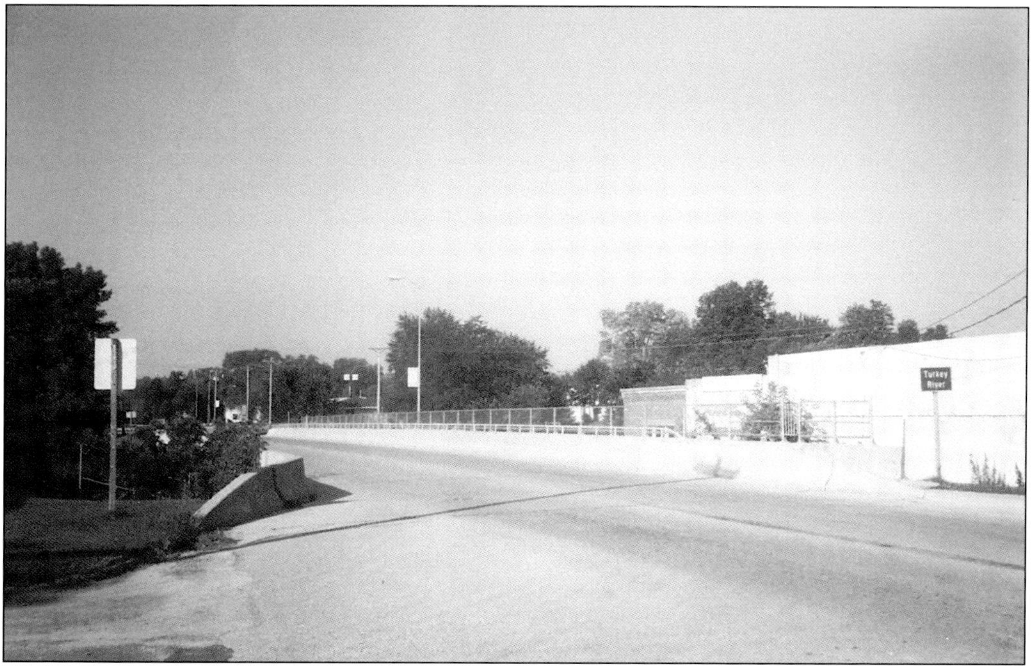

View of Current Bridge. The new bridge was constructed in 1987.

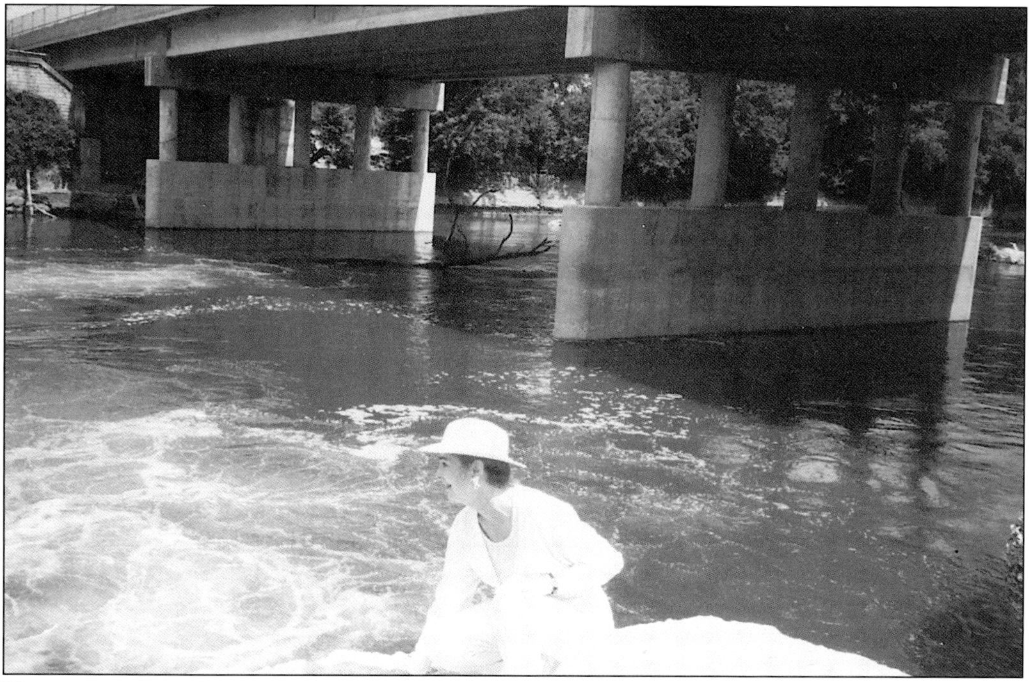

Under the New Bridge, c. 1991. Here is a great view of the bridge and the Turkey River. This is the same girl on page 23, Judy Jurgens, on another visit. She has grown up!

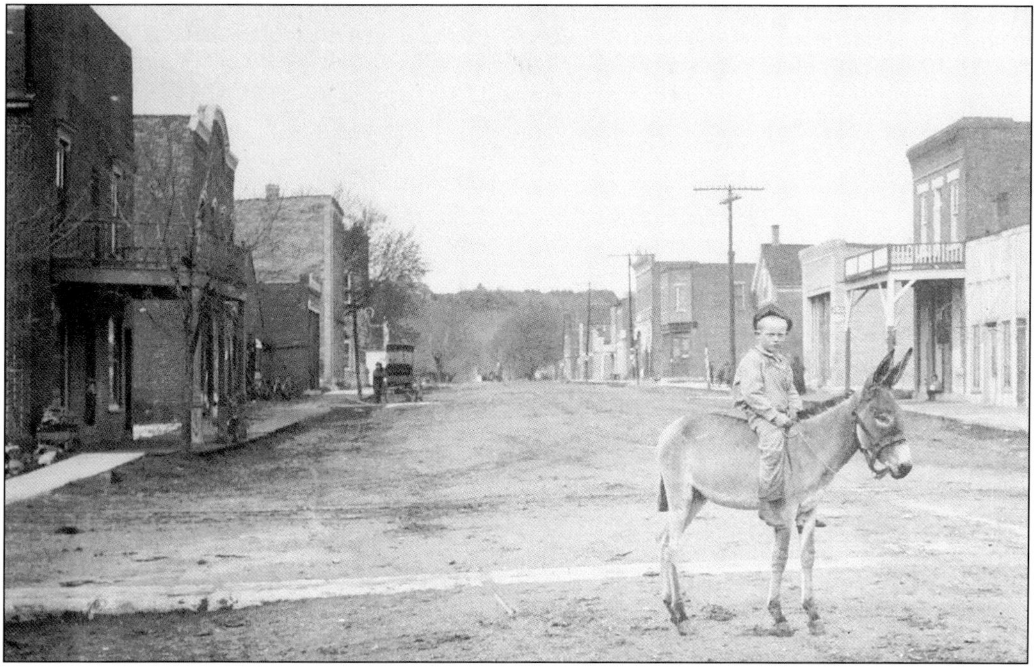

BOY ON DONKEY, MILL STREET, C. 1895.

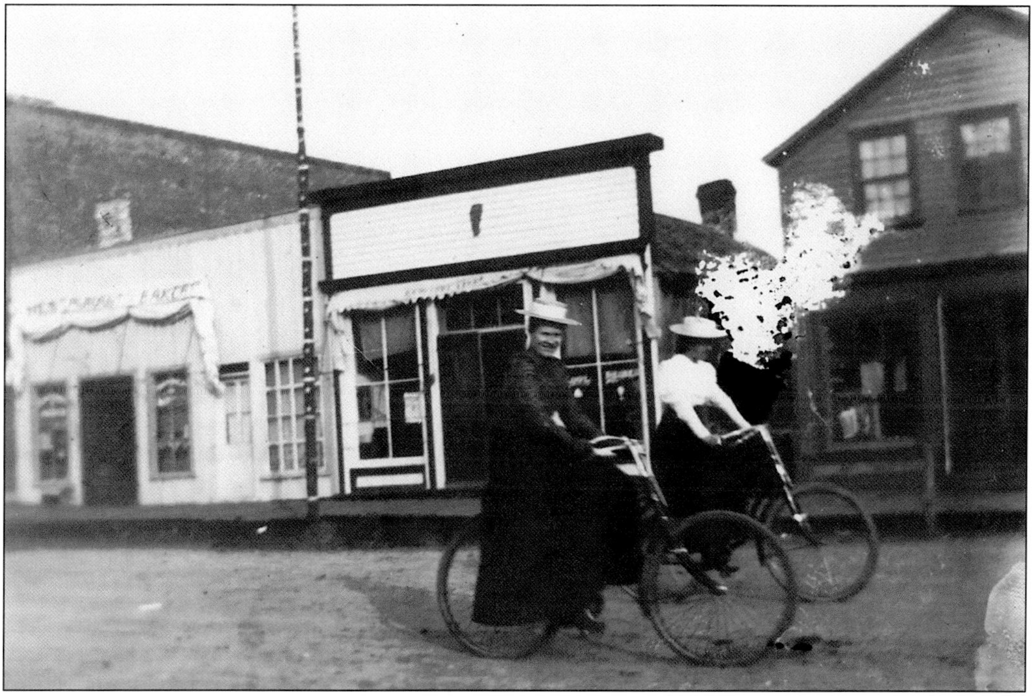

PEOPLE ON THE MOVE, MILL STREET, C. 1900.

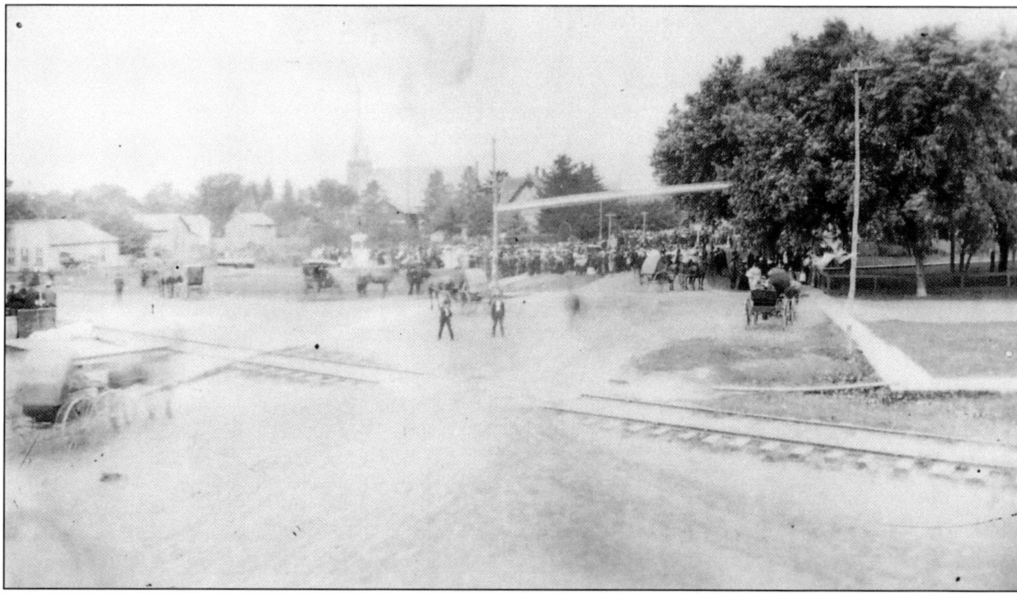

VIEW OF CLERMONT, C. 1904. The gathering may have been the dedication of the Lincoln and Henderson statues. The spire of the Catholic church and the Lincoln Statue as well as the rail lines are visible.

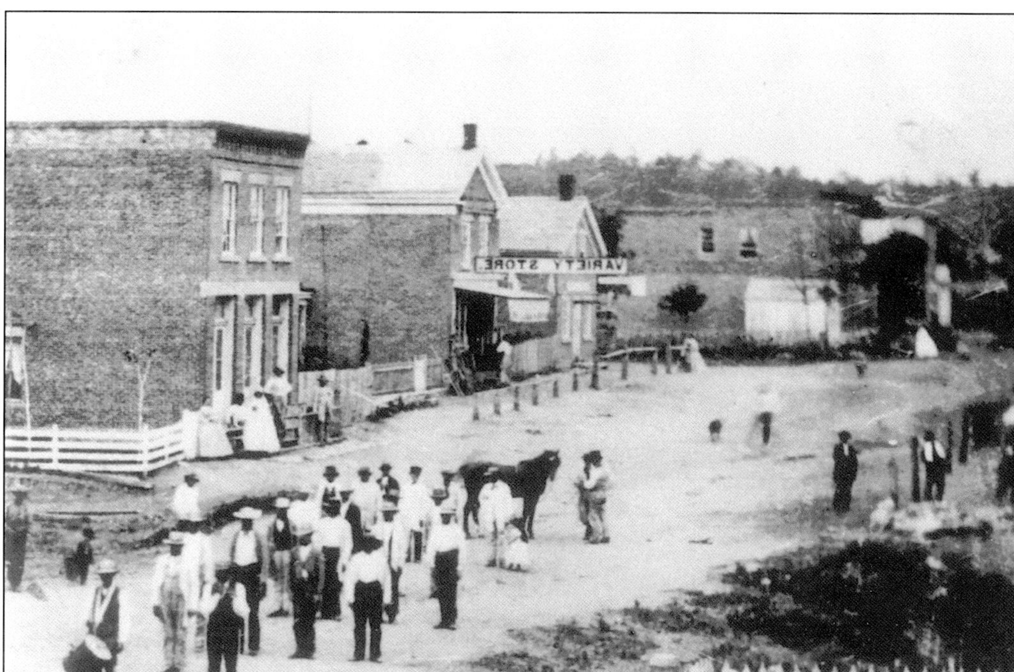

EARLY VIEW OF MAIN STREET. The people and the event are unknown. The photograph is actually reversed and the figures should be going northeast. Note the figure in the foreground who is holding a drum and the sign "Variety Store."

Two

The River, the Dam, and the Mill

Clermont was the ideal site for a dam and mill along the Turkey River. In 1849, the firm of C.D. Carlton and John Thompson of Elkader, Iowa, constructed a log dam and sawmill along the river. A brickyard was also constructed as plans for the future flour mill took shape. Irish immigrants were most likely hired at the McGregor Landing to dig and fire bricks for the mill. The construction of the new mill was completed in 1854, and the first flour was milled in 1855. A cooper mill was also constructed across the street, which made the barrels for shipping the flour. Barrel hoops were made of small hickory poles (not iron) and the staves were mostly of oak. The finished barrels slid to the mill across the street on a wire stretched from one of the top stories. Until the coming of the railroad in 1871, the flour was packed in barrels and transported to McGregor and Clayton, Iowa, where it was shipped by flatboats to various destinations. William Larrabee purchased the Clermont Mills in 1857 and sold it in 1874. The mill passed through the hands of several businessmen until 1901, when Christian C. Miller purchased it. Miller converted the mill into a power plant for generating electricity in 1909–10. The Power Plant operated as C.C. Miller & Sons, then the Turkey River Light and Power Company, and finally it reorganized as the Northeast Iowa Light and Power Company. NILPC supplied hydro power for most of northeastern Iowa with several other plants on the Upper Iowa, Turkey, and Volga Rivers. The plant was eventually closed in 1963.

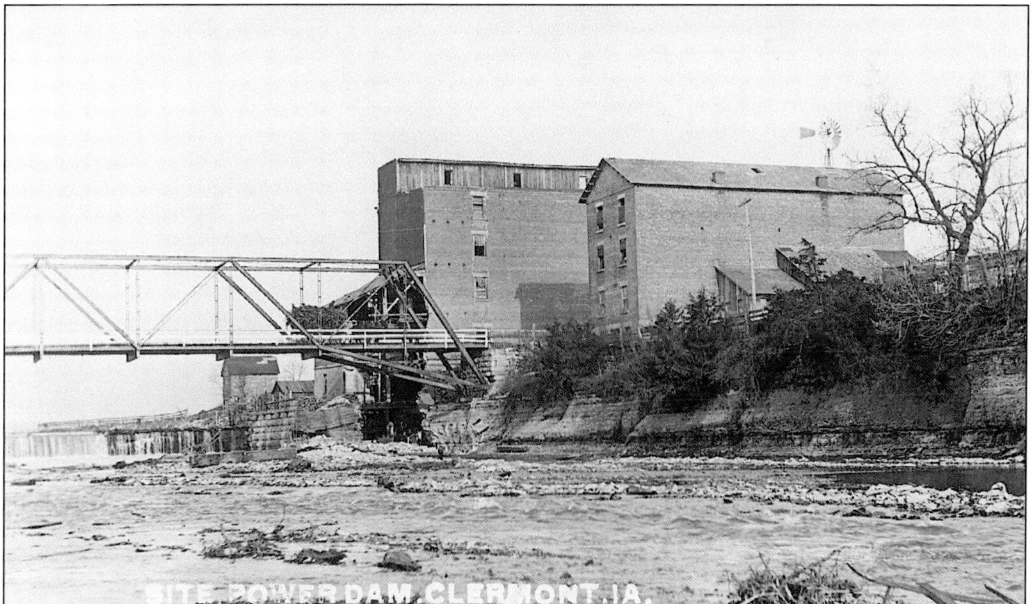

The Site of the Future Power Plant.

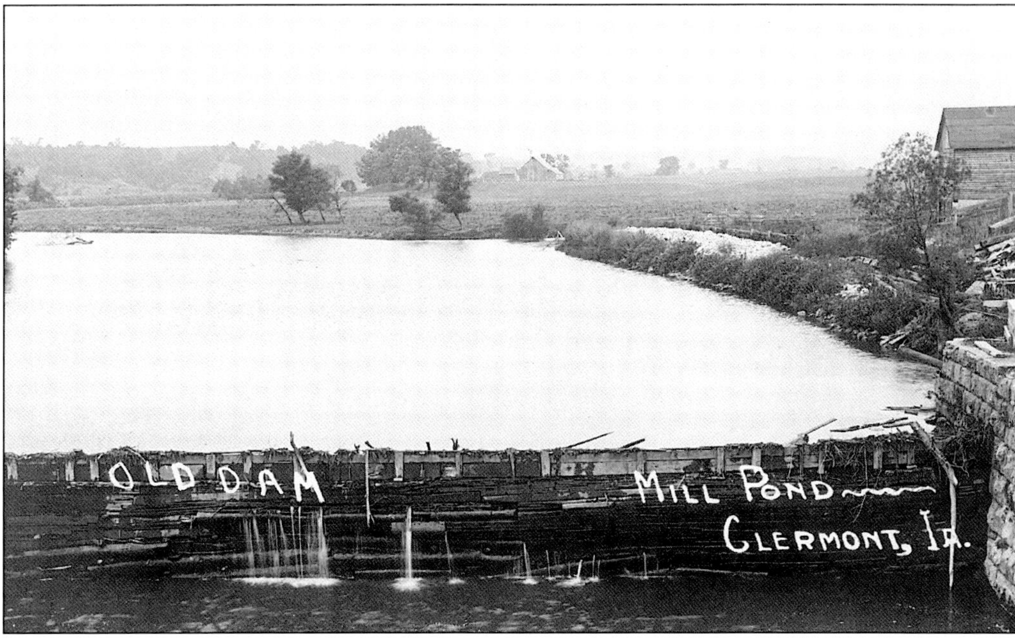

VIEW OF THE OLD LOG DAM AND MILL POND ON THE TURKEY RIVER, C. 1890S.

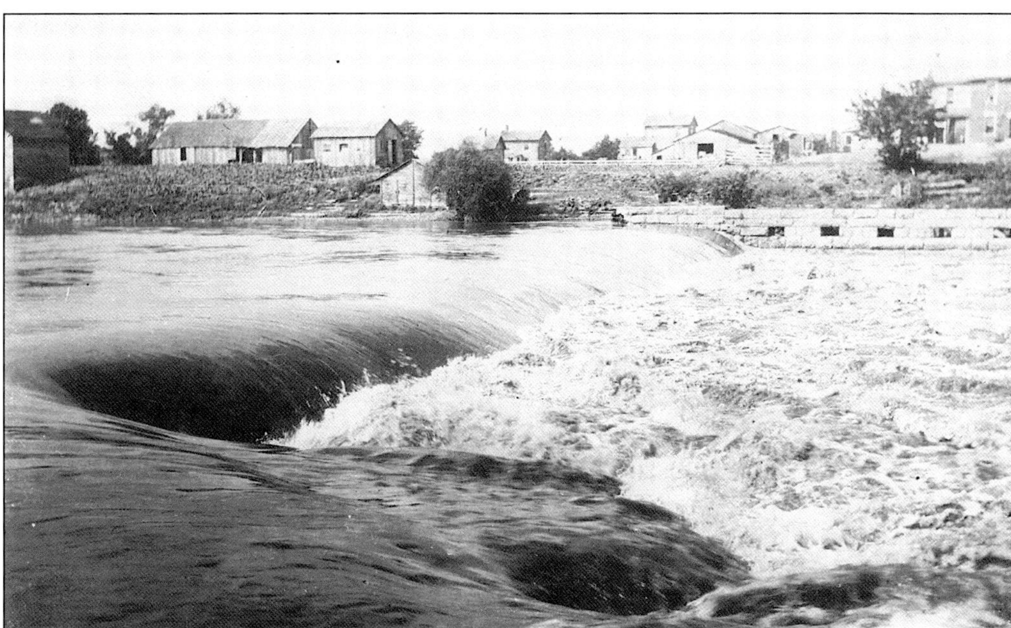

FLOOD WATERS OVER THE OLD LOG DAM. The picture also shows a view of early Clermont.

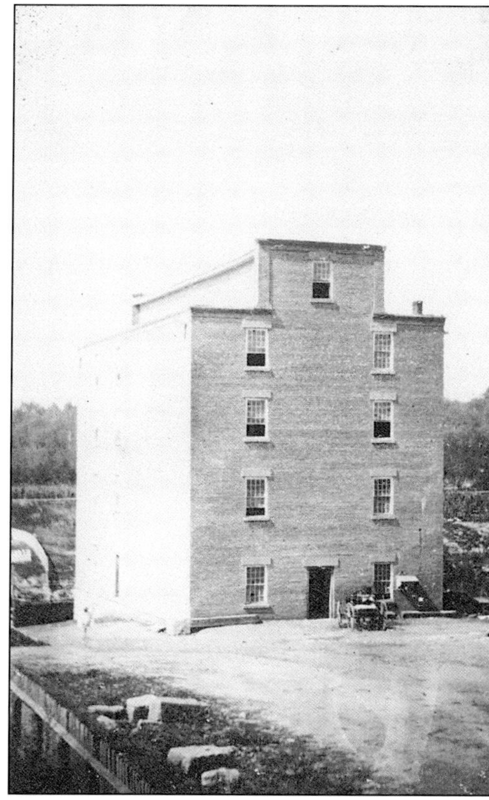

OLD MILL, C. 1890. The mill, built in 1854, was a brick building that replaced an old frame structure. It was five and a half stories. The basement, cut of solid stone, was 40 feet wide and 80 feet deep. It was capable of grinding 900 bushels of wheat in 24 hours.

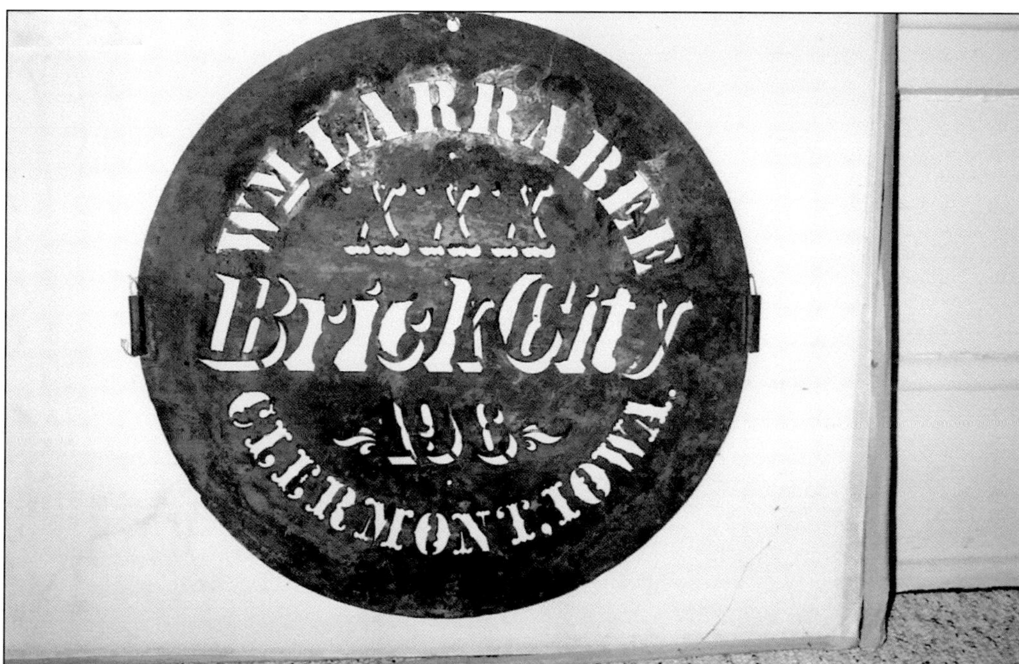

WILLIAM LARRABEE'S TIN STENCIL FLOUR LABEL. William Larrabee shipped flour from Clermont to various locations. The destination of each barrel was labeled on the lid.

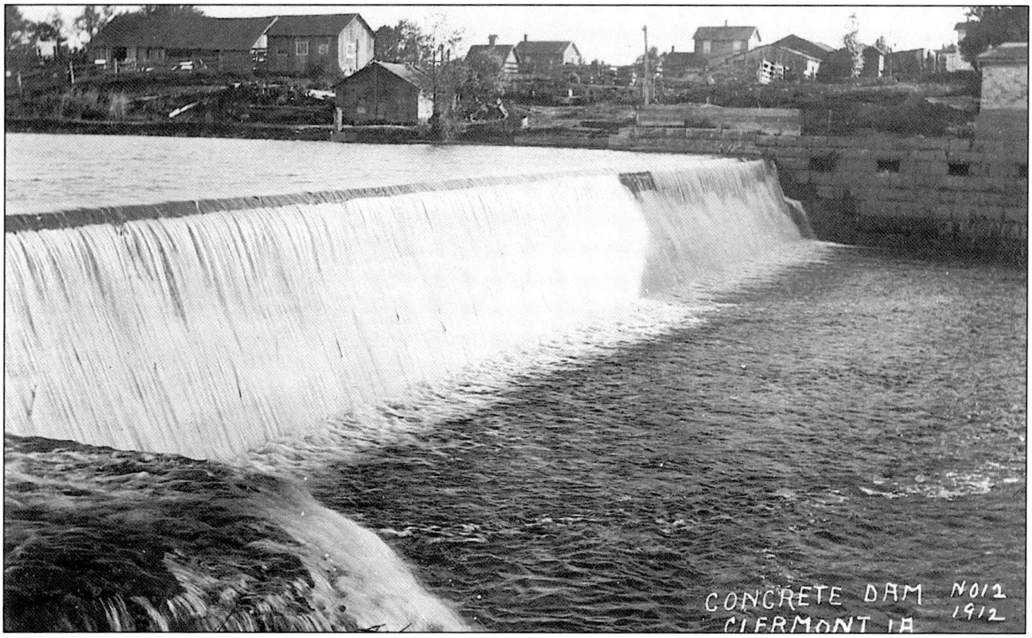

CONCRETE DAM, c. 1912.

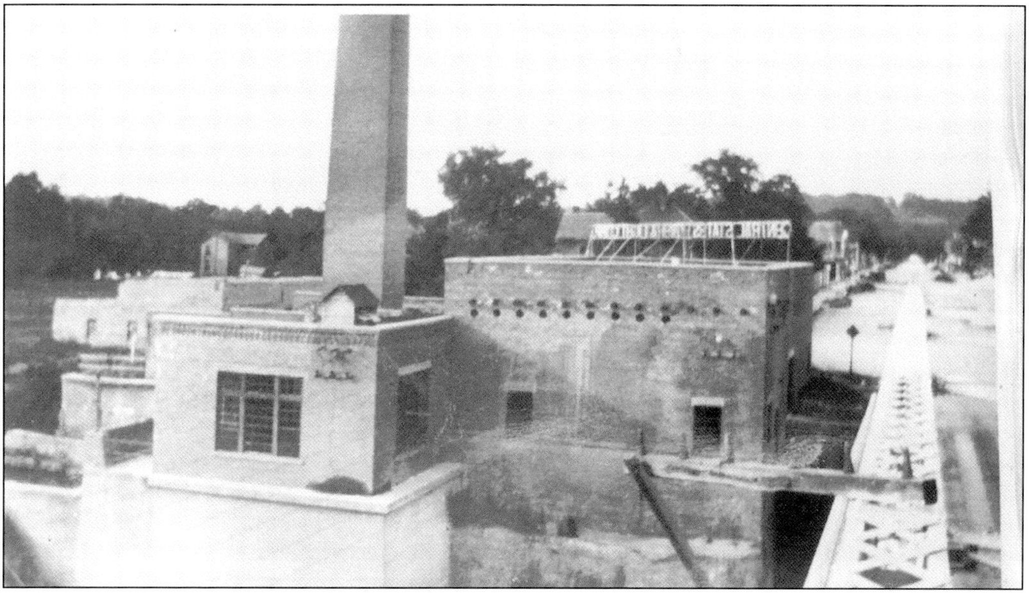

POWER PLANT, BETWEEN 1938–1940.

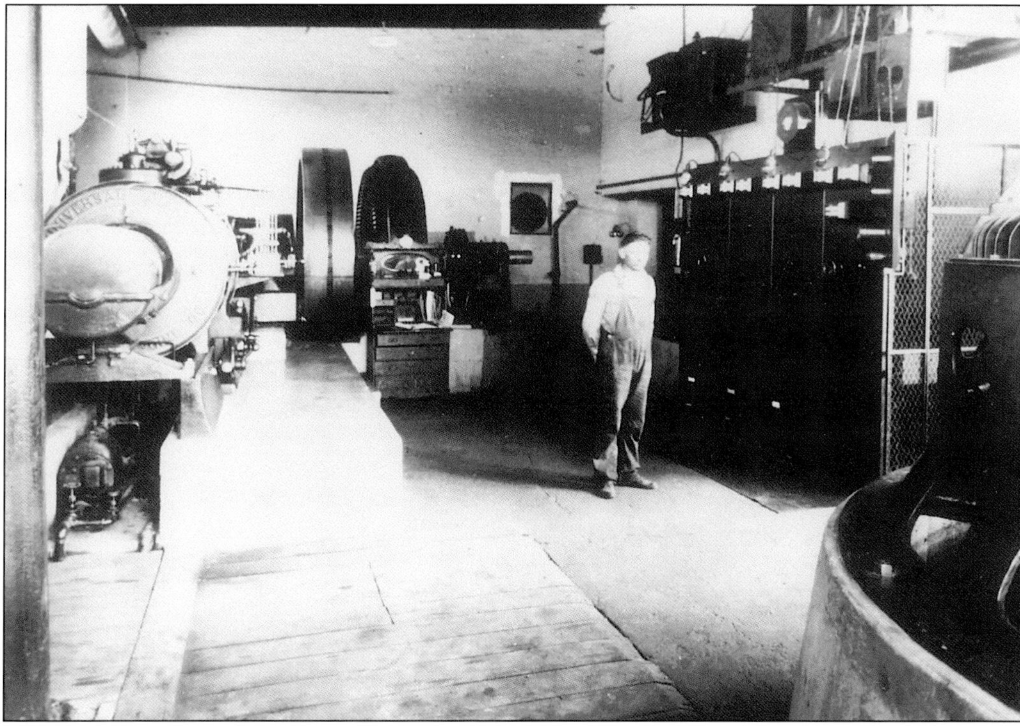

View of the Interior of the Power Plant. The wooden door to the mill wheel is clearly seen in the foreground. The man in the photograph is probably Art Simpson. Mr. Simpson, an employee at the plant who at one time ran the telephone office, fell to his death probably through this very door when he lifted it up to show a visitor the water wheel under the plant.

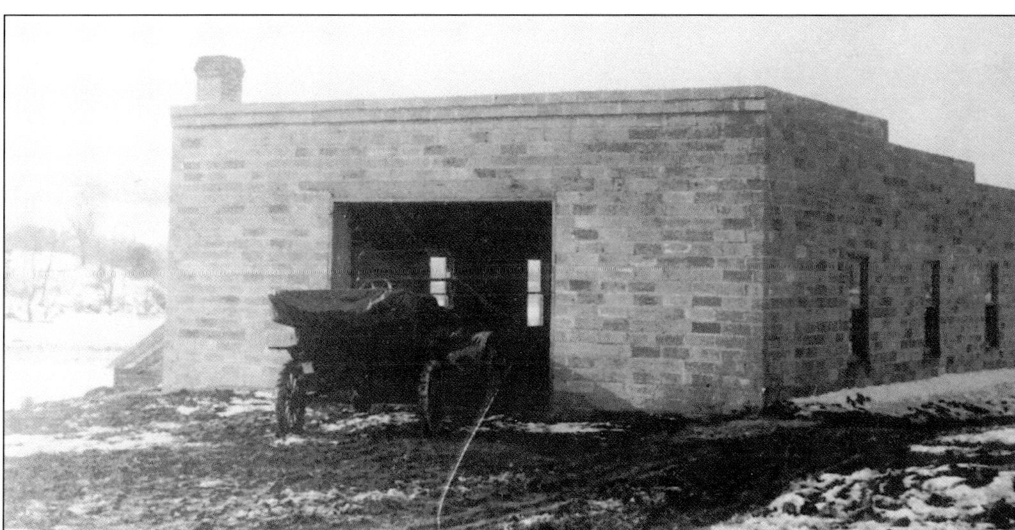

Garage at the Power Plant, c. 1915 or later.

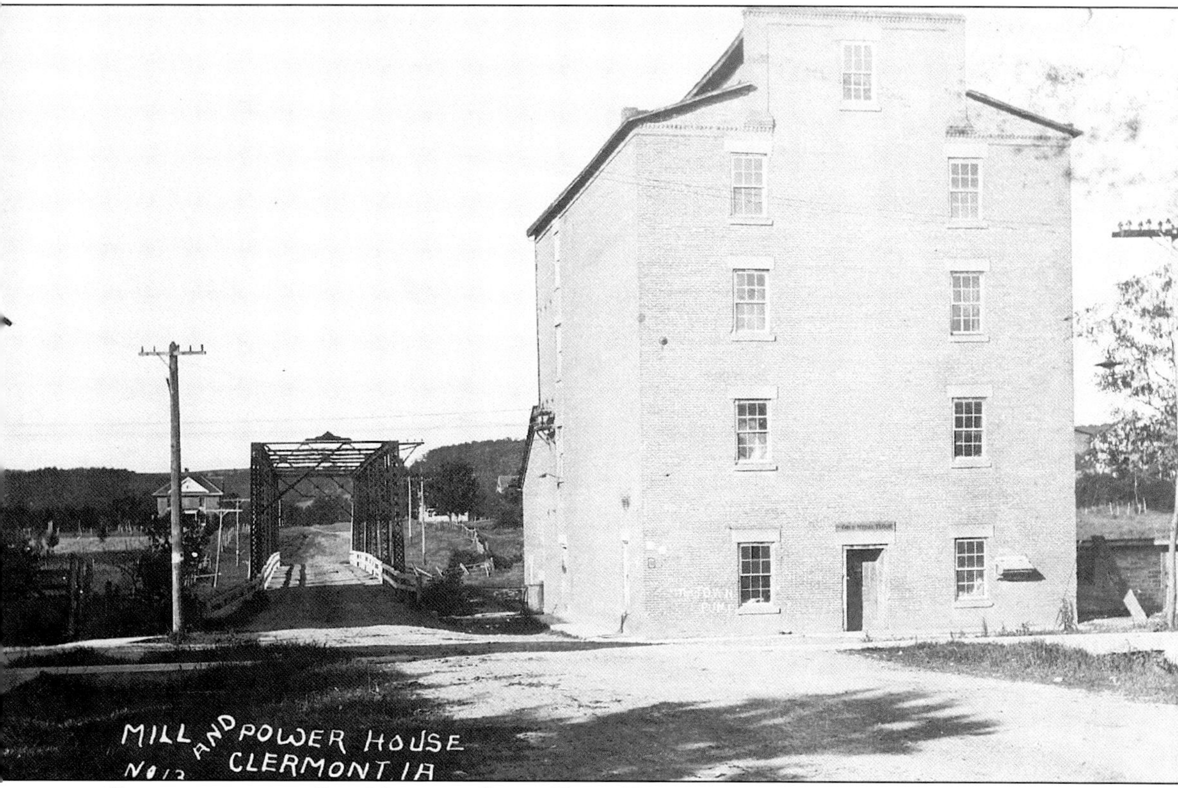

REMEMBERING THE OLD MILL AND STEEL TRUSS BRIDGE.

Three

THE "BRICK CITY"

Brickmaking in Clermont was one of the town's oldest and longest-lived industries. Clermont brick became so famous in the second half of the nineteenth century that the town earned the name "Brick City." White, red, and blue clay deposits were in abundance around the town. Many of the most enduring and unique buildings in Clermont are built of the native brick, and more than one brickyard seems to have existed. Carlton & Thompson had a brickyard, and the bricks from this yard were probably used in the construction of the old mill. Ezra H. Dibble and his sons Martin V. Dibble and B.F Dibble were early "dabblers" in the brickmaking business and established a brickworks near their farm, eventually constructing an establishment just west of town. They manufactured red and the celebrated hard, white, "Milwaukee" brick. Clermont bricks were eventually shipped by rail all over the state.

A brickyard was located at the northeast end of town (Block 66), and in this yard local businessman C.C. Miller turned the brick business into a leading industry in Clermont. Miller set up the Brick & Tile Company that eventually became the Brick & Sand Company with offices on Main (Mill) Street. The yard must have been a bustling place with the round kilns, brick dryers, brickmaking machines, gravel pits, men with wheelbarrows, and teams of horses hauling brick and loading boxcars that would carry the brick to distant places.

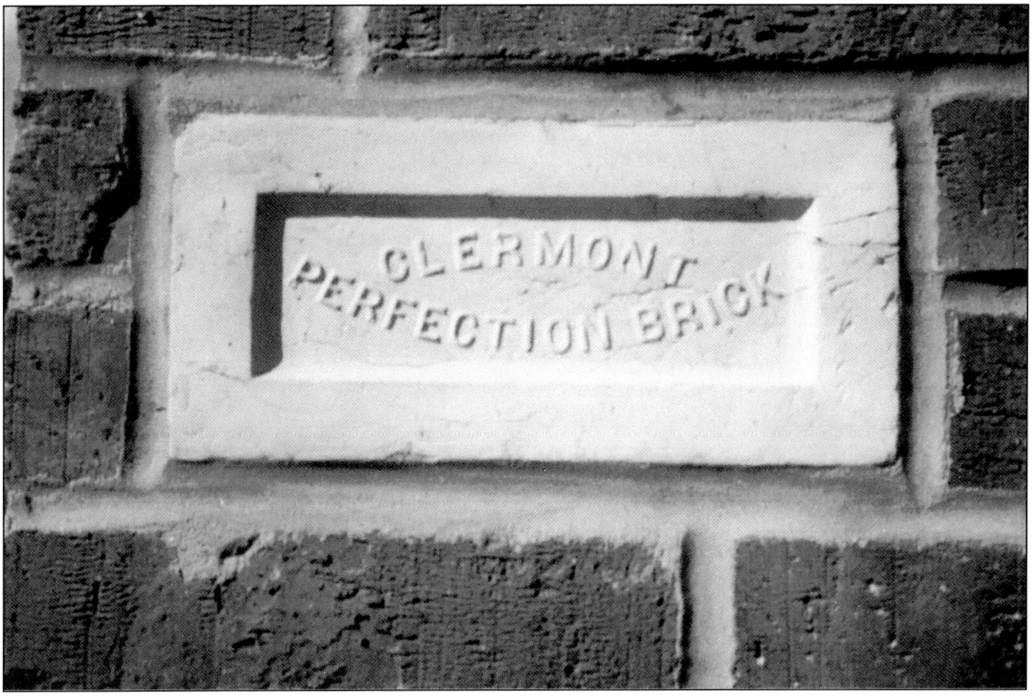

CLERMONT "PERFECTION" BRICK. White and red brick was produced at Clermont as well as hollow and block tile.

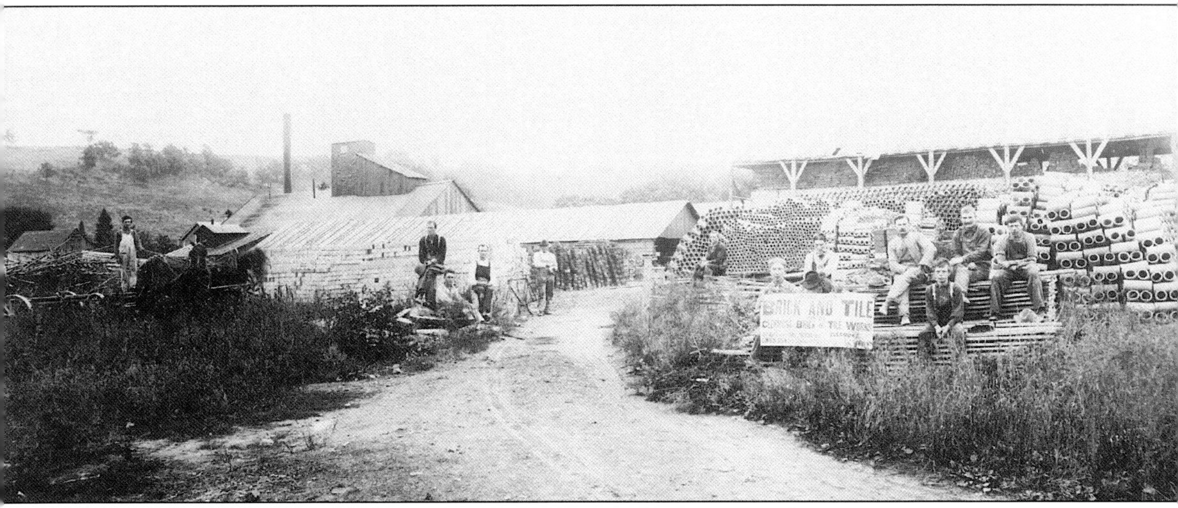

WORKERS IN THE CLERMONT BRICK AND TILE WORKS OWNED BY C.W. MILLER, DATE UNCERTAIN. The yards were located at the east end of town. Note the hollow tile and hollow block brick neatly stacked in the shed. The photograph just barely reveals the old stone barn (far right in the distance), which is still standing today.

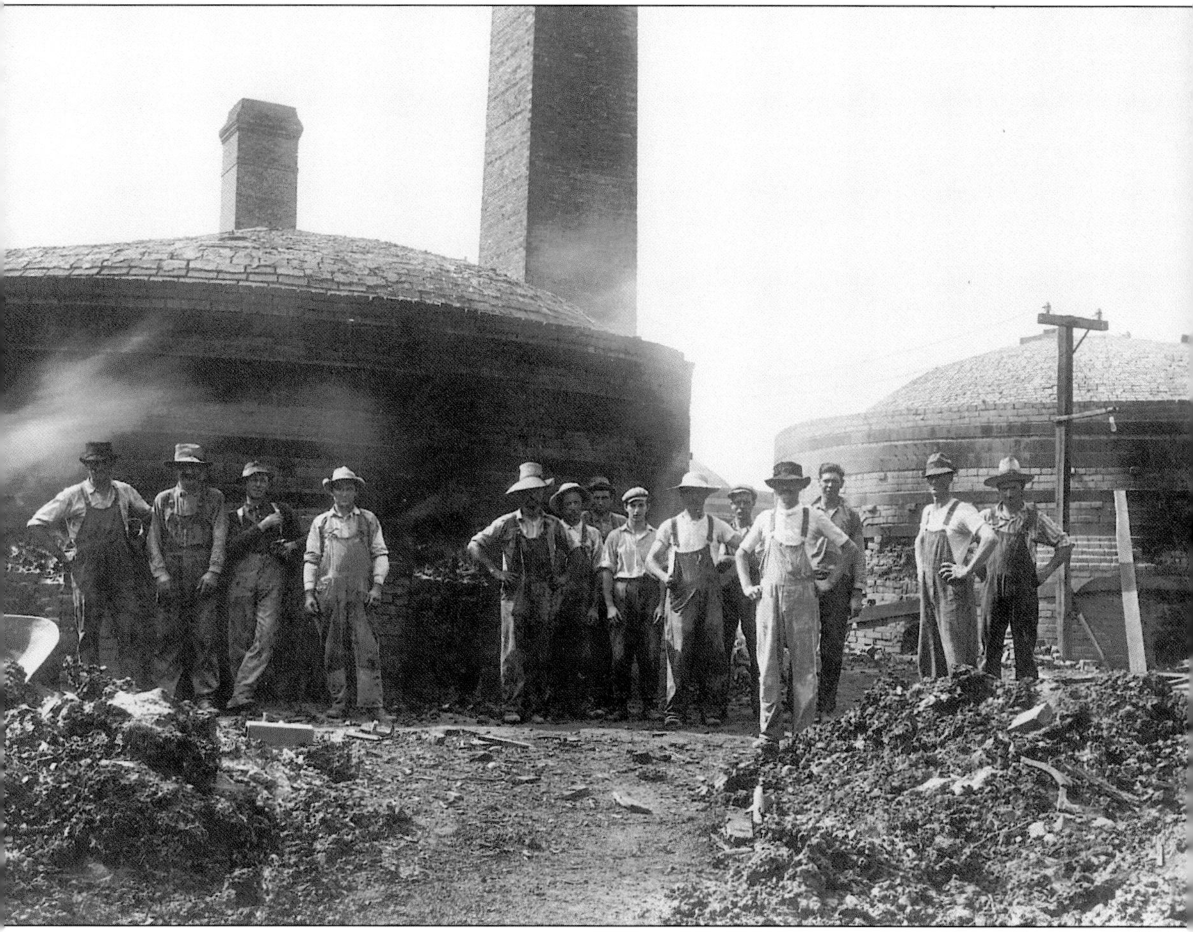

Workers and Kilns, Clermont Brick & Sand Company, 1920. The Clermont Brick & Tile Company eventually reorganized as the Clermont Brick & Sand Company with offices on Main Street. The photograph provides a rare glimpse of the round kilns used to fire the bricks. From left to right are, Phil Steffens, Fred Schave, Alfred Miller, ? Dryer, Roy Meyer, Christ Nelson, Fred Grossman, Truman Shaffer, unidentified, Christ Peterson, Joe Gress, Charlie Cupps, Claude Gress, and George Cook. (Courtesy of Historic Clermont.)

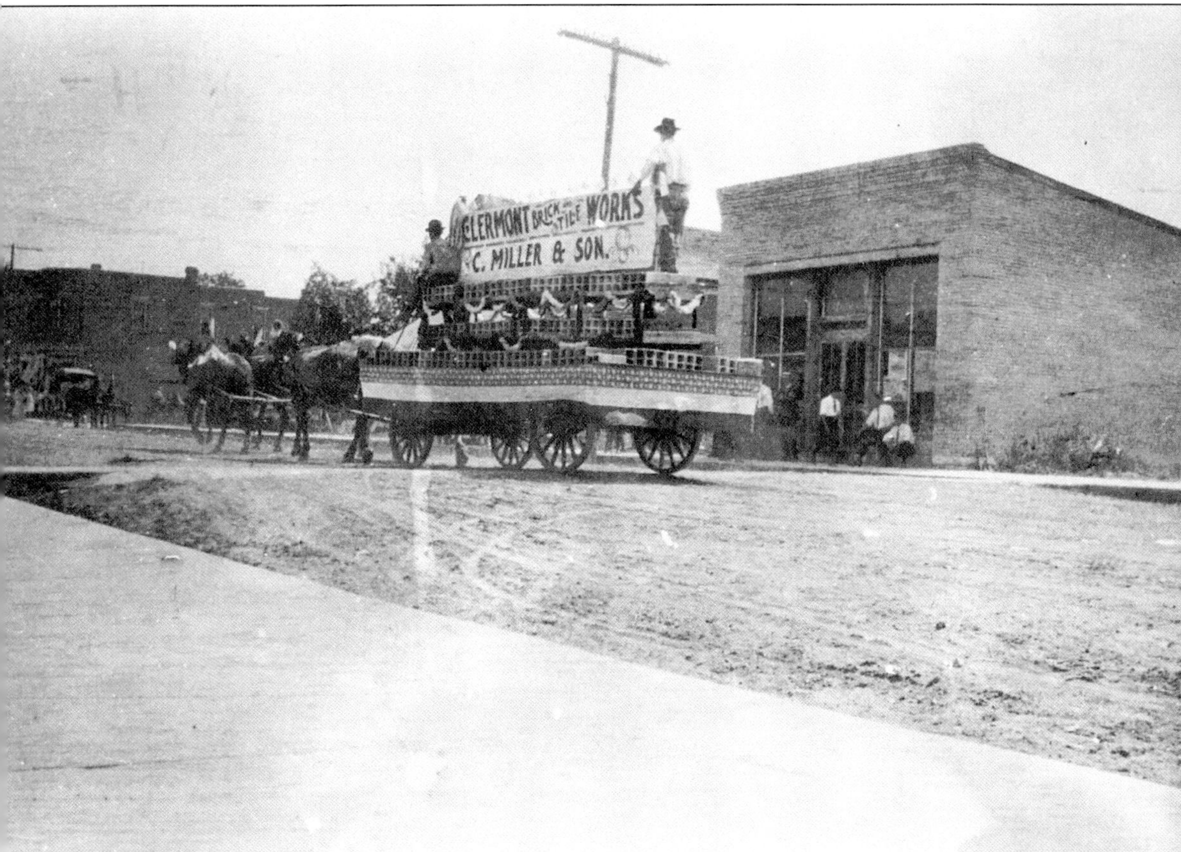

Hauling Brick, C.C. Miller & Son. Workers from the brickyard are pictured here hauling brick down Main Street. From the banner and the decorations on the wagon, the occasion may have been a parade on the Fourth of July. The name of "C.W. Miller" is clearly displayed.

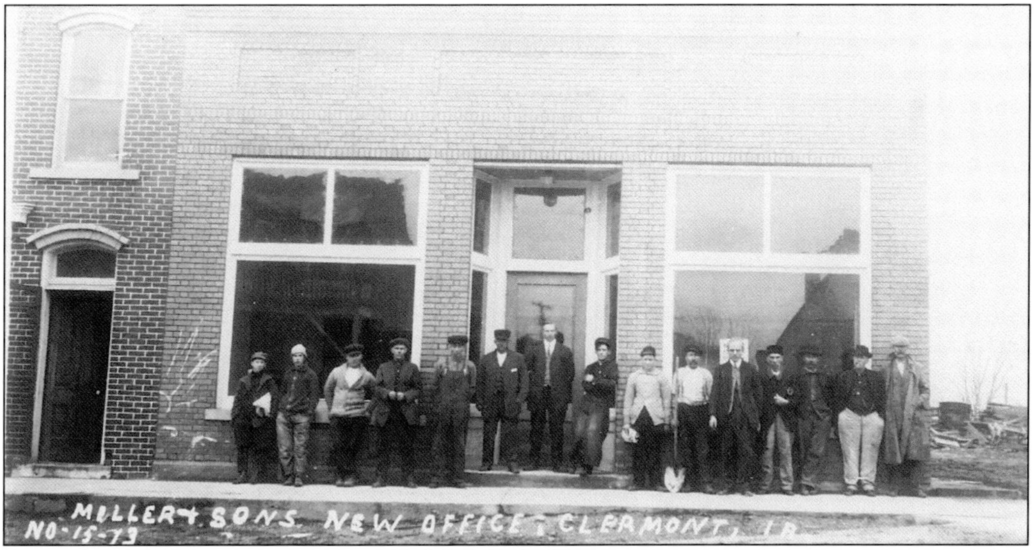

OFFICES OF C.C. MILLER & SONS. The Clermont Brick & Sand Company set up offices on Main (Mill) Street. C.W. Miller is in the center.

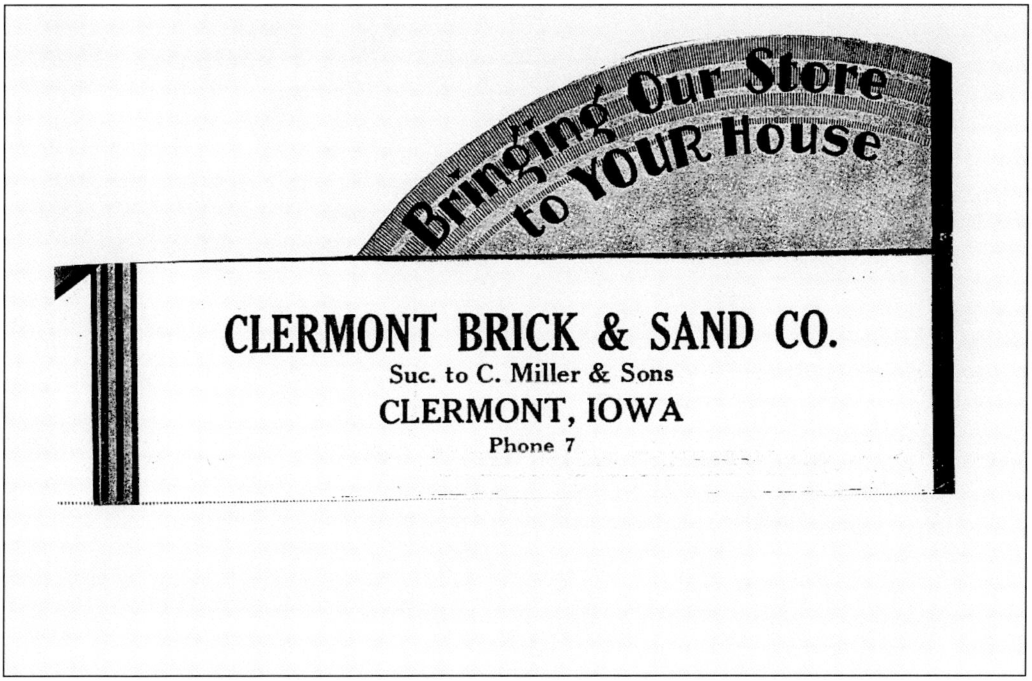

PART OF THE FALL CATALOG OF THE CLERMONT BRICK & SAND COMPANY, C. 1920S.

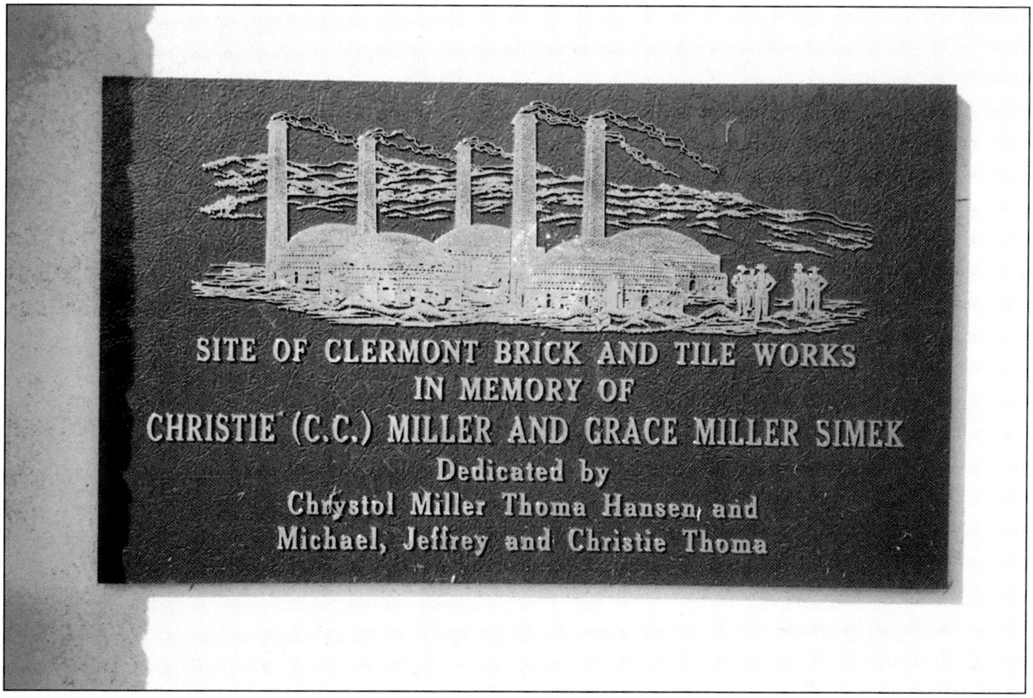

Plaques Commemorating the Site of the Clermont Brick and Tile Works. The plaque at top remembers Christian "Christie" Miller and Grace Miller Simek.

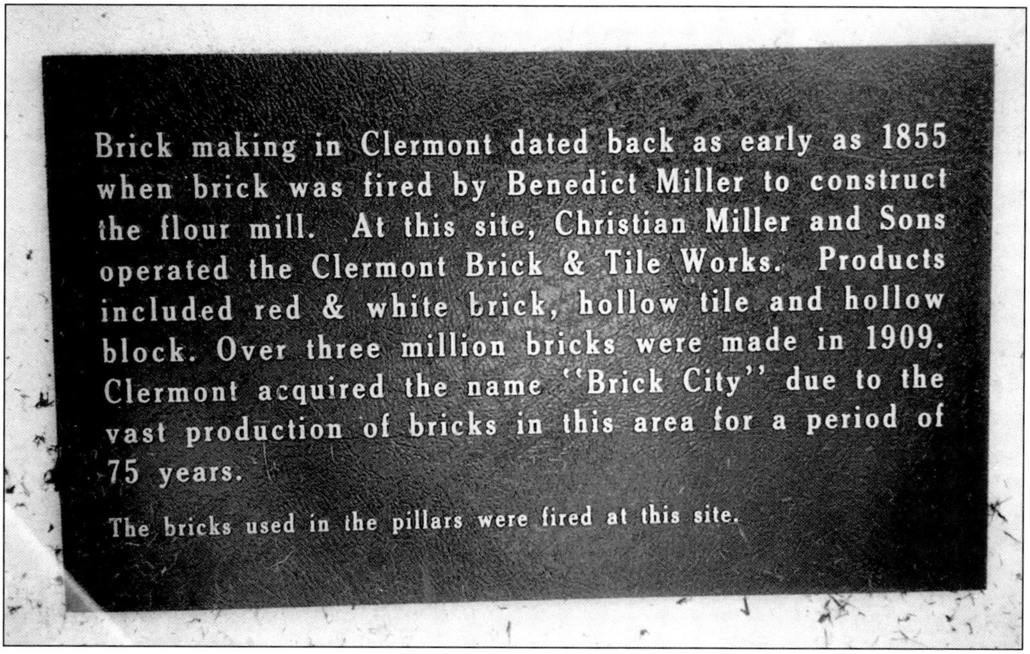

Four

THE LARRABEES

The town of Clermont is often remembered as the home of the 12th governor of Iowa, William Larrabee, a "Connecticut Yankee," who arrived in the vicinity of Clermont in the mid-1850s. He taught school, engaged in milling and in land speculation, and later entered politics on the Republican ticket. He married Anna Matilda Appelman, the daughter of Captain G.A. Appelman, an early settler of Clermont, in March 1862. The couple raised seven children, who all received their early education in the public schools at Clermont. The family lived at more than one location in town before moving into Montauk. The Larrabees called Clermont home for many years, and the influence of this amazing family is still visible in the town.

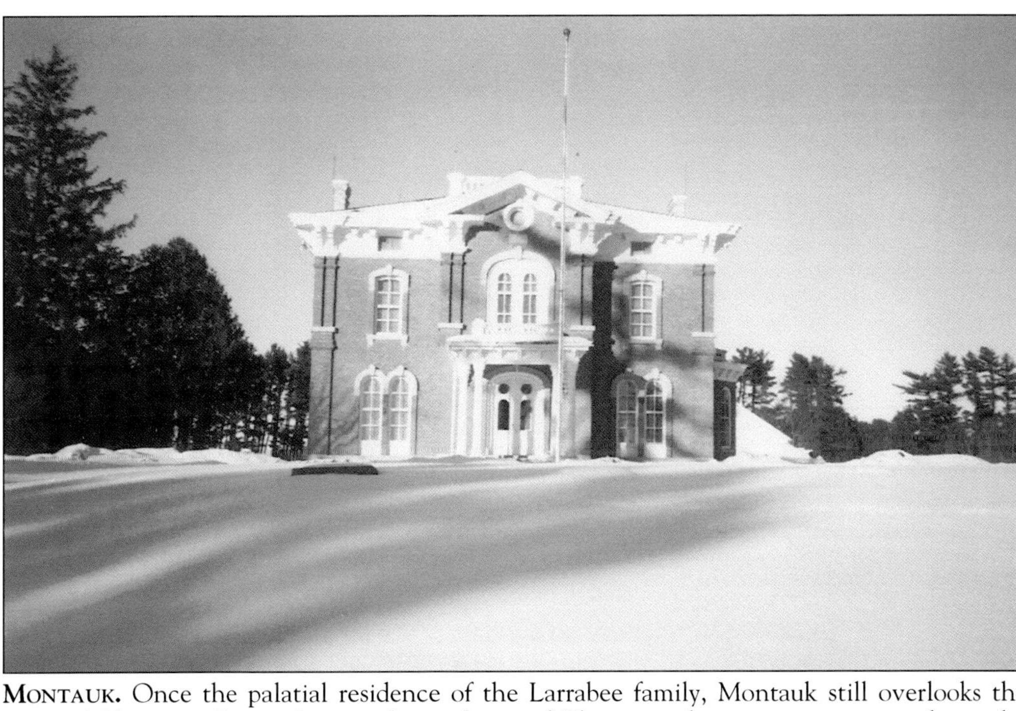

MONTAUK. Once the palatial residence of the Larrabee family, Montauk still overlooks the town of Clermont. Located one mile northeast of Clermont, the mansion is currently on the National Register of Historic Places in Iowa.

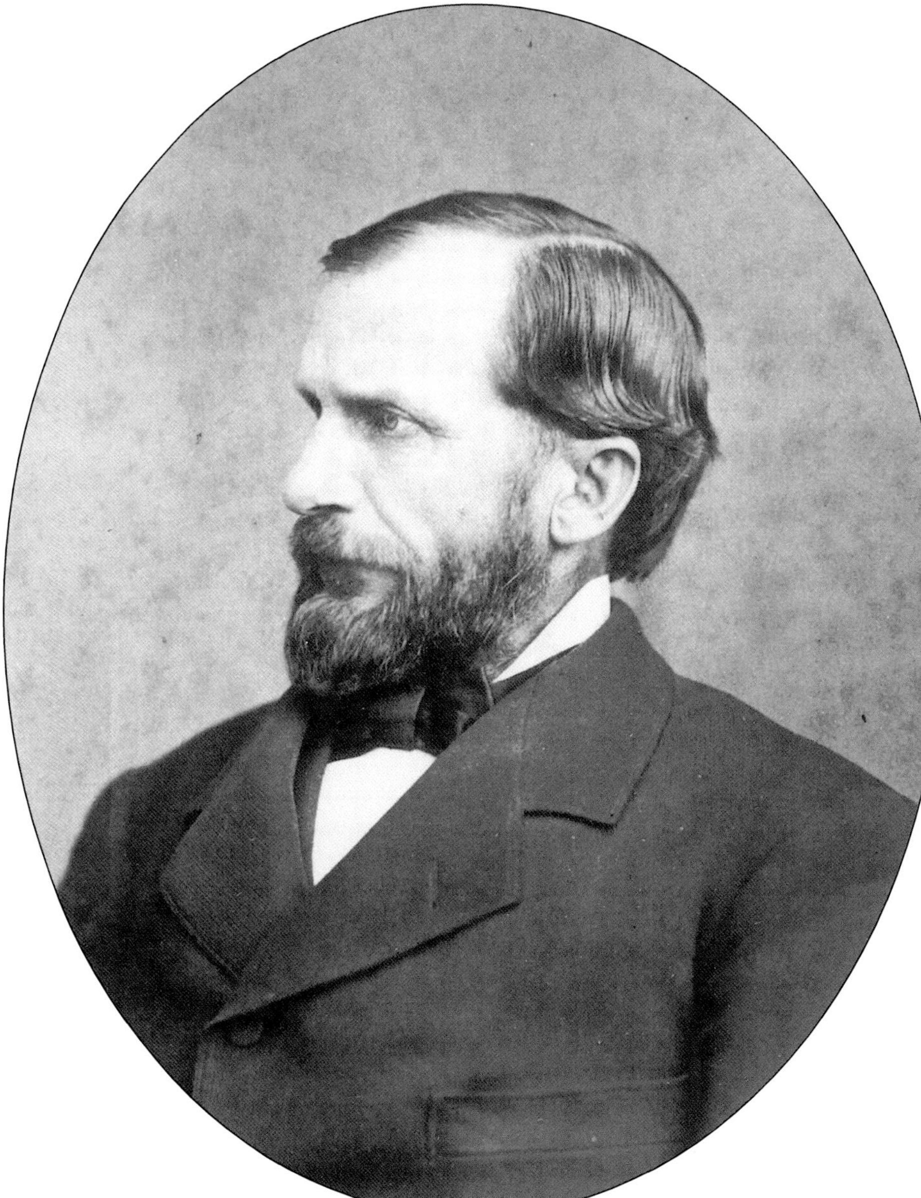

William Larrabee, 1832–1912. Farmer, miller, railroad promoter, banker, and politician, Larrabee served two terms as the 12th governor of Iowa from 1886 to 1890. Short in stature (just over 5 feet) and blind in one eye, he cast a long shadow over the political arena of the day. Larrabee was elected to the state senate in 1868 and remained in the office for 17 unopposed years before resigning to seek the office of governor. He earned recognition for his support of railroad regulation, temperance, votes for women, and educational reform.

NEWSPAPER CLIPPINGS ON WILLIAM LARRABEE. Although the incident reported in the newspaper is probably fictional, it does illustrate the personal interest Larrabee always took in the welfare of the people of Clermont.

Beginning at Home

THE late Governor Larrabee, the Grand Old Man of Iowa, was extremely fond of children. One day, while looking over his mill at Turkey River, he found an urchin, dirty and ragged, sound asleep near the waterwheel. The boy was Mickey Burke, son of a poor family in the neighborhood.

The governor asked the boy why he was so dirty and ragged. The boy explained his mother had a large family and had to work hard and could get him no better clothes.

"But you can keep clean," exhorted Larrabee. "You could wash your face and hands if you wanted to. That costs nothing."

Mickey said he would try.

"Well," said the governor, "now is the time to begin."

He procured a washbasin, some soap and a towel, and watched Mickey scrub himself until he shone. Then the governor got Mickey some clothes and dressed him neatly. Mickey looked fine.

"Now," said Larrabee, "we'll see about getting you a job."

He took Mickey to the store of an old German of whom the governor was very fond. Mr. Schneider had no place for Mickey.

"But you must have!" expostulated Larrabee. "Just look at him and see what a nice boy he is. He is clean and neat; he is a good talker and would make a good clerk. There is no finer boy, Mr. Schneider, than Mickey here."

Schneider was obdurate. He had no place.

The governor and Mickey walked out of the store, much disappointed. As they reached the sidewalk Mickey turned to his benefactor and asked: "Mr. Larrabee, if I am such a darned fine boy as you say, why don't you give me a job yourself?"

Iowa's Next Governor.

The time is fast approaching when the call will be issued by the State Central Republican committee to place in nomination a candidate for the position of Governor. Among the different candidates mentioned up to this time we notice that State Senator Larrabee, of Clermont, Fayette county, is well spoken of. He is chairman of the Ways and Means committee and well acquainted with the State's affairs and her wants and needs. Without committing ourselves to the cause of any one candidate, we say it is for the interest of Sioux county, and the whole northwest for that matter, to support that candidate that resides the nearest to us as having a tendency to do this portion of Iowa the most good. We also want another "business" governor, of the make-up of Gov. Gear.

ENDORSEMENT OF LARRABEE FOR GOVERNOR OF THE STATE.

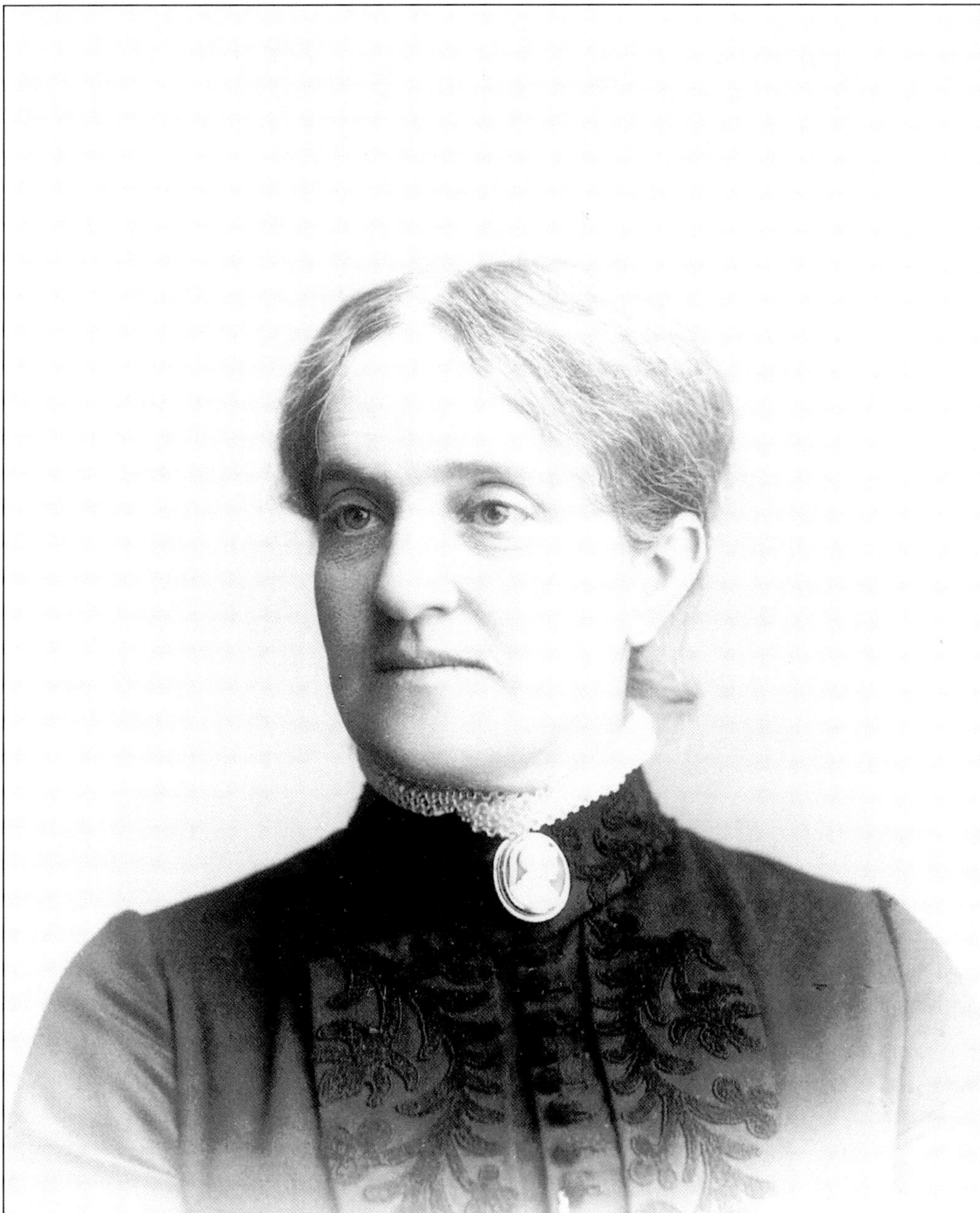

Anna Matilda Appelman Larrabee, 1842–1931. As the active, independent, and outspoken wife of William Larrabee Sr., Anna Larrabee is remembered especially for her devotion to her family, and her generous contributions to Clermont. One of her most ambitious projects was planning a new school building for the town of Clermont between 1912 and 1913. "Mrs. Larrabee is one of Iowa's self-made women. Her predominant traits are of the intellectual and social order. Her motto in life has been 'Act well thy part, where're thy duty lies,' and whether in the care of a large farm and household, when Gov. Larrabee's public life calls him from home, or when filling not less onerous but more public duties, the same self-possession characterizes this Iowa woman." (Source unknown.)

E MESSENGER & CHRONICLE

Widow of Former Gov. Larrabee Serves Hot Coffee to Road Gang

CLERMONT, Dec. 10—The traits of character which have made Mrs. William Larrabee, widow of the former governor of Iowa, beloved throughout northeastern Iowa, where she is best known, have not been dimmed by the years.

A few mornings ago when the thermometer registered below zero, a gang of twenty workmen labored in the icy blast, grading the famous Larrabee hill, one of the steepest grades in northeast Iowa, situated in front of Montauk, the Larrabee home. Mrs. Larrabee's heart was touched by the thought of these men working there and she resolved to do something for them.

About 10 o'clock the workmen were surprised to see a man appear carrying a huge coffee pot and a pitcher of cream. With him was another man carrying cups, sugar and spoons. Work stopped, the coffee was poured, and all hands were warmed as the hot liquid was consumed.

The kindness displayed by the 87-year-old woman, still exerting her influence for good from her commanding site over Clermont, made a profound impression on the men and seemed to inject a new spirit in their work.

NEWSPAPER CLIPPING ON ANNA MATILDA LARRABEE. Here she is shown bringing coffee for the workers.

WOMEN NOT PREPARED TO VOTE, SAYS MRS. WILLIAM LARRABEE.

Wife of President of Iowa Commission at World's Fair Asserts Men Have Been Conducting Government Satisfactorily All These Years—Her Model Is Helen Gould — Thinks Clubs Have Good Purposes Which Are Not Always Filled—Politics Should Be Barred.

HER STAND WITH REGARD TO VOTES FOR WOMEN.

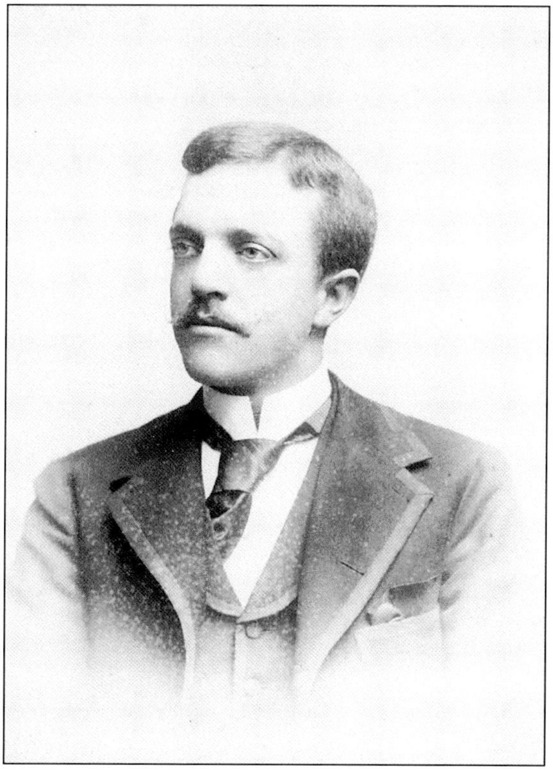

CHARLES LARRABEE (JUNE 13, 1862–MARCH 4, 1943). Charles was the eldest son of Governor and Mrs. William Larrabee. He graduated from Iowa State University at Ames in 1881 with a degree in agriculture. He married Charlotte Winston Osborn on May 8, 1901, and the union produced three children: Charles Jr., Fredric Osborn, and Anna. The family resided in Armstrong and in Fort Dodge, Iowa, where Charles served as the vice president and director of the Iowa Savings Bank, *c*. 1913. He was also known as an educated farmer and a breeder of thoroughbred cattle.

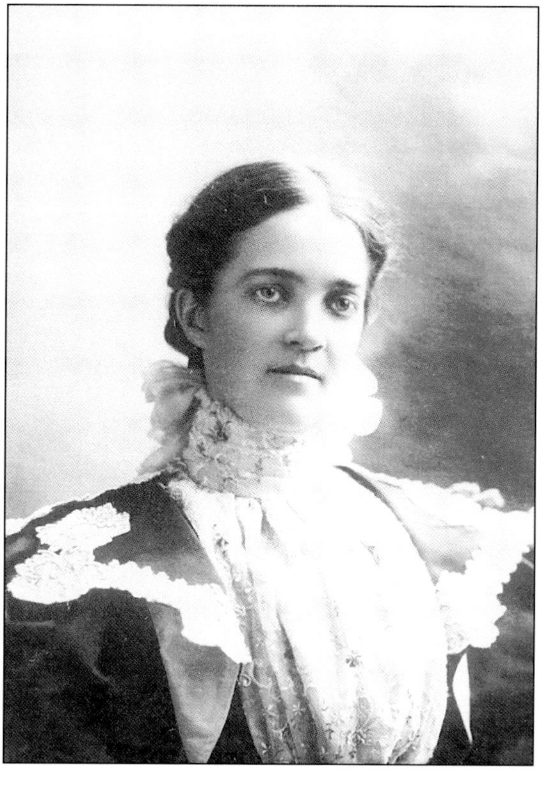

AUGUSTA LARRABEE (1864–1897). Augusta was the second child of William and Anna Matilda. She studied in Clermont schools and at Iowa State University. She was a talented artist who exhibited her paintings at art shows. She married Victor Brown Dolliver on March 14, 1897. The couple moved to Minneapolis where Augusta died soon after at the age of 33 years.

JULIA (1867–1937). Julia was the third child of William and Anna Matilda. She attended Clermont schools and Iowa State University. She married Don Lathrop Love on August 20, 1890. The couple made their home in Lincoln, Nebraska.

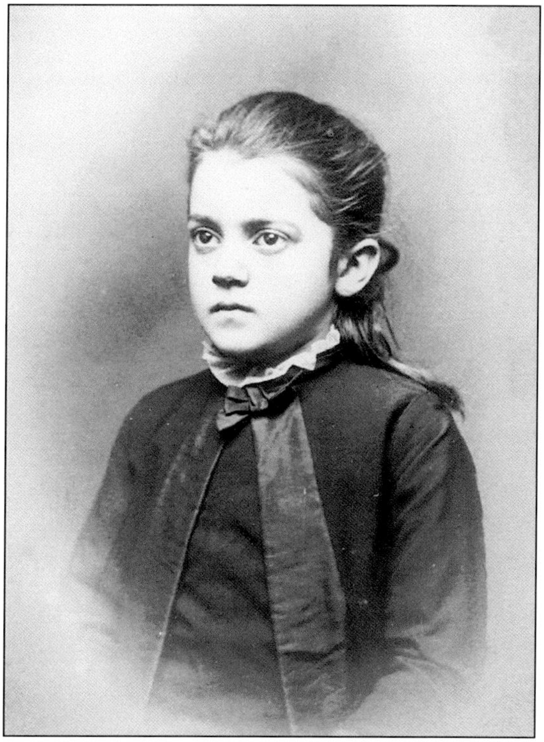

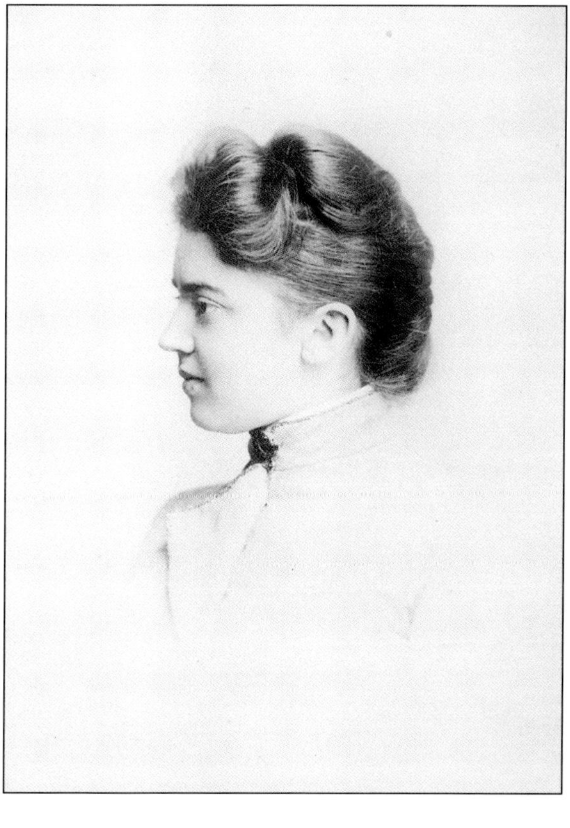

ANNA (1869–1965). Anna was the fourth child of William and Anna Matilda. Anna is known to have had great musical talent, and she taught voice and violin at Clermont. For 60 years, she played the pipe organ at the Union Sunday School service, and she continued to live at Montauk until her death. She would approve of the fact that Montauk is being kept as a "living home."

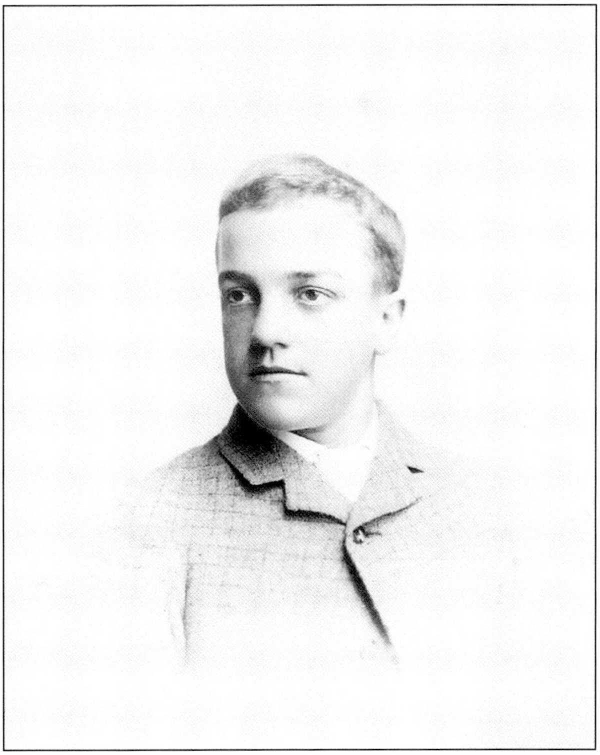

William Larrabee Jr. (1870–1933). William was the fifth child born to William and Anna Matilda. William graduated from Iowa State University in 1896 with a degree in law, and returned to Clermont to set up a law practice. He married Lillian Grey Inglis in 1901 and made his home at Montauk until 1913. That same year he built a house at the bottom of Montauk hill, where his children were born: William Inglis (1902), William III (1904), Lillian Innes (1906), Helen Augusta (1911), and twins, Janet and James (1915). William was elected a representative of Fayette County for the 29th General Assembly (1902) and again for the 33rd, 34th, and 35th General Assemblies. He also served as the vice president of the Clermont Bank.

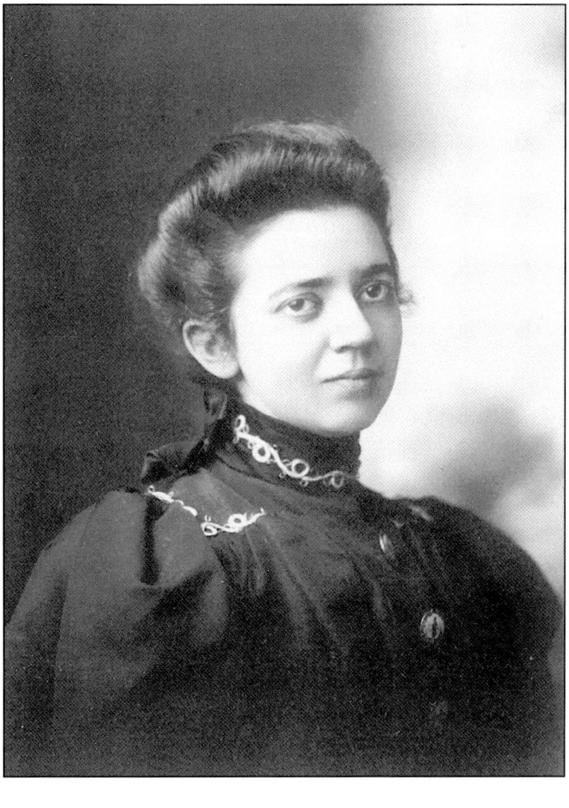

Helen (1876–1919). Helen was the youngest child of William and Anna Matilda. She attended Clermont schools and graduated from Iowa State University in 1899. She married Charles Burton Robbins on September 9, 1903. Her three children were Anna Marcella (1906), Julia Larrabee (1909), and Lewis Frederic (1911).

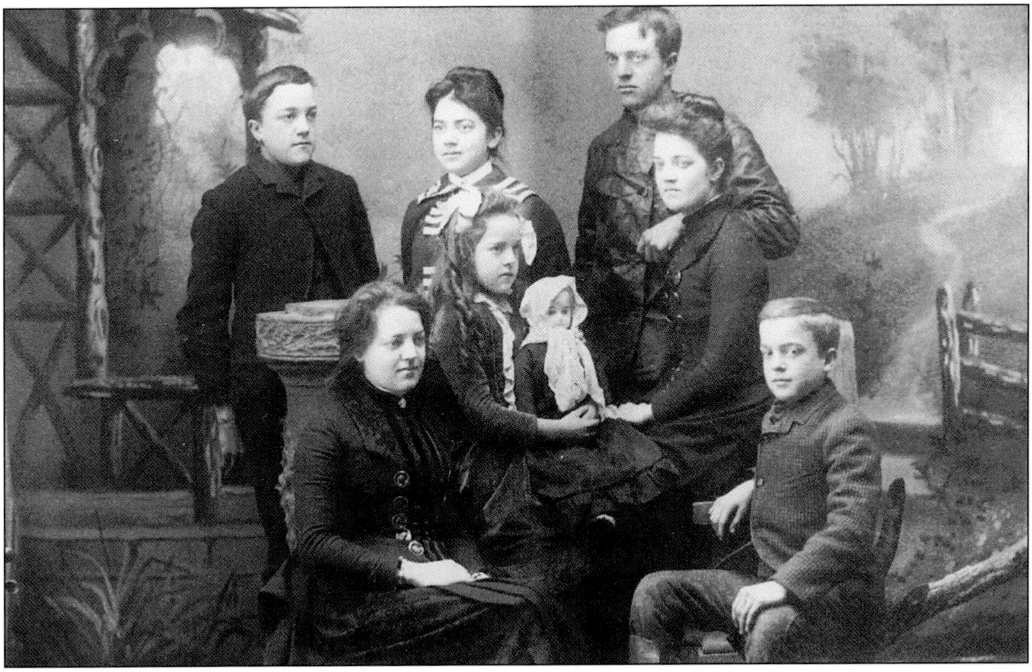

Larrabee Children. They are from left to right, (top row) William Jr., Anna, and Charles; (seated) Jullia, Helen (with doll), Augusta, and Frederic. Frederic Larrabee (1873–1959), who is not featured in the portraits, was the fifth child of William and Anna Matilda. He graduated with a degree in law from Iowa State University. He was elected state senator in 1908 for the 33rd, 34th, 35th, and 36th sessions of the general assembly.

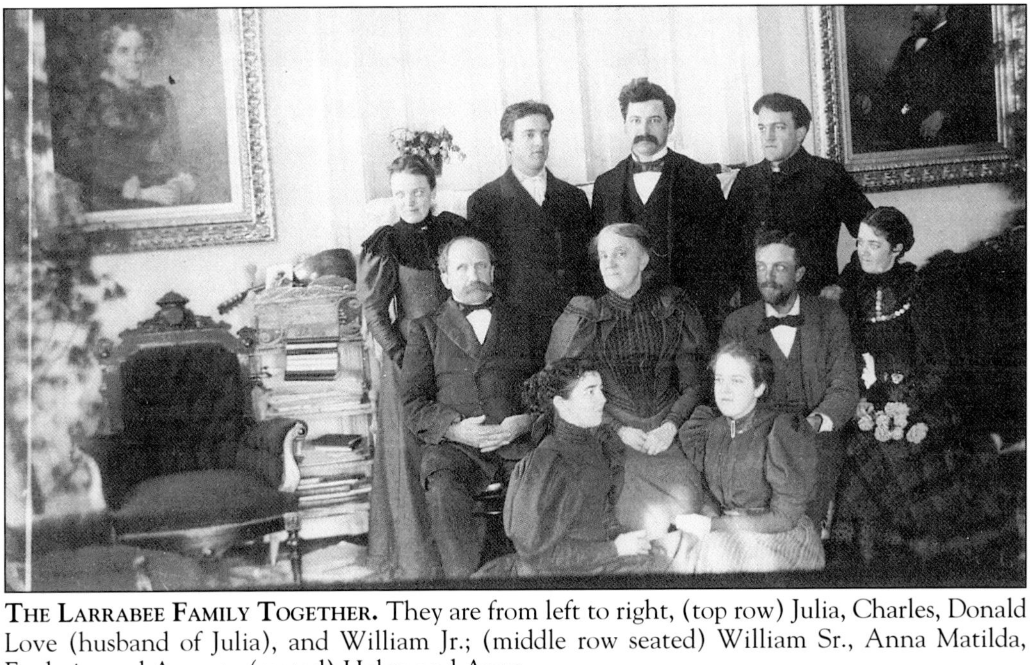

The Larrabee Family Together. They are from left to right, (top row) Julia, Charles, Donald Love (husband of Julia), and William Jr.; (middle row seated) William Sr., Anna Matilda, Frederic, and Augusta (seated) Helen and Anna.

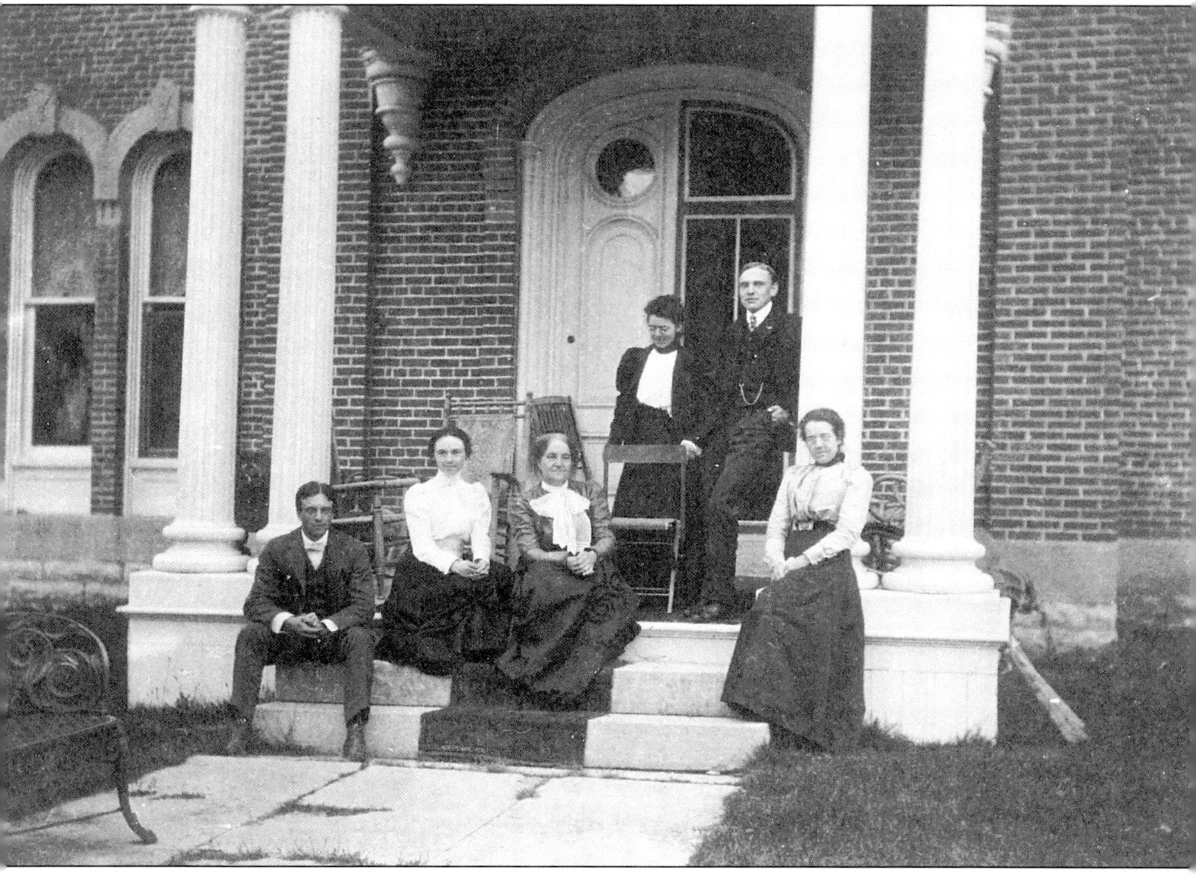

MEMBERS OF THE LARRABEE FAMILY ON THE STEPS OF MONTAUK. From left to right are William Jr., Mrs. William Jr., Mrs. William Sr., Helen, unidentified gentleman, and Anna.

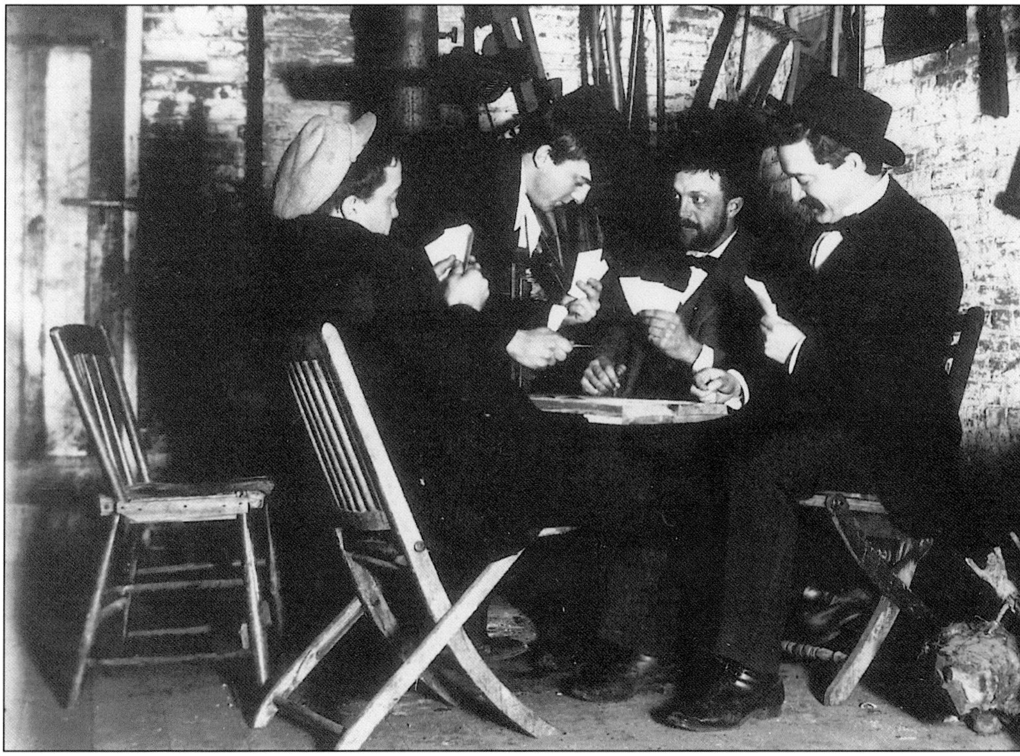

LARRABEES IN THE "WORKSHOP" AT MONTAUK PLAYING CARDS. From left to right are: Charles ?, William Jr., and Frederic and Don Love (husband of Julia).

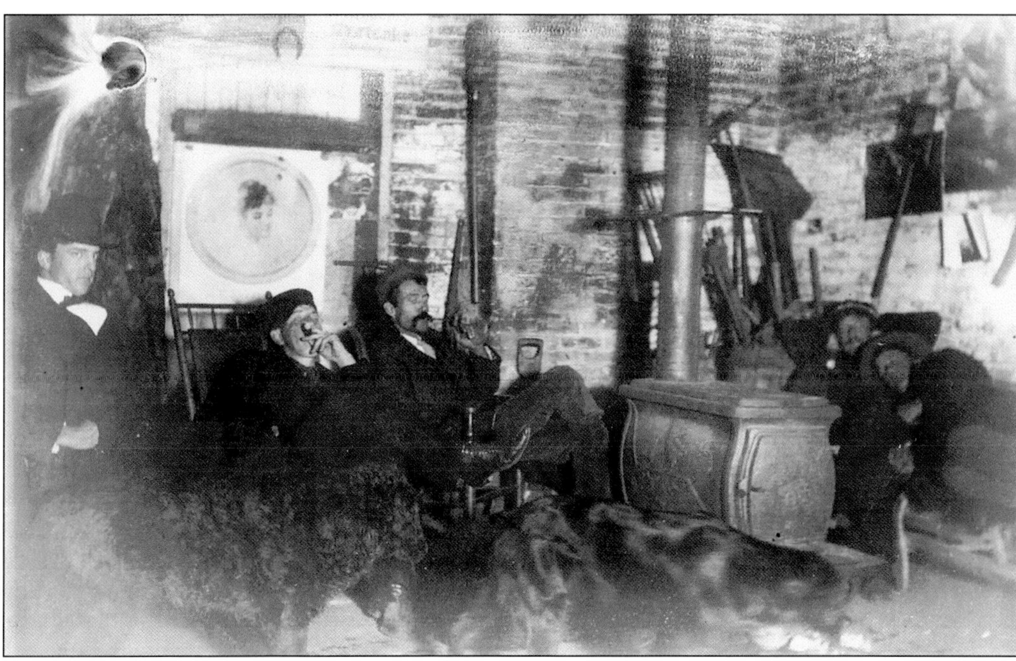

WILLIAM LARRABEE JR. (FAR LEFT) WITH FRIENDS AT MONTAUK.

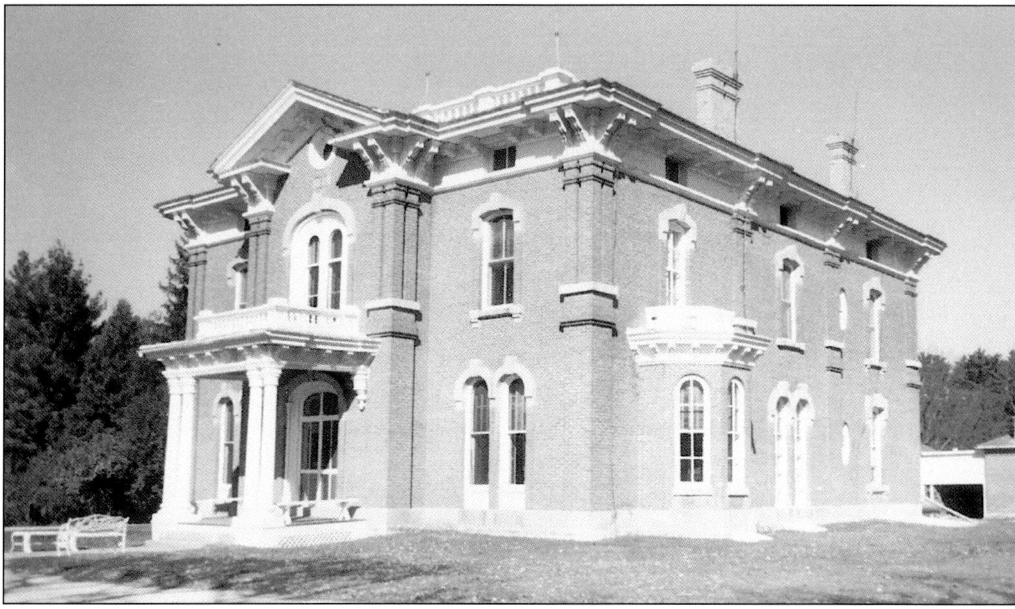

MONTAUK. Montauk is a large two-story brick house in the Italianate style designed by Milwaukee architect E.T. Mix. The 14-room house, built of native brick and limestone, sits on 46 acres surrounded by over 100,000 pine trees. The outbuildings and structure on the grounds include a laundry and summer kitchen, a creamery/ice house, a workshop and wood shed, a water tower with windmill, barn and carriage house, machine shed, outhouse, chicken house, corn cribs, and a hog house.

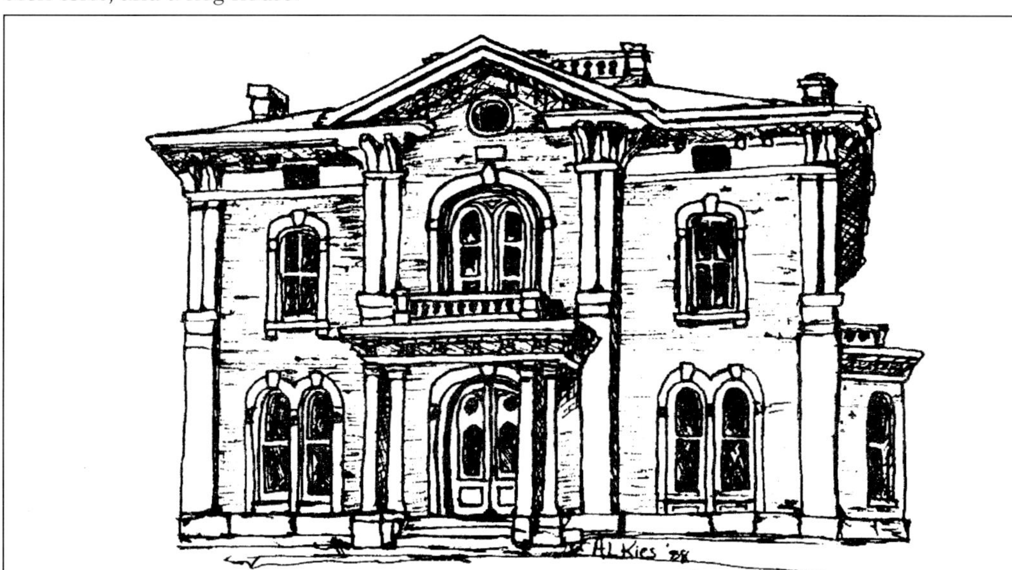

SKETCH OF MONTAUK. Montauk was donated to the State Historical Society of Iowa in 1976. Visitors to this "living home" are treated as honored guests as they tour the elegant rooms of the mansion and investigate the out buildings. The lovely flower gardens are enjoyed, and turkeys are still seen strutting on the grounds.

Bronze Statues of Civil War Heroes on the Grounds at Montauk. Larrabee, a student of the Civil War, commissioned the statues in New York and subsequently had them shipped directly to St. Louis for display at the St. Louis World's Fair Exposition of 1904. When they returned to Clermont, Larrabee wanted to place them in the town street corners, but the townsfolk objected and they were placed up at Montauk. Admiral David Glasgow Farragut is at right. Farragut is noted for the saying, "Damn the torpedoes, full speed ahead!"

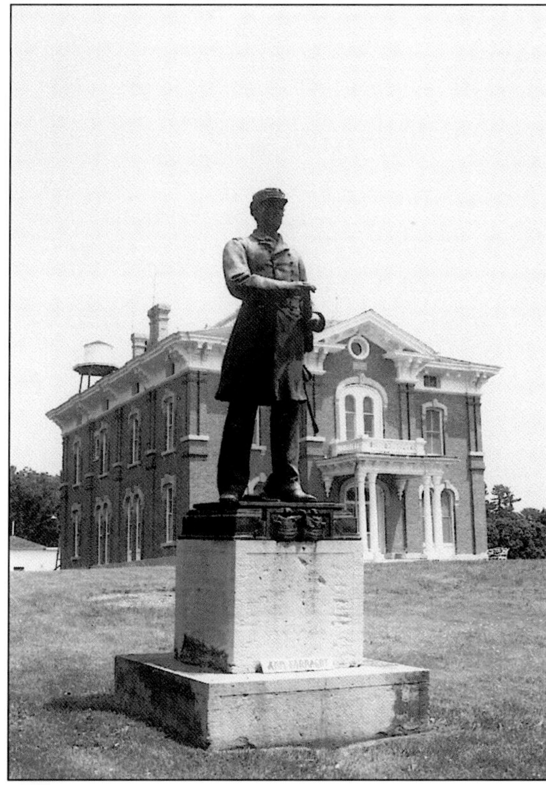

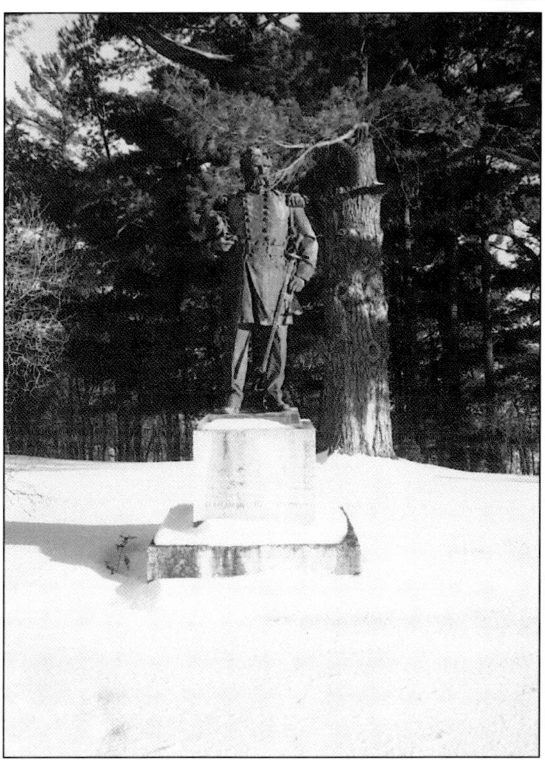

Admiral George Cleveland Dodge.

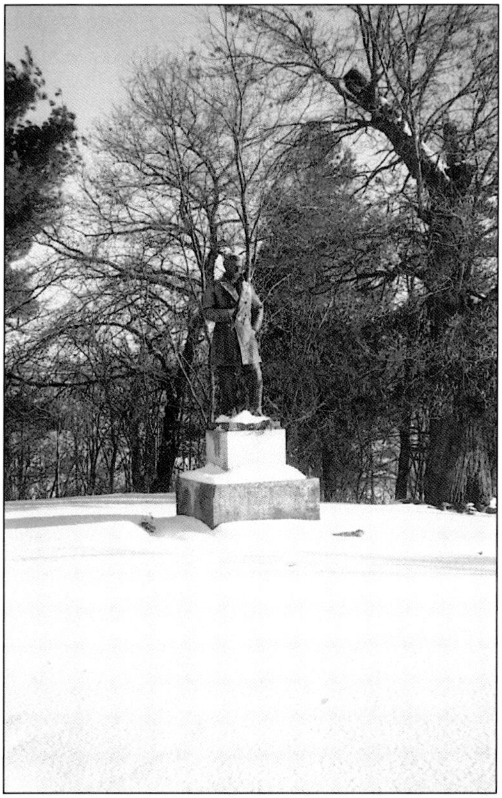

General Ulysses S. Grant.

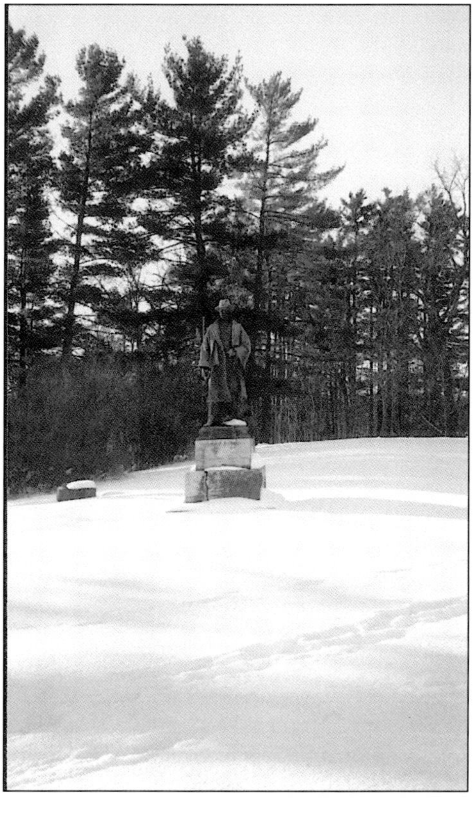

General William Tecumseh Sherman.

Admiral Farragut Looking over the Valley from his Perch at Montauk.

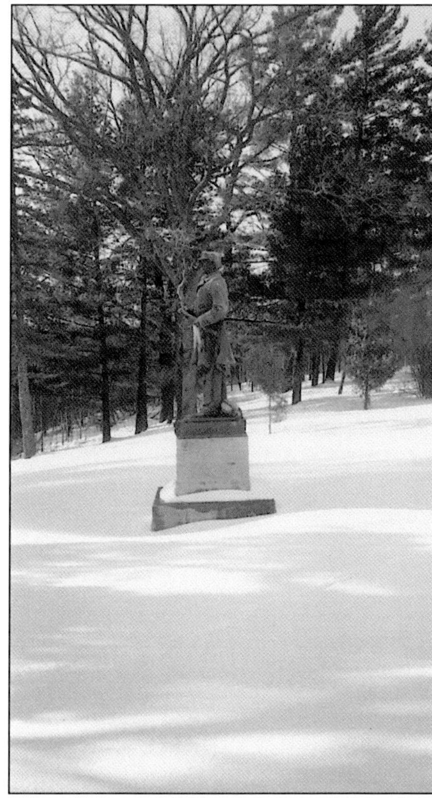

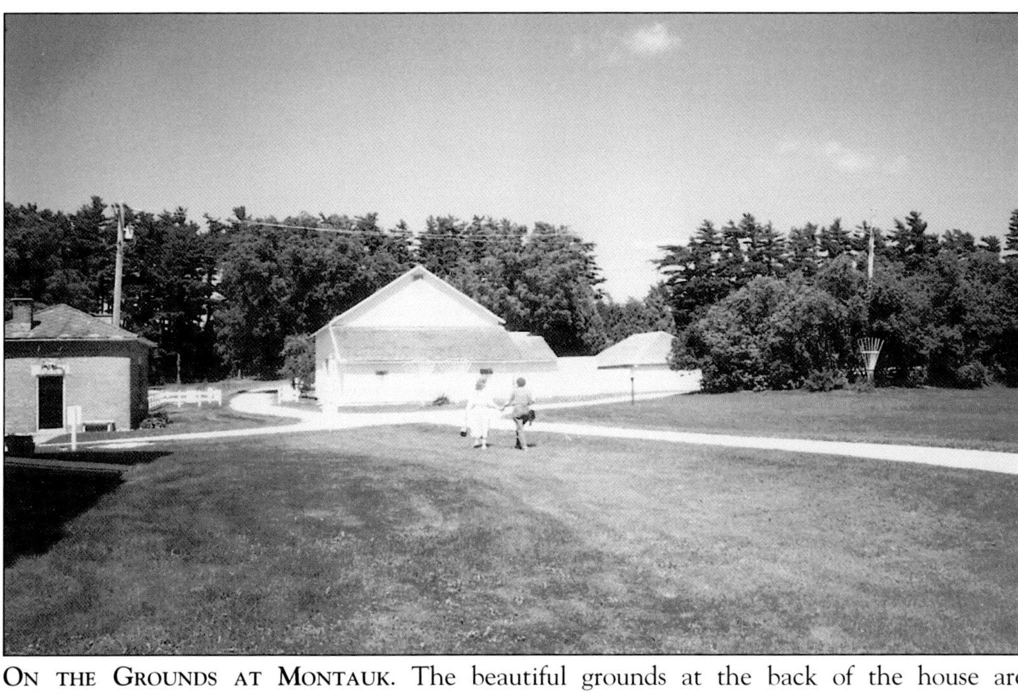

On the Grounds at Montauk. The beautiful grounds at the back of the house are clearly seen.

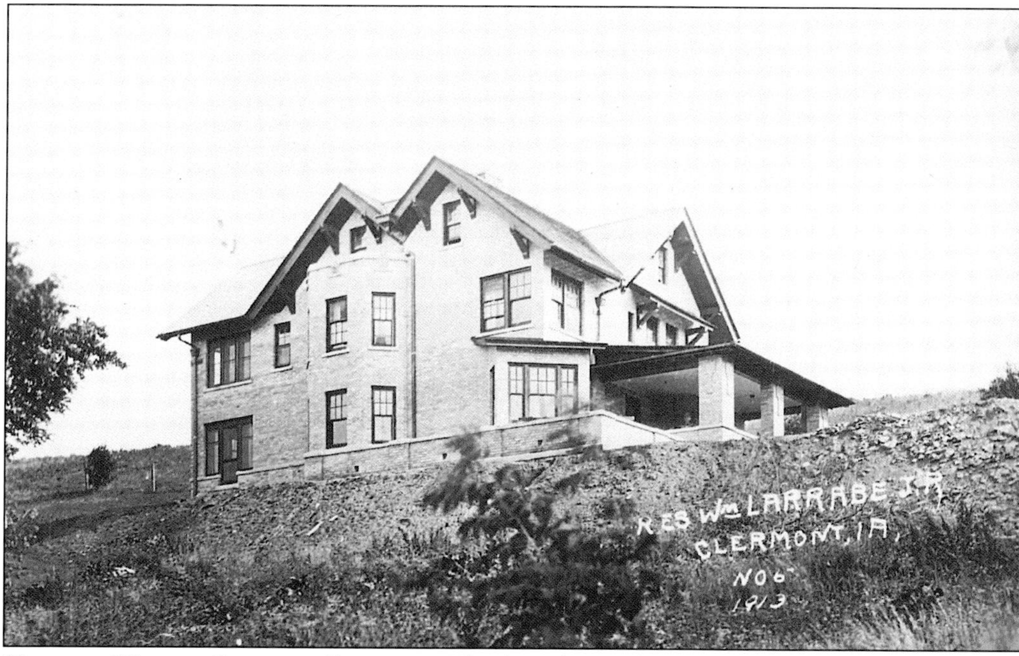

House of William Larrabee Jr., 1913. This large house, built by the son of William Larrabee Sr., is located just below Montauk.

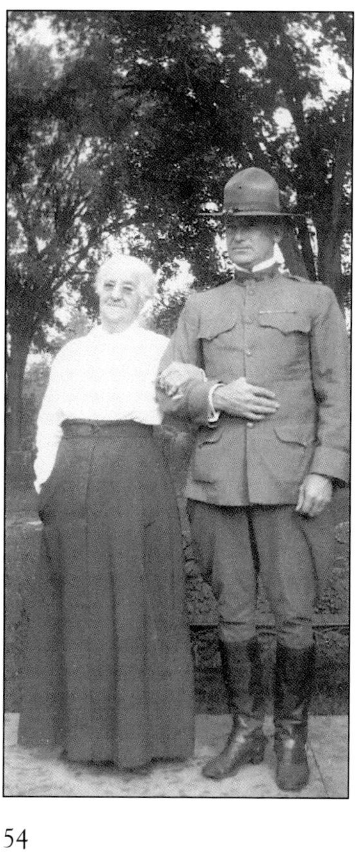

Mrs. William Larrabee Sr. with Colonel C.B. Robbins on the Grounds of Montauk. Robbins, the husband of Julia Larrabee, served in the First World War.

Governor and Mrs. William Larrabee Sr. on their 50th Wedding Anniversary.

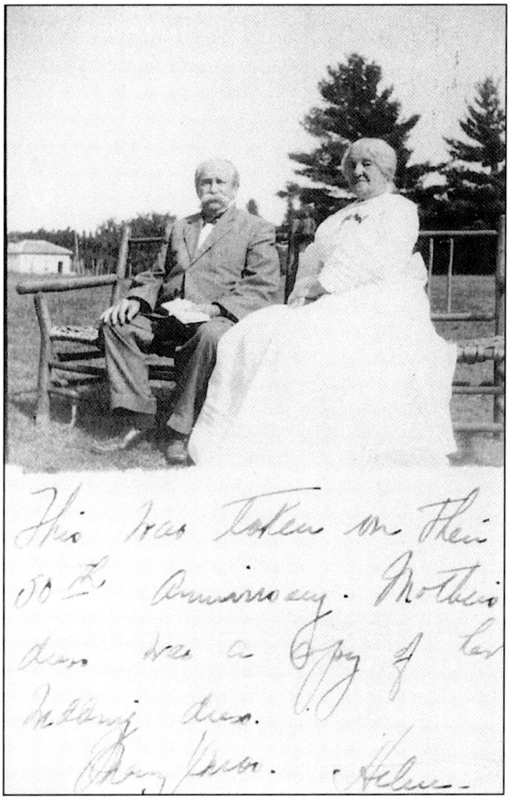

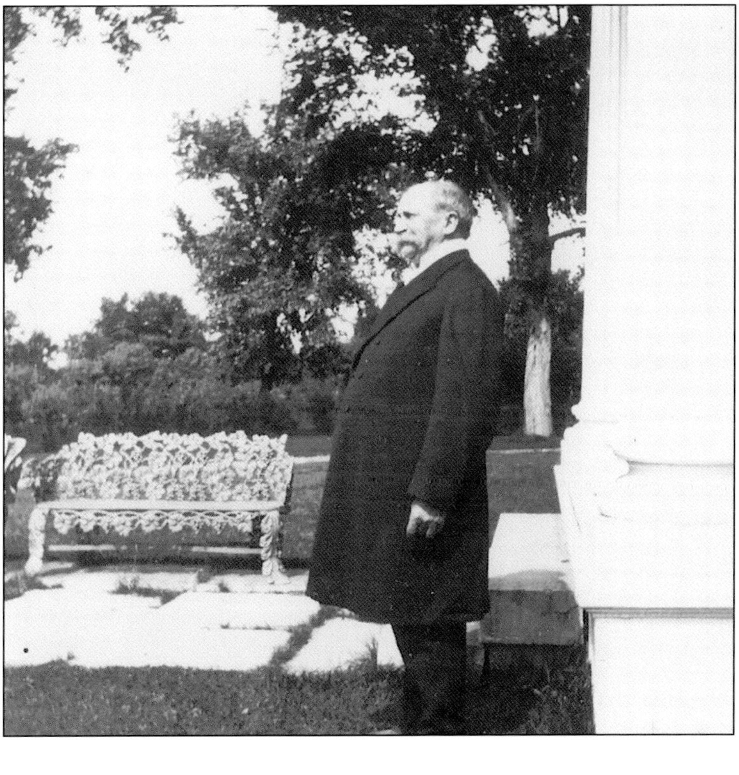

Governor William Larrabee on the Front Porch at Montauk.

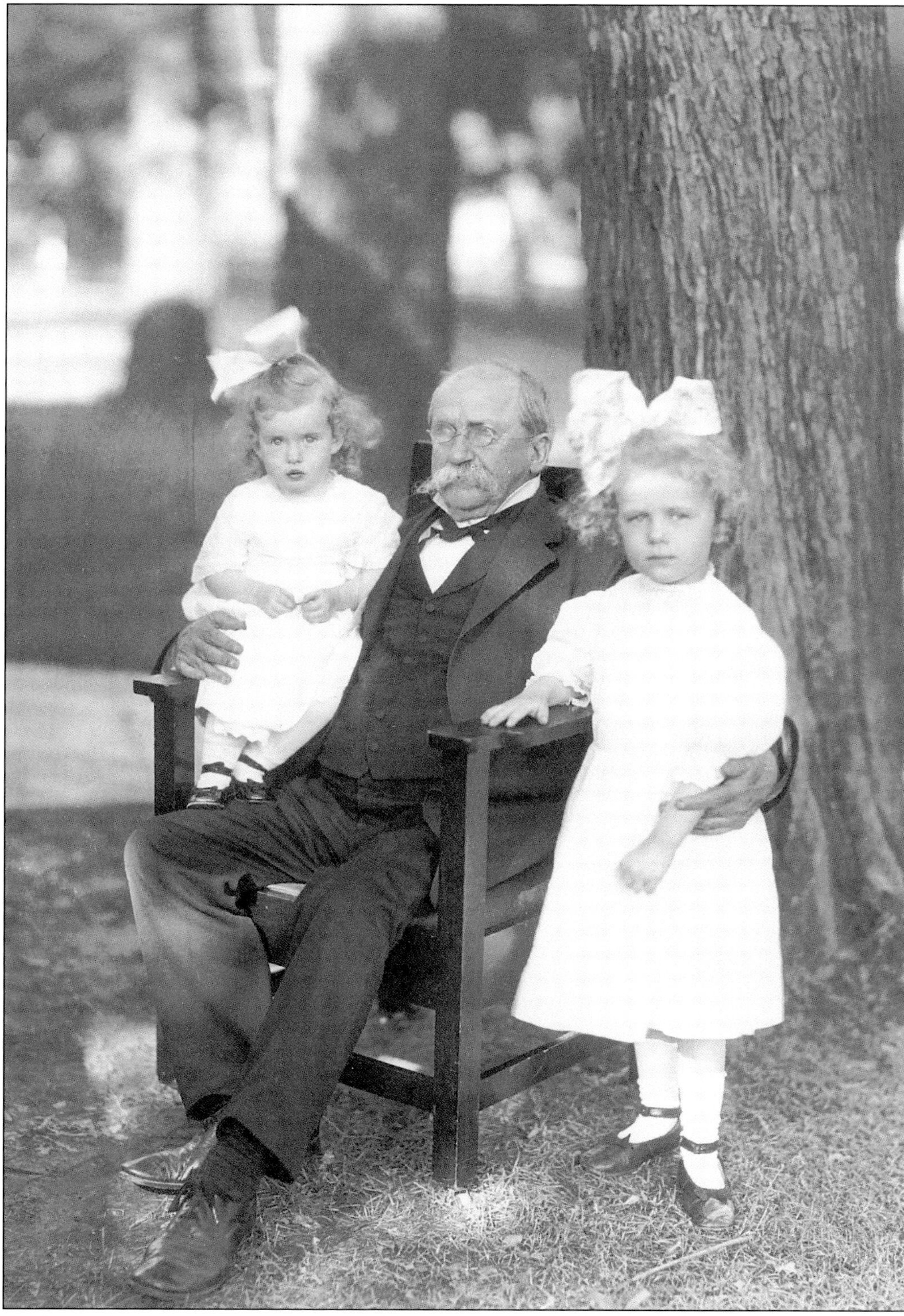

EX-GOVERNOR WILLIAM LARRABEE WITH TWO OF HIS GRANDCHILDREN ON THE GROUNDS AT MONTAUK.

Five

Churches and Schools

Churches and schools figure very early in the history of Clermont. Religious organizations and education helped define the town and the people. Early church buildings included St. Peter's Catholic Church, the Episcopal Church of the Saviour, West Clermont Lutheran Church, East Clermont Lutheran Church (outside of Clermont), the Methodist church, and the Union Sunday School.

Clermont pupils probably first attended school in a log cabin as early as 1850 with Mrs. Edwin Stedman as their teacher. Between 1852 and 1854, school was probably taught in a two-story frame structure near the river (also the former residence of Chris Miller) with Miss Laura Hotchkiss as teacher. In 1854 a brick structure was built on Vine Street near the Methodist church. The Independent School District of Clermont was formed in 1860, and a new building replaced the old between 1867–68. A new grade school was completed as well; a new high school building replaced this structure in 1914. The Larrabee School building, financed by William Larrabee Sr., was completed in 1912 and was considered the "ideal school." Both the high school and the Larrabee buildings are still very much a part of Clermont.

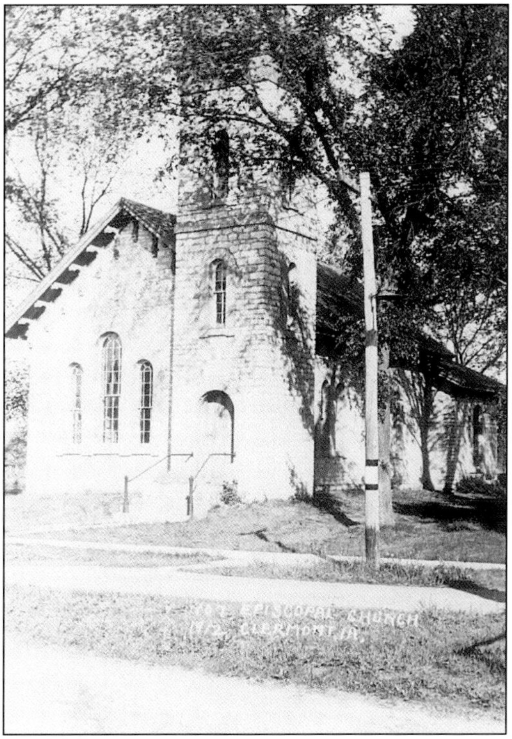

EPISCOPAL CHURCH OF THE SAVIOUR, 1912.

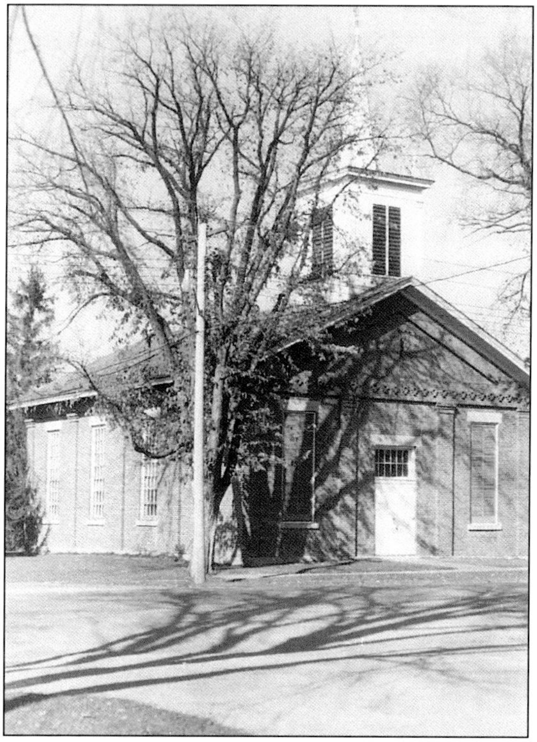

Presbyterian Church and Union Sunday School. The Clermont Presbyterian Church was built in 1858. In the 1870s the church became non-denominational and renamed the Union Sunday School. It is now the property of the Iowa State Historical Society and is listed on the National Registry of Historical Places. It is currently used as a community meeting place.

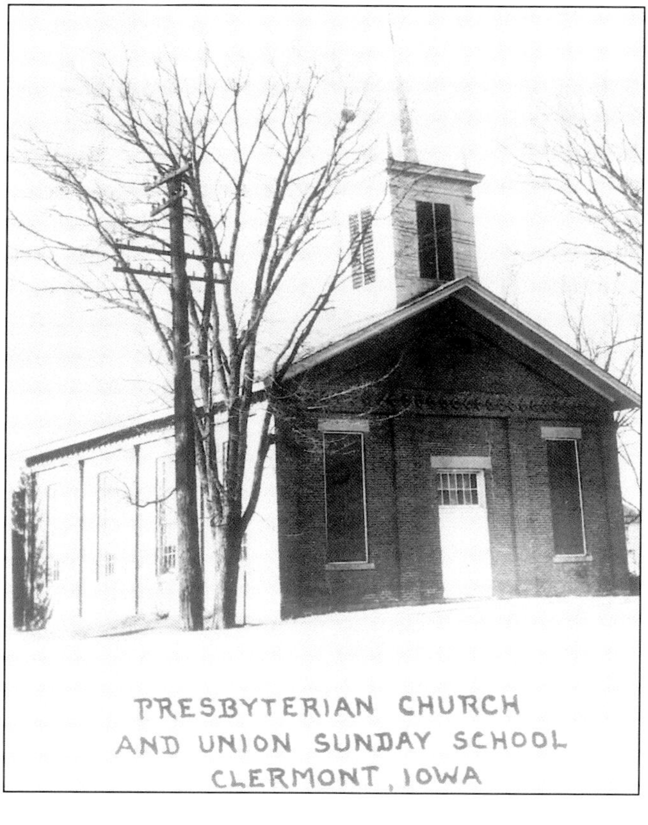

Presbyterian Church and Union Sunday School.

ORGAN IN THE UNION SUNDAY SCHOOL. In 1896, the Larrabees ordered a magnificent organ from the Kimball Company in Chicago for the Union Sunday School. It measured 22 feet wide, nine feet six inches deep, and over 19 feet high. Now completely restored and completely operational, it remains a showpiece of the town.

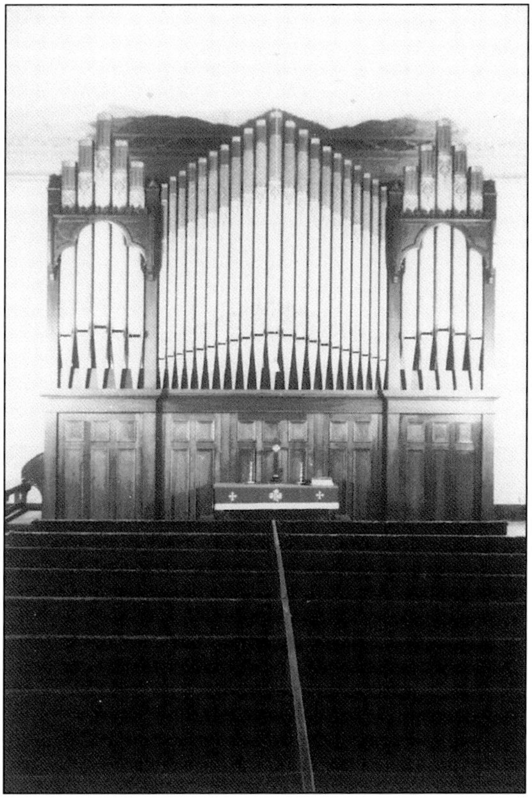

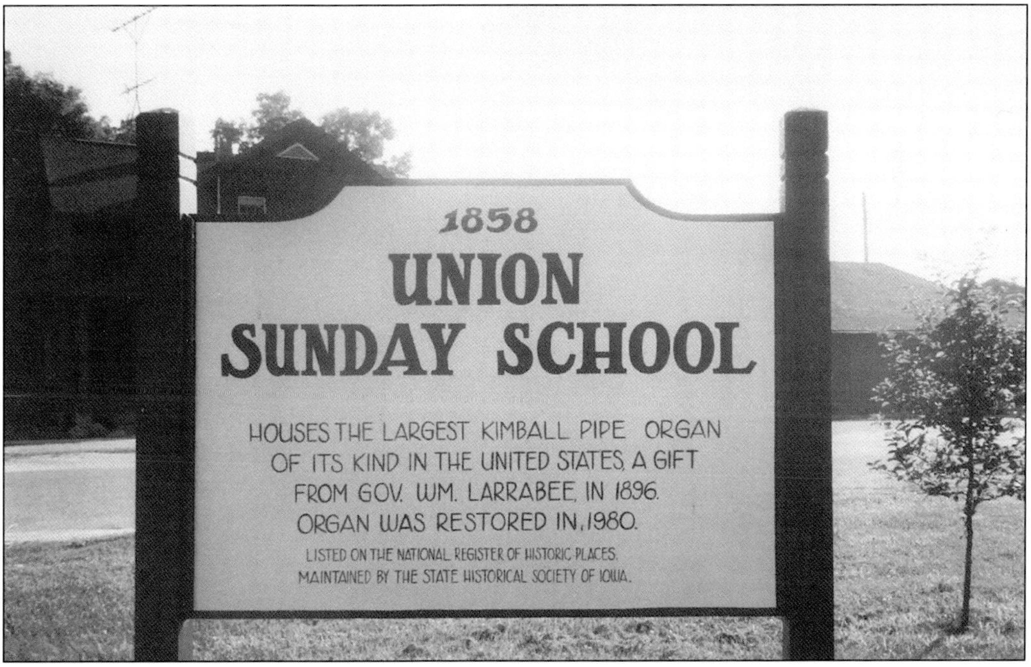

UNION SUNDAY SCHOOL. This building houses the largest Kimball pipe organ of its kind in the United States.

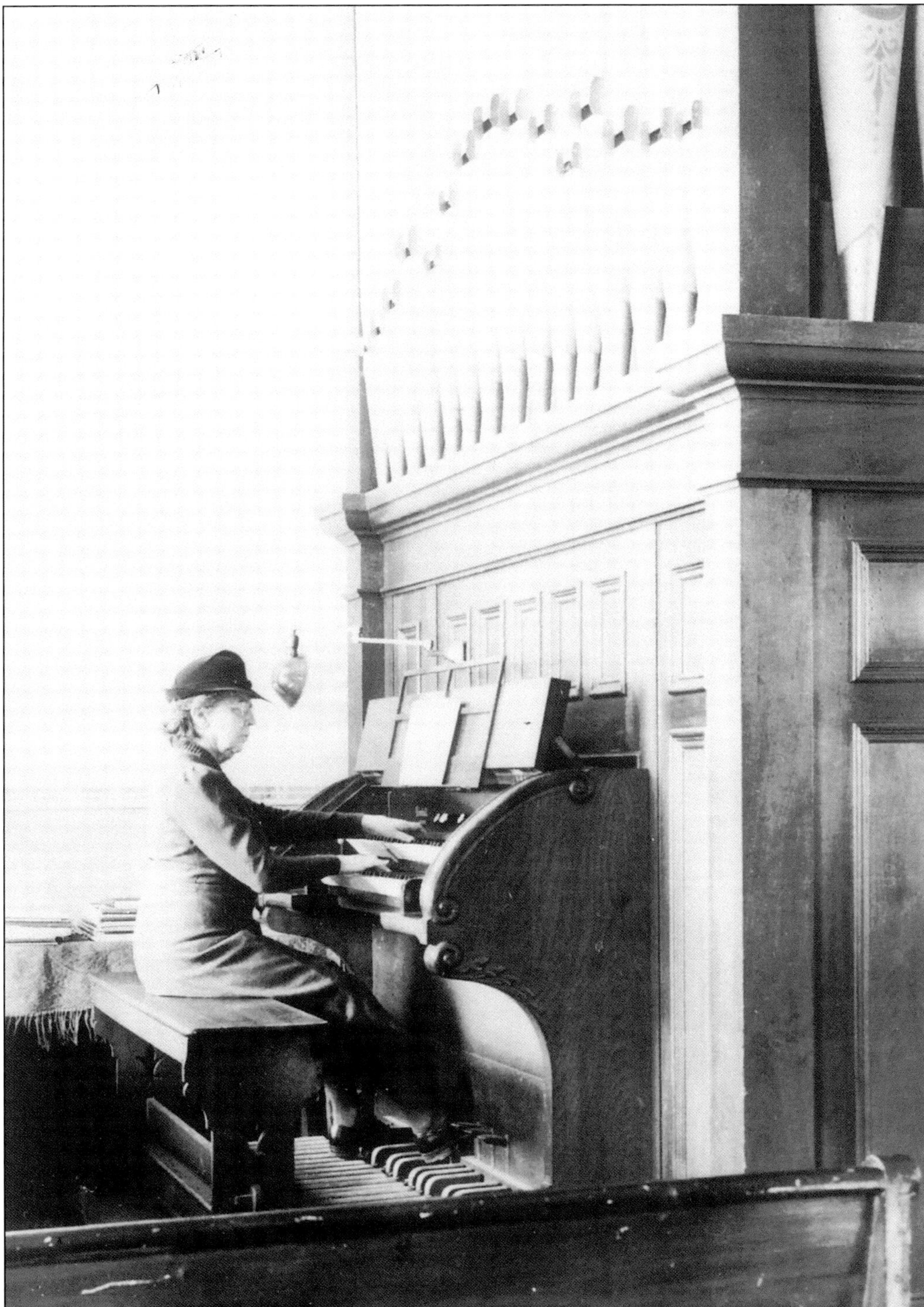

ANNA LARRABEE AT THE ORGAN. The Larrabee family were prominent members in the Clermont Presbyterian Church. Anna Larrabee was organist of the church for many years until her death in 1965.

St. Peter's Catholic Church. The church was founded by Irish immigrants in 1842. A small frame church was built in 1860 and was replaced by a new masonry structure (this photograph) completed in 1882. The church was rebuilt after it was destroyed in the tornado of 1913.

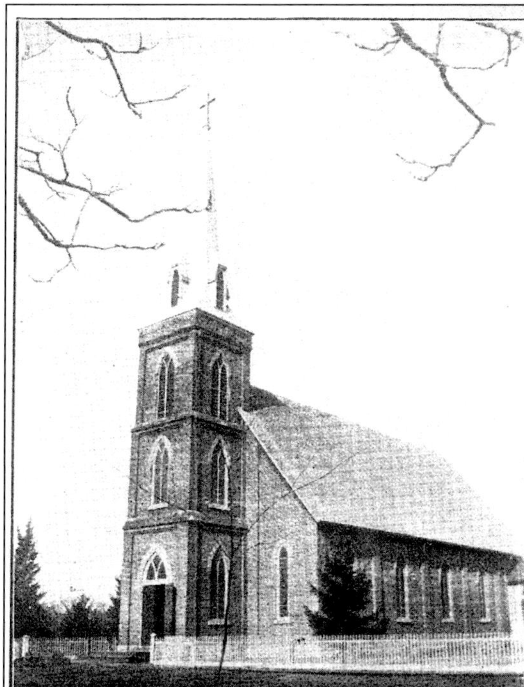

ST. PETER'S CATHOLIC CHURCH, CLERMONT, IOWA

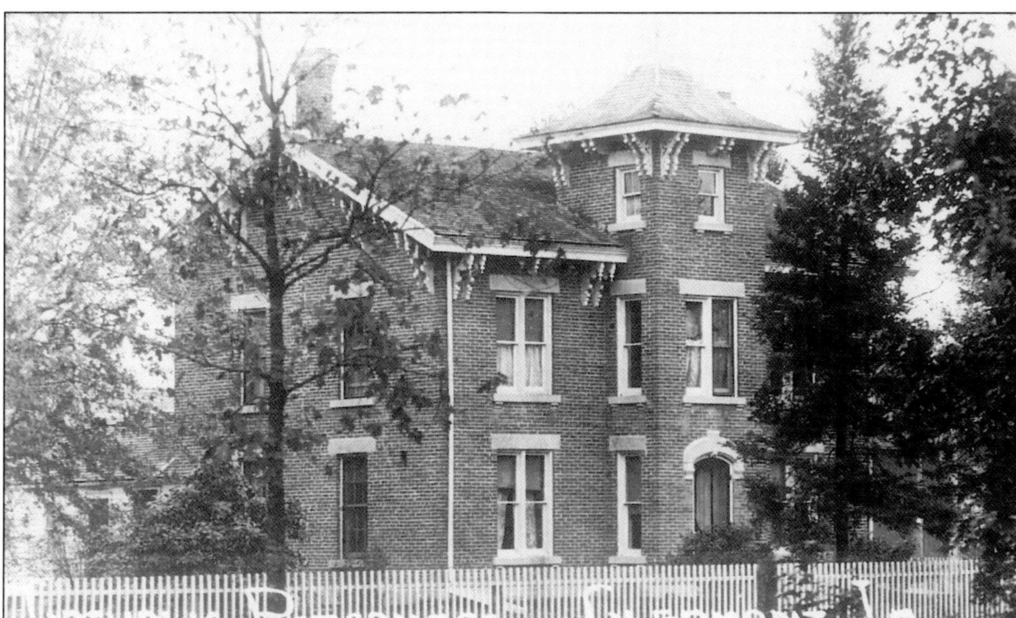

View of Catholic Parsonage. The Parsonage was completed in 1872 at the cost of $5,000.

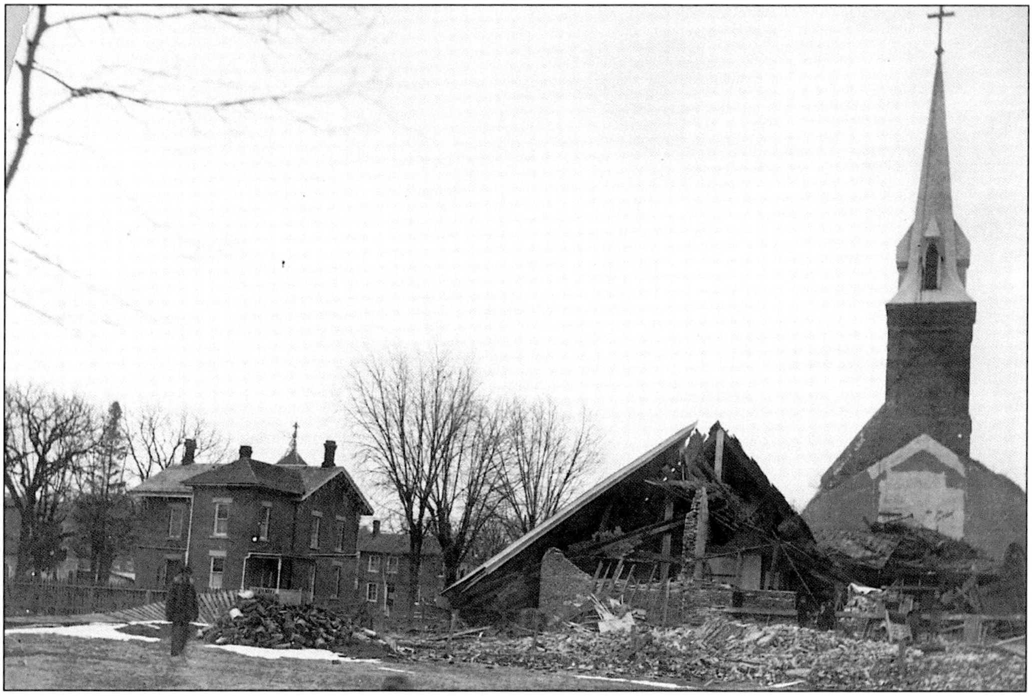

St. Peter's Catholic Church after the Tornado, March 23, 1913. "Word from Clermont is that the storm of Sunday evening did much damage to Fayette County . . . The storm's chief damage was at Clermont where the Catholic church was totally destroyed. A $3,000 pipe organ, a gift of the late Governor Larrabee, was reduced to a heap of kindling wood. The total loss of the church is estimated at $25,000." (Courtesy of *Free Irish*, Webster City, IA, 1913.)

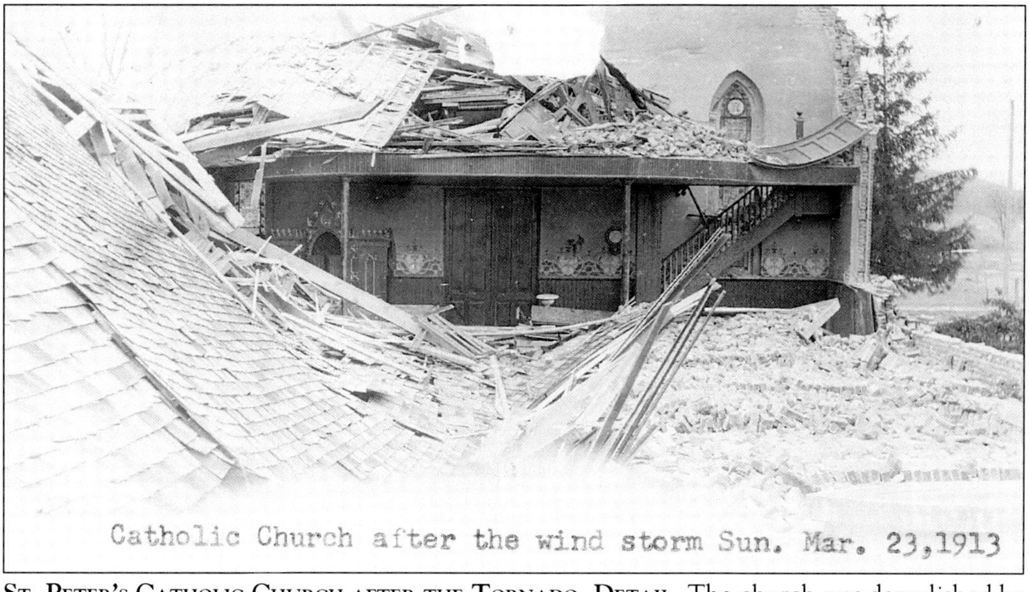

St. Peter's Catholic Church after the Tornado, Detail. The church was demolished by the tornado with the exception of the vestibule and the tower. The tower and the basement foundation were used in the construction of a new church.

EPISCOPAL CHURCH OF THE SAVIOUR. "Age and weather have turned the rough stones to a beautiful soft gray. The long narrow windows and the tall square tower add much to the beauty of this 'Little Stone Church.'" (From *Stories of Early Fayette County History* by Grace Roark, 1938.) The church was built in 1867 from stone quarried from Williams's quarry east of the town. This unique structure is one of three similar churches in the United States built by Mrs. Frances Vinton.

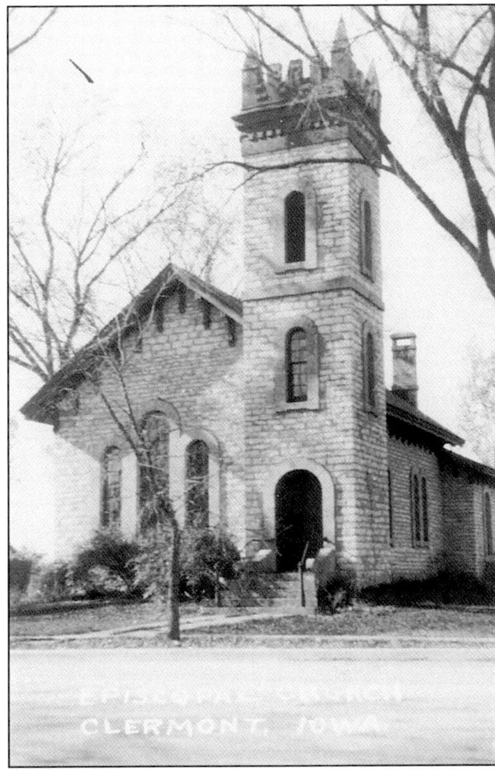

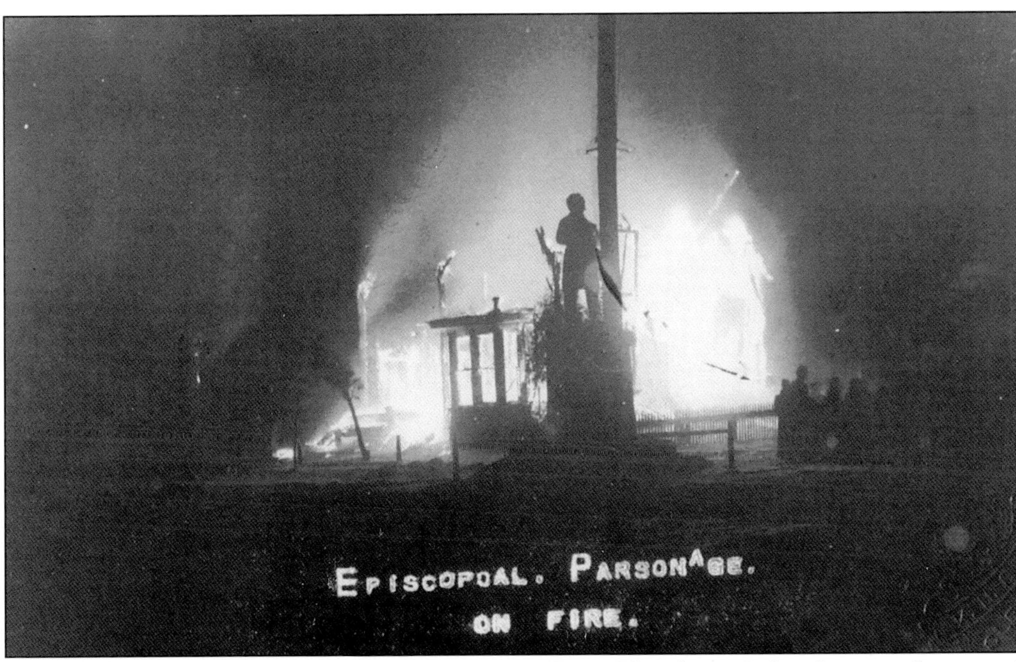

DRAMATIC SHOT OF EPISCOPAL PARSONAGE ON FIRE. The date of this fire is unknown. A photograph of the Episcopal parsonage before is unfortunately not available. The statue of David Henderson is vividly outlined by the flames. Kettle Groth, a photographer who owned a shop in Clermont, took this photograph.

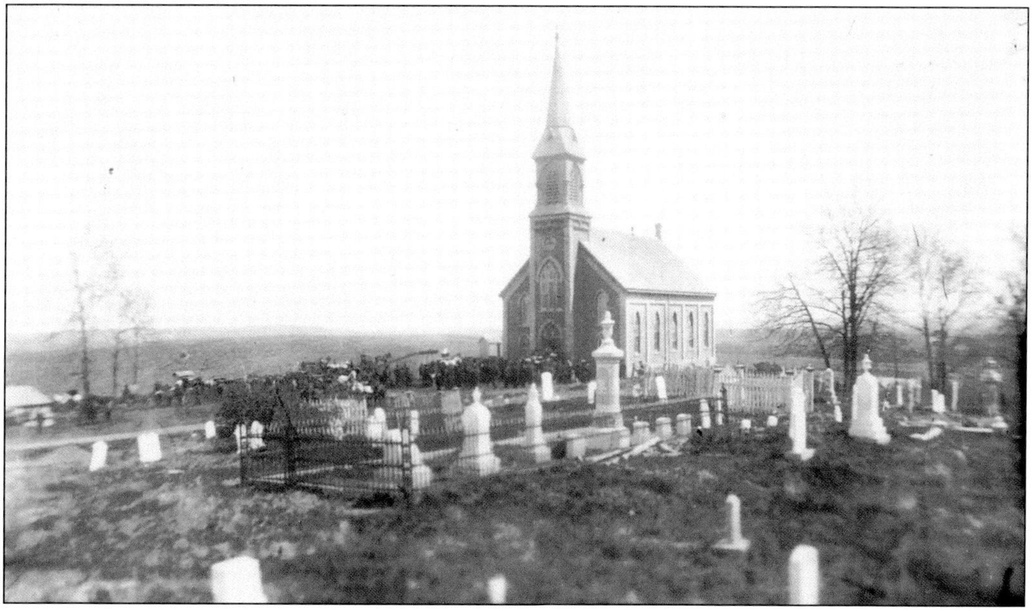

East Clermont Lutheran Church. The East Lutheran Congregation organized outside of Clermont. This remarkable stone church is located on the road to Gunder.

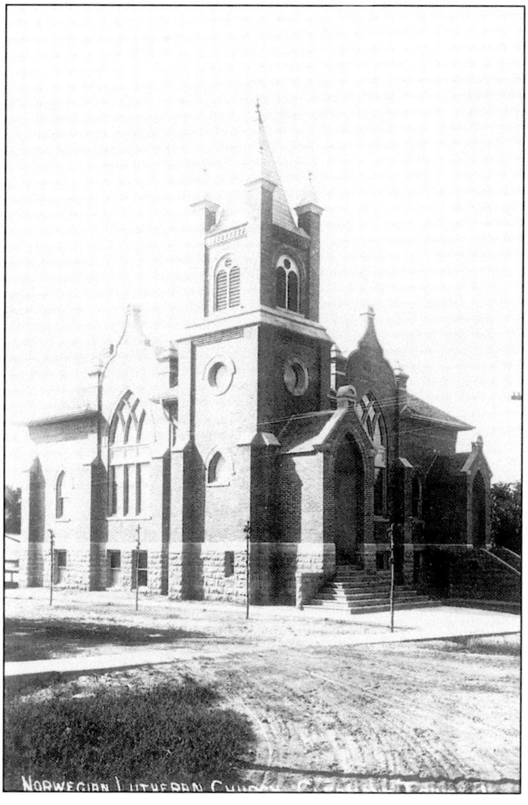

West Clermont (Norwegian) Lutheran Church. The Lutherans of Clermont who were attending the East Clermont Lutheran Church decided to build a new church in 1915. The church was constructed at the cost of $15,000 and remained unchanged until 1962.

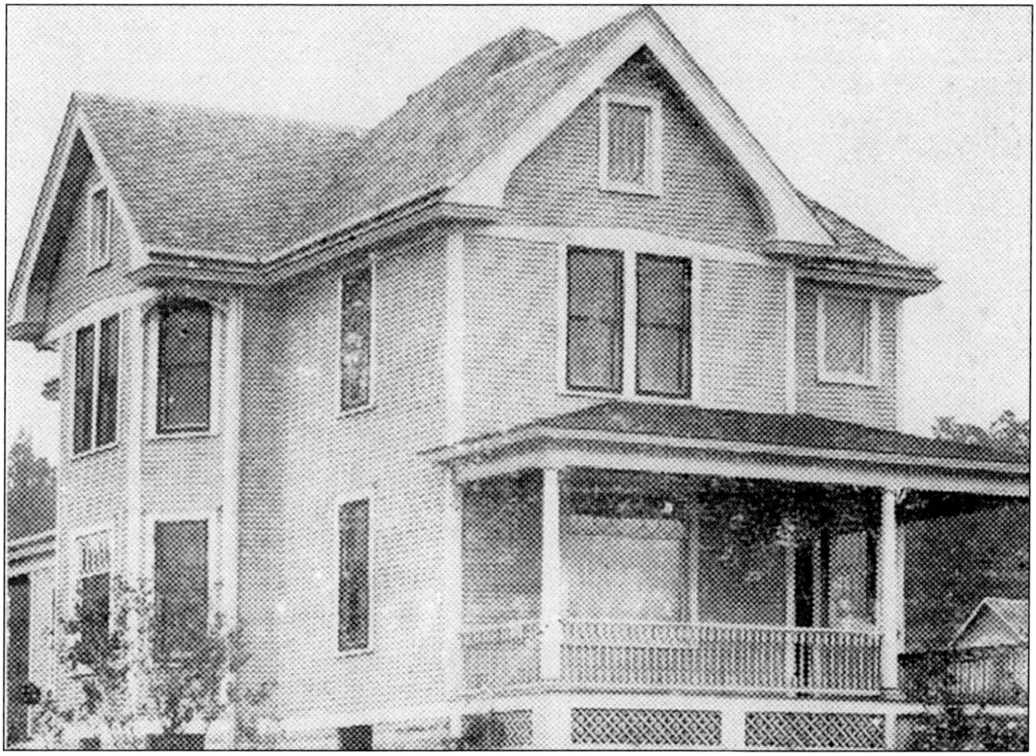

NORWEGIAN LUTHERAN CHURCH PARSONAGE. The date of completion and cost of the parsonage is not known.

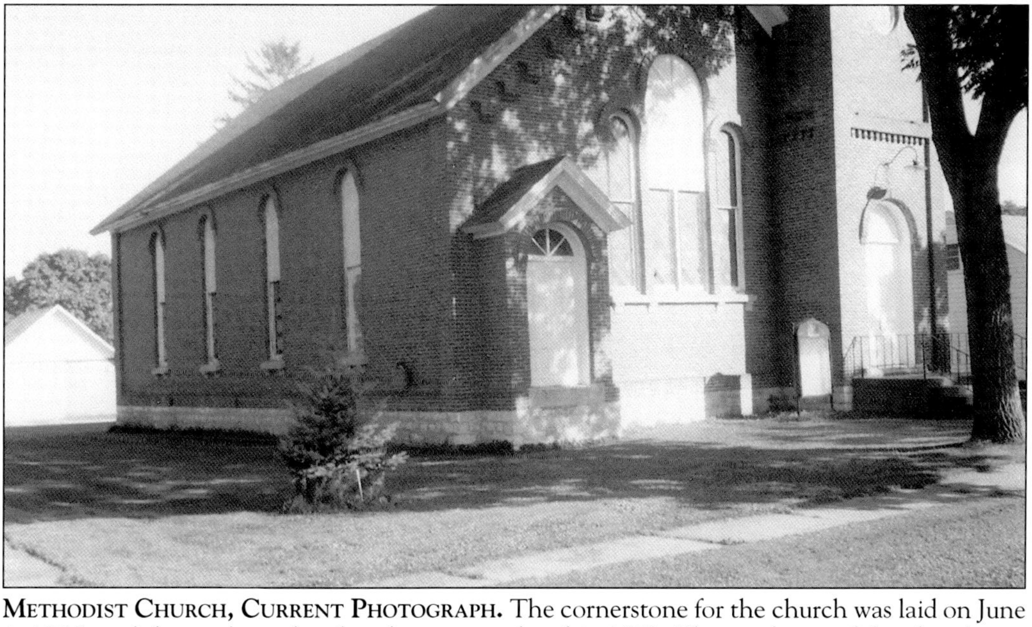

METHODIST CHURCH, CURRENT PHOTOGRAPH. The cornerstone for the church was laid on June 4, 1866, and the work on the church was completed in 1873. The total cost of the church was $5,432.94. Members closed the church in 1913 due to lack of support. Eventually the church building became a Masonic Lodge in 1925.

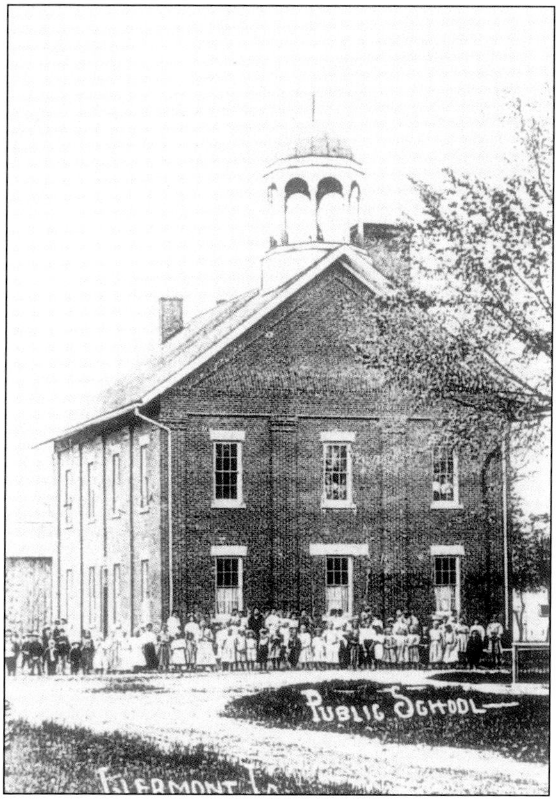

Clermont Public School Building. The distinctive round cupola of the "new" brick schoolhouse built between 1867–68 is visible in the lithograph of Clermont in 1875. The building was used until 1913. It was eventually torn down and replaced with the new high school.

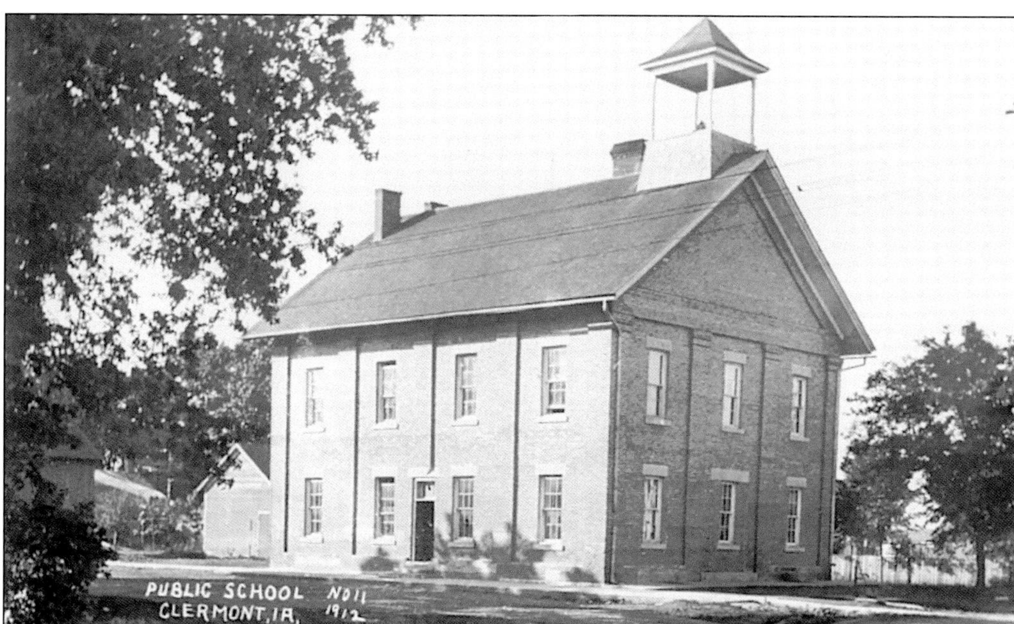

Public School, c. 1912. Here is the Public School with a different style cupola.

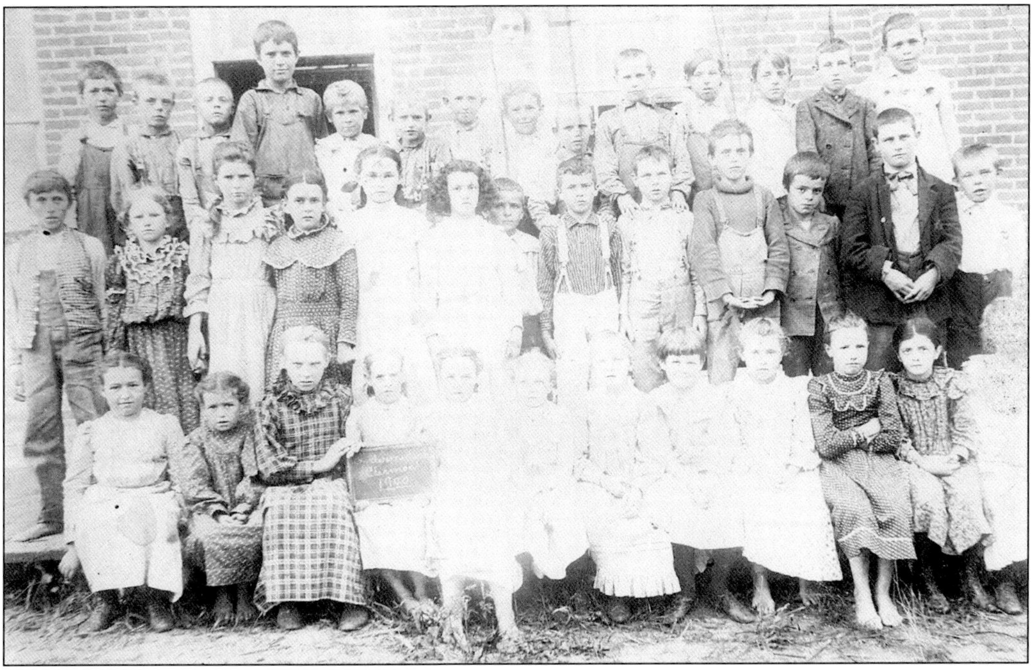

Class Portraits at the Public School. This is a class portrait in front of the Public School, Intermediate Class, 1900.

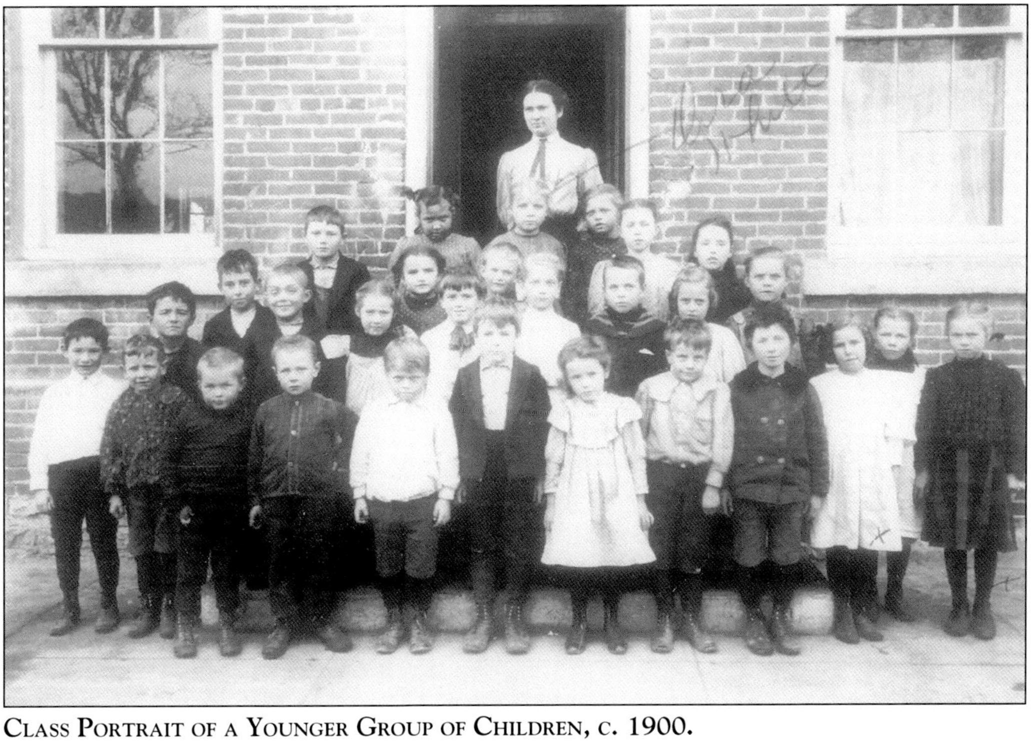

Class Portrait of a Younger Group of Children, c. 1900.

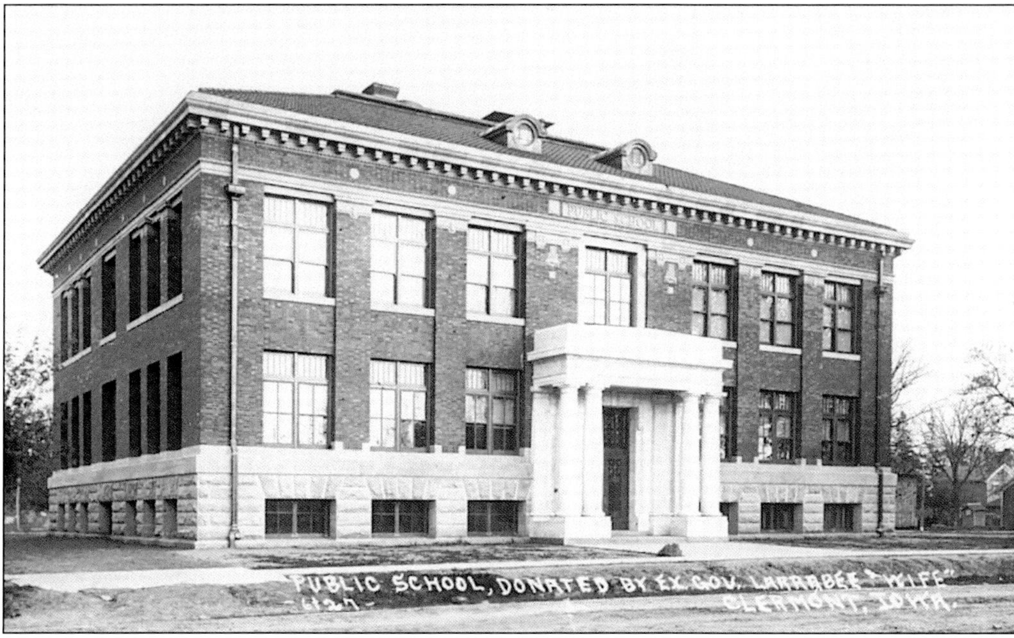

LARRABEE SCHOOL, 1912. The building, donated by the Larrabees, was the most modern of its time. Mrs. William Larrabee Sr. was a driving force behind this project. This magnificent building, a massive structure of steel, marble, stone, and brick, included many up-to-date features including an auditorium on the second floor equipped with piano, stage, and curtains. It was also fireproof. The structure remains a monument to the progressive views on education held by the Larrabee family.

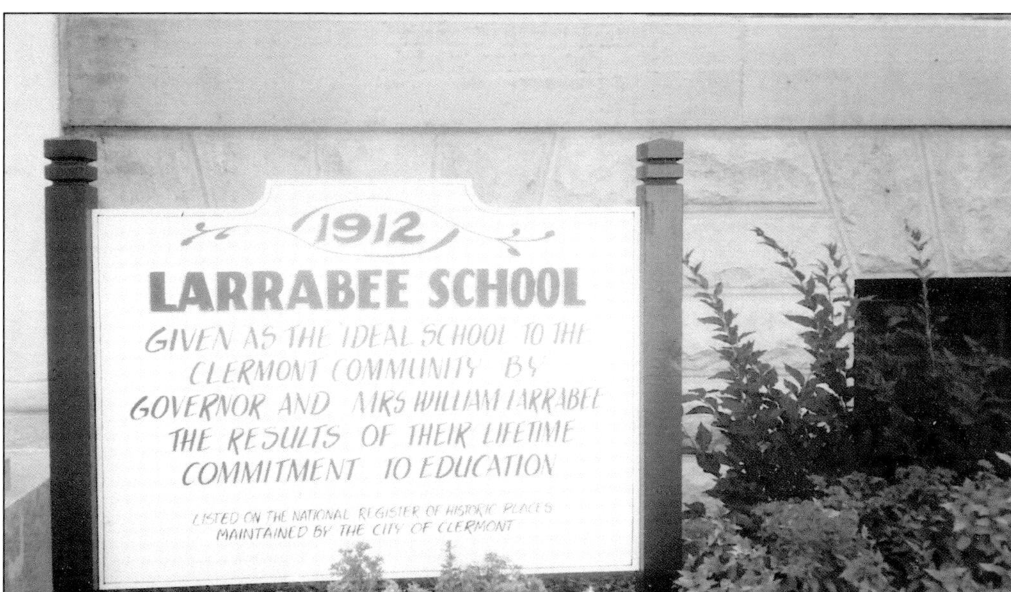

THE IDEAL SCHOOL.

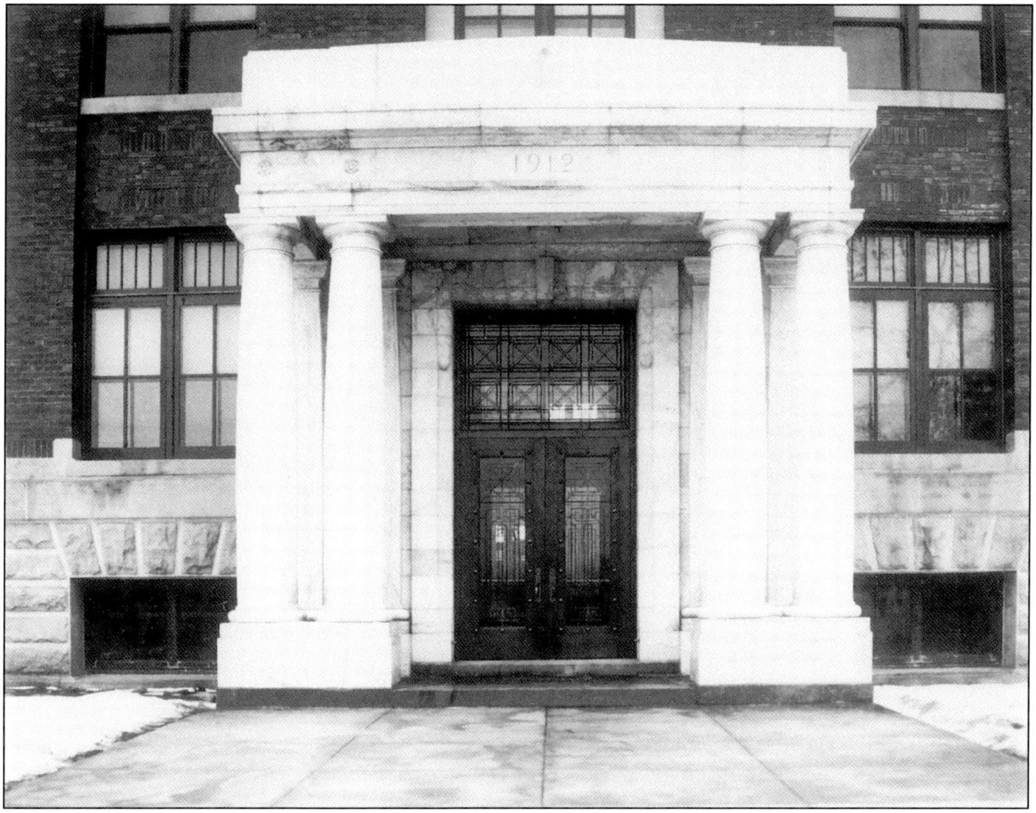

Entrance to the Larrabee School Building. The distinctive marble facade of the Larrabee School is a showcase piece.

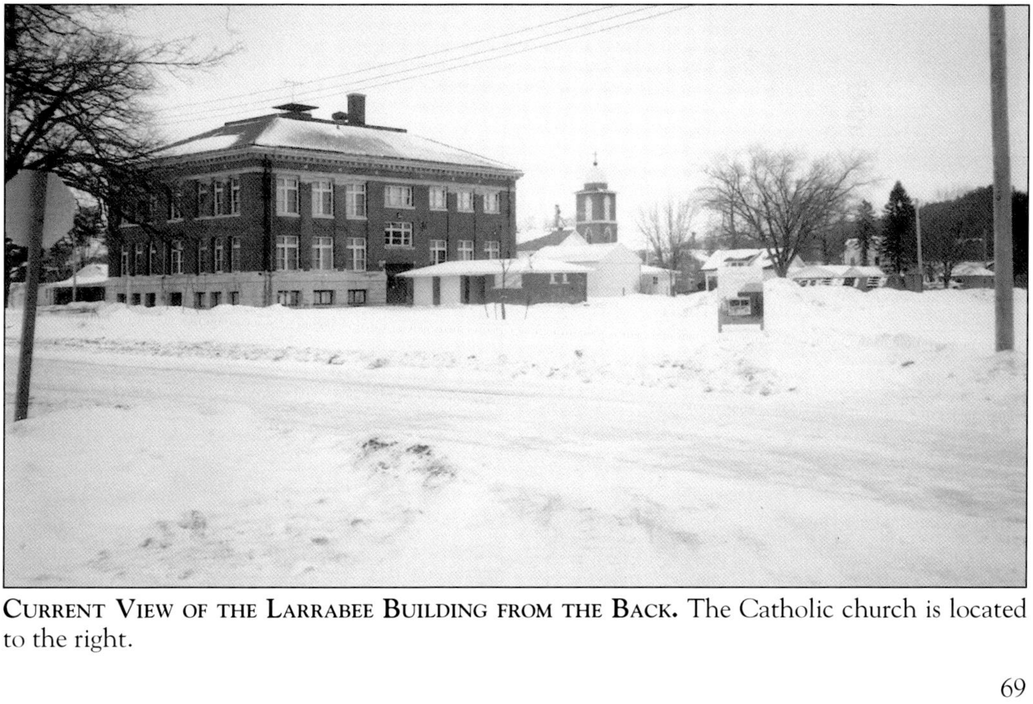

Current View of the Larrabee Building from the Back. The Catholic church is located to the right.

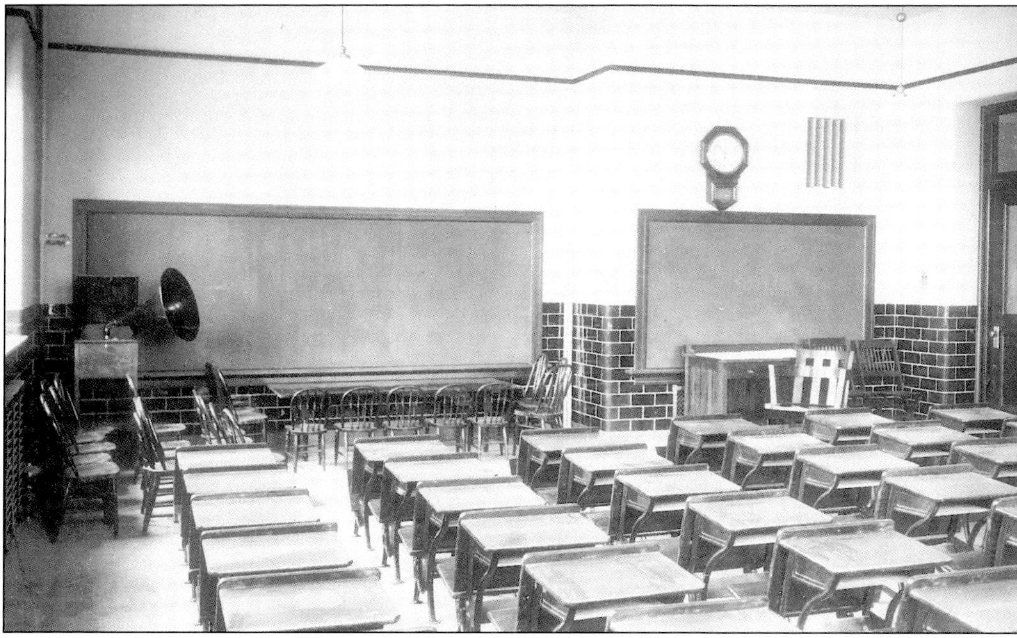

INTERIOR OF ONE OF THE SCHOOL ROOMS IN THE LARRABEE BUILDING.

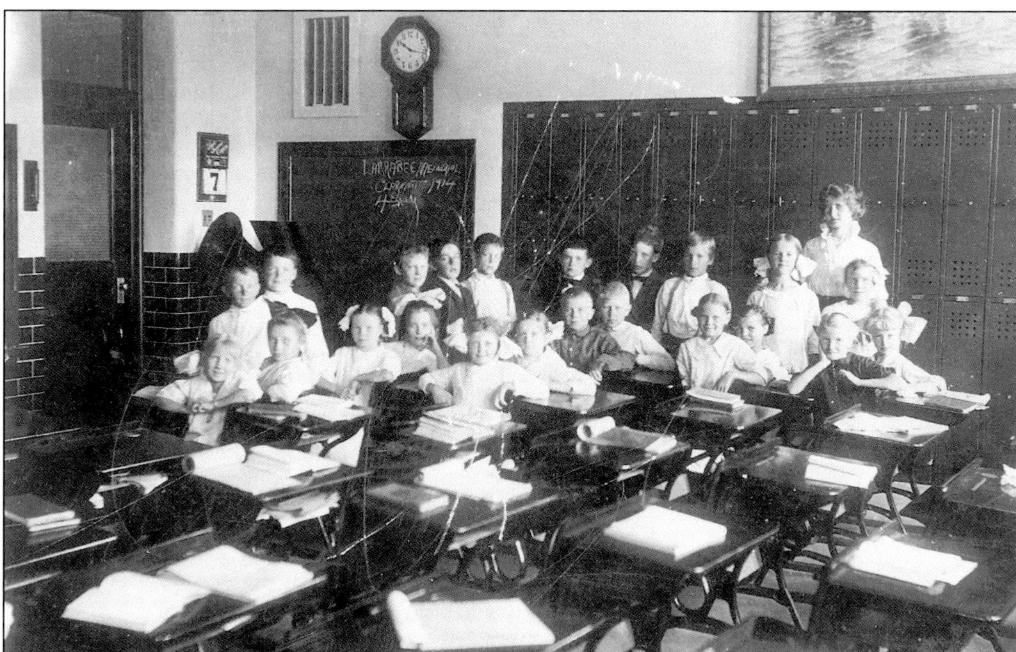

INTERIOR OF LARRABEE BUILDING WITH STUDENTS, FOURTH GRADE CLASS, 1914. Some of the children are identified from left to right: Charlie Sullivan, Clarence Mecklenburg, Gilbert ?, Richie ?, Bernard Callahan, Harvey Shipten, Ester Hauge, Melta Busser, Irene Howard, Marjorie Sullivan, Alta Olson, Florence Weden, Grace Miller, Vivian Johnson, Chris Gutcher, Bill Paulson, Gladys Guss, Vera Gruver, Grace Martin, and Alma Koland. The teacher is Miss Nina Kroeg (?).

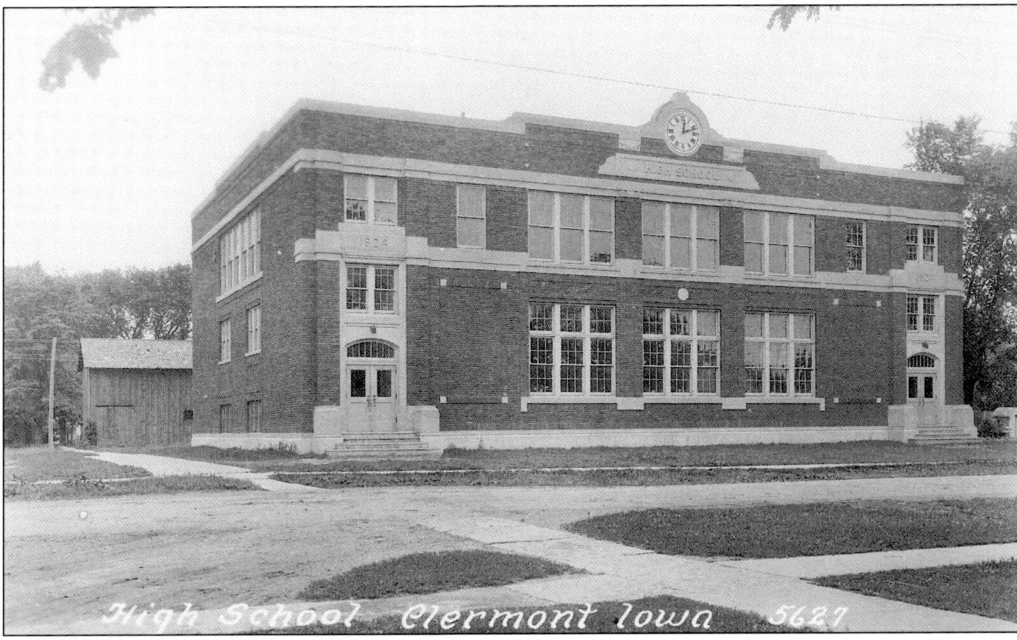

High School with Distinctive Tower Clock. The building was completed in 1922 and replaced the old Public School.

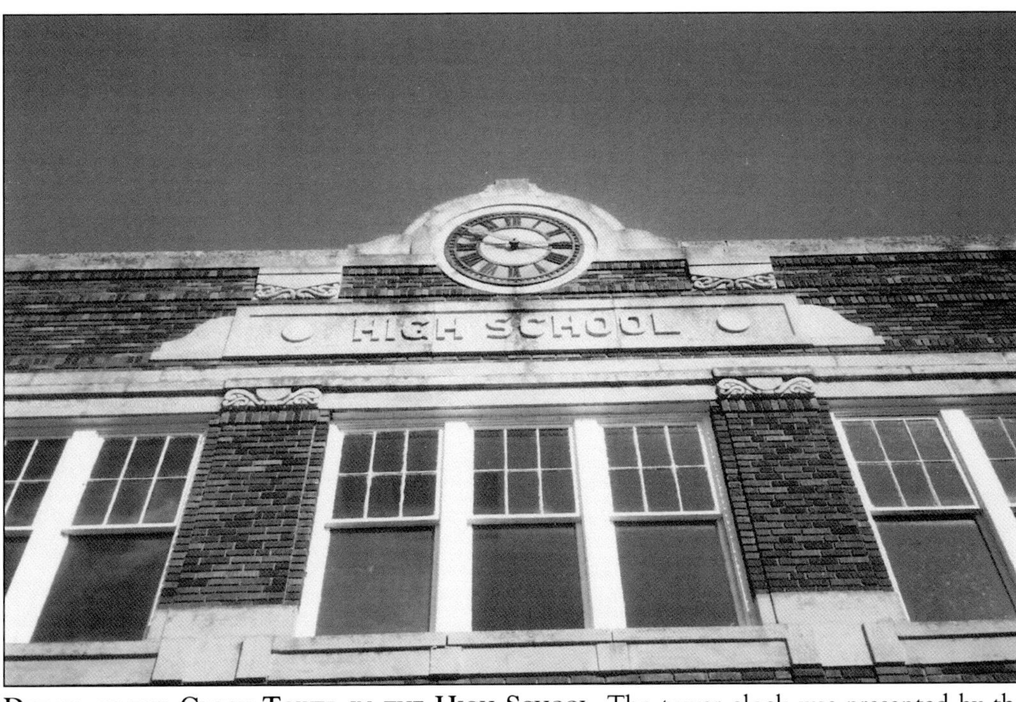

Detail of the Clock Tower in the High School. The tower clock was presented by the Ladies Aid Society in 1925.

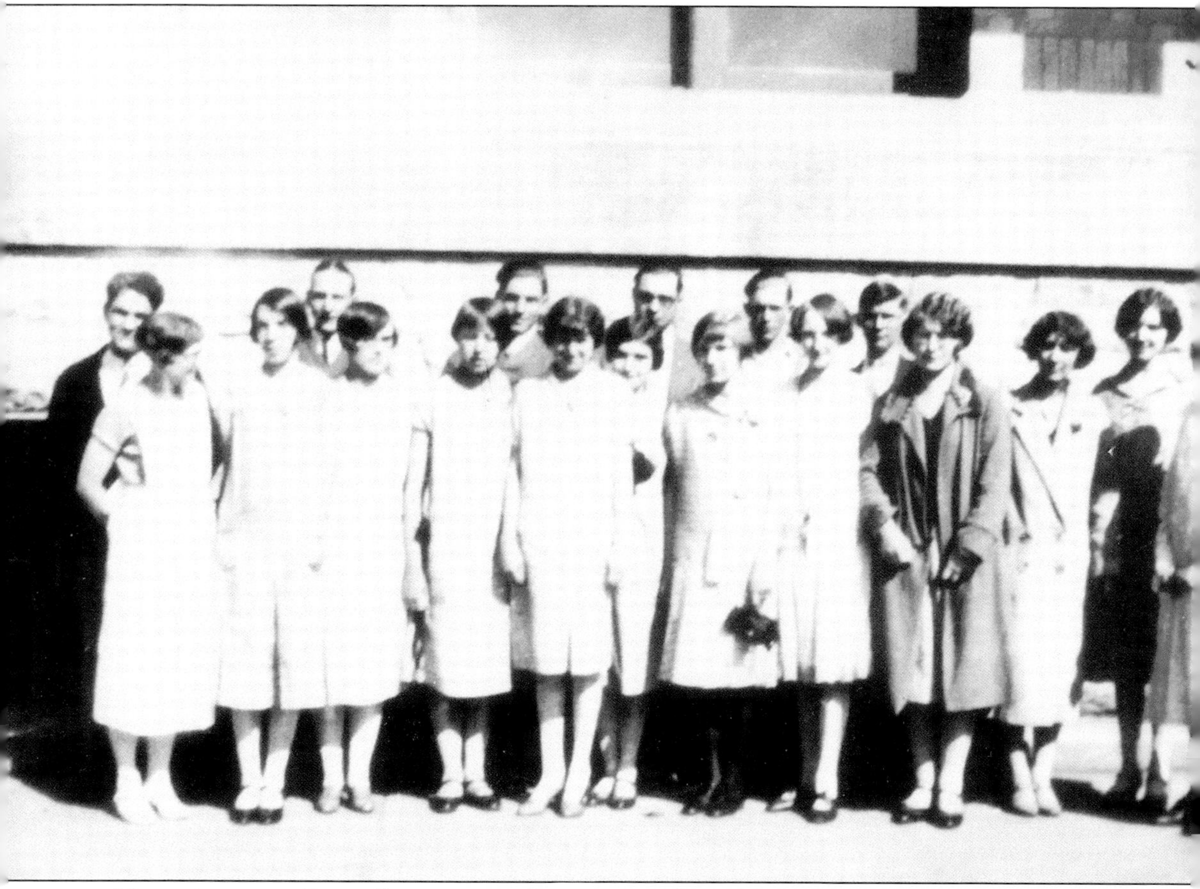

MEMBERS OF THE FIRST GRADUATING CLASS OF THE NEW HIGH SCHOOL, 1926. They are from left to right, Eddie Busser, Miss Kerr (teacher), Anna Ruth Simpson, Archie Rolfs, Miss Parker (teacher), Mabel Christensen, Millerd Nelson, Bess Peters, Anna Bigler, Mr. Tate (teacher), Elizabeth Skarshaug, Lyle Gress, Ellen Bilden, Mr. Hungerford (superintendent), Alta Larson, Teacher (?), and Mrs. Hungerford (?). Members who were not present are Jim Powers and Magdeline Olson.

Class of 1926 Reunion

The Clermont high school class of 1926 held a reunion in the play room at the Larrabee building Saturday evening. The evening started out with a three-course dinner supervised by Mrs. Herbert Martin assisted by Mrs. Floyd Bergeson and Mrs. Vernon Meyer.

Represented at the dinner were: Mr. and Mrs. N. B. Jurgens (Anna Bigler), Minneapolis, Minn.; Mr. and Mrs. Julian Moe (Ellen Bilden), Decorah; Mr. and Mrs. Archie Rolfs (Magdaline Olson), Wenatchee, Wash.; Mr. and Mrs. James Barrett, Oregon, I..; Anna Simpson Barrett, Chicago; Bess Peters Tschantz, Independence; Elizabeth Skarshaug, Ames, and Mr. and Mrs. Millard Nelson.

Class members missing from the roll were: Alta Larson Blood, Catherine Kloster Halverson, Ed Buser, Lyle Gress, Mabel Christianson and Aubrey Guyer.

Supt. and Mrs. M .H. Moore were guests.

It was noted that only Millard Nelson and Bess Tschantz had children graduating from the alma mater.

The high school girls' clarinet quartette composed of Kathryn Larson, Judy Swenson, JoAnn Moore and Joan Swenson, gave two numbers and Romona Olson entertained with her reading, "Patsy". Falshlight pictures were taken and the group then gathered around the piano for a session of singing of songs of yesteryear and now.

CLASS OF 1926 REUNION. MEMBERS OF THE CLASS MET IN CLERMONT TO CELEBRATE THEIR 25TH ANNIVERSARY.

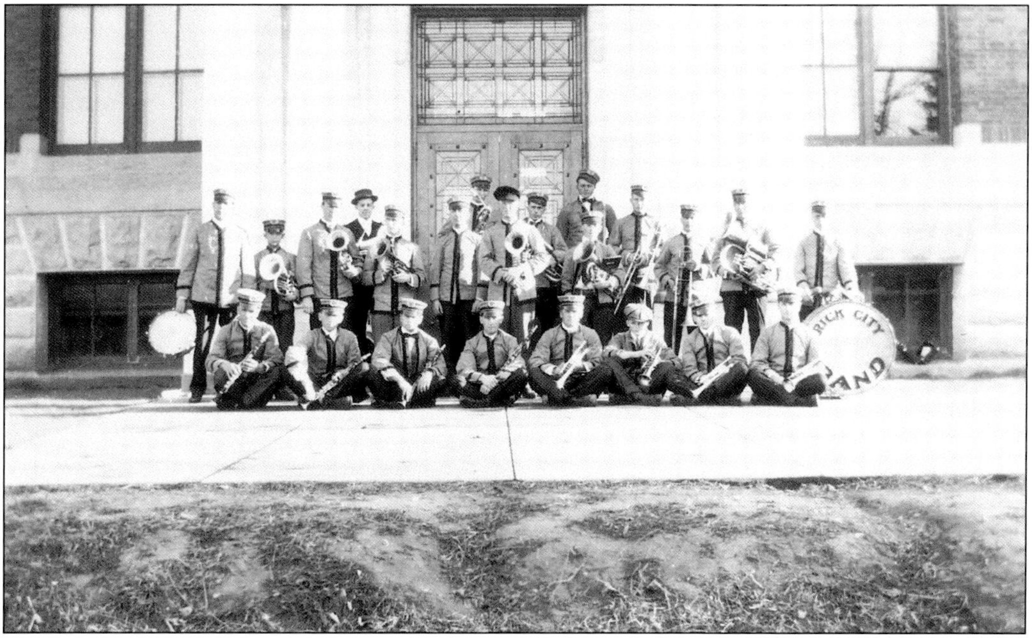

Brick City Band in front of Larrabee Building, c. 1915.

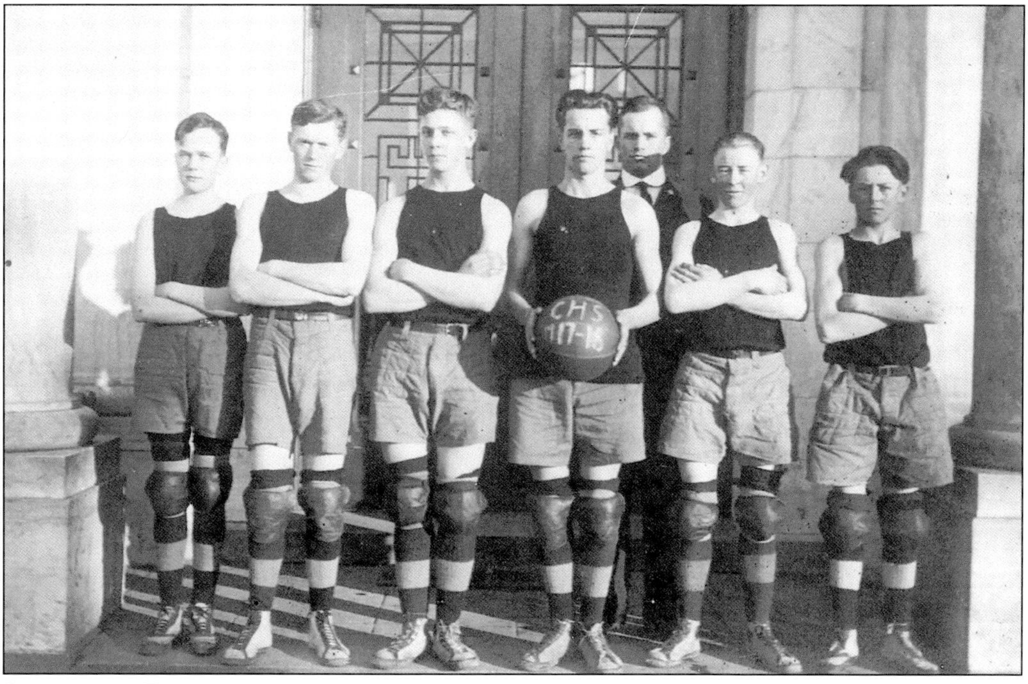

Basketball Team in front of Larrabee Building, 1917–18.

Six

Railroads, Banks, and Private Enterprise

Clermont grew substantially between 1850 and 1920. With the coming of the railroad after 1870, Clermont saw rapid economic development. A number of industries and support businesses grew up in the town including the Clermont Iron and Foundry Company (1873), the State Bank of Clermont (1905), the Farmer's Savings Bank (1913), Clay-Loid Manufacturing Company (1919), and the Clermont Printing Company (1873). A variety of small shops and stores continued to thrive in Clermont during these years. They included a blacksmith shop, creamery, cooper's mill, a harness shop, grocery store, dry goods store, ice cream and confectionery store, a drugstore, a furniture store whose owner was also in the undertaking business, a "double store" that sold dry goods and farm implements, and a hardware store. At one time there appeared to be at least two or even three barbershops in town!

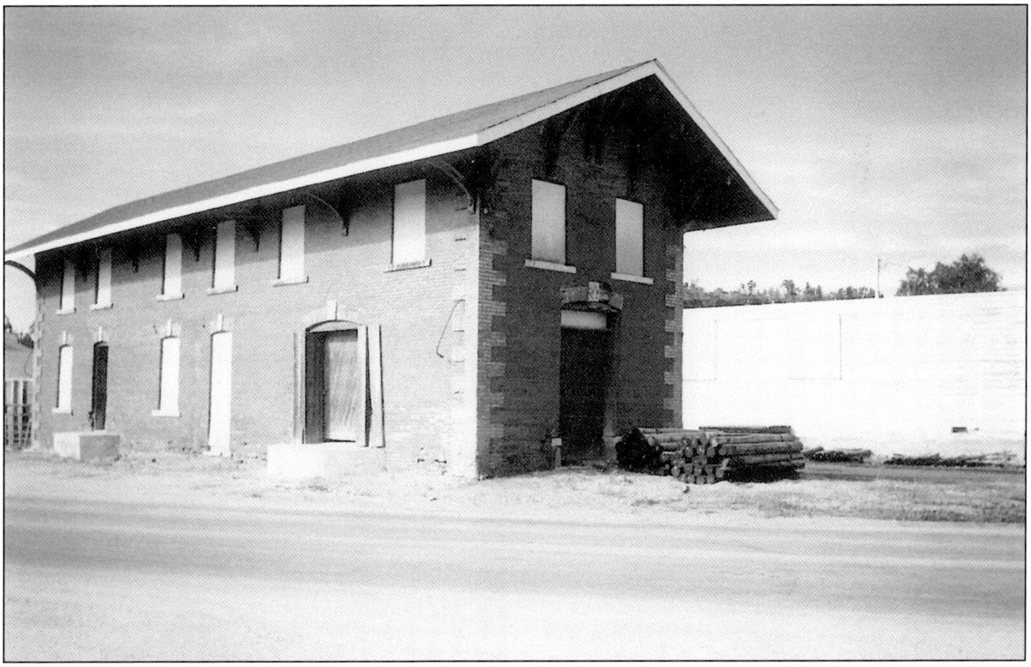

Rock Island Railroad Depot, Current View. The Depot was constructed in 1871 entirely out of native red brick. The first train rolled into the station on September 5, 1872.

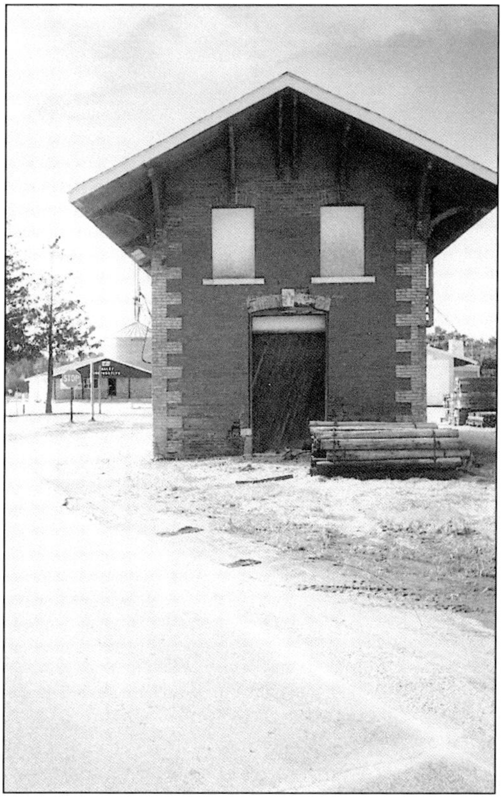

Additional Views of Railroad Depot, Details.

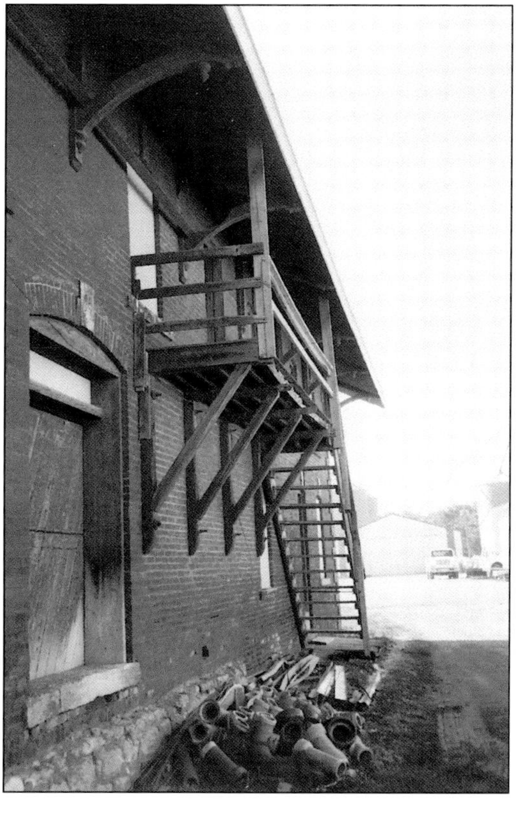

View of Depot, Details.

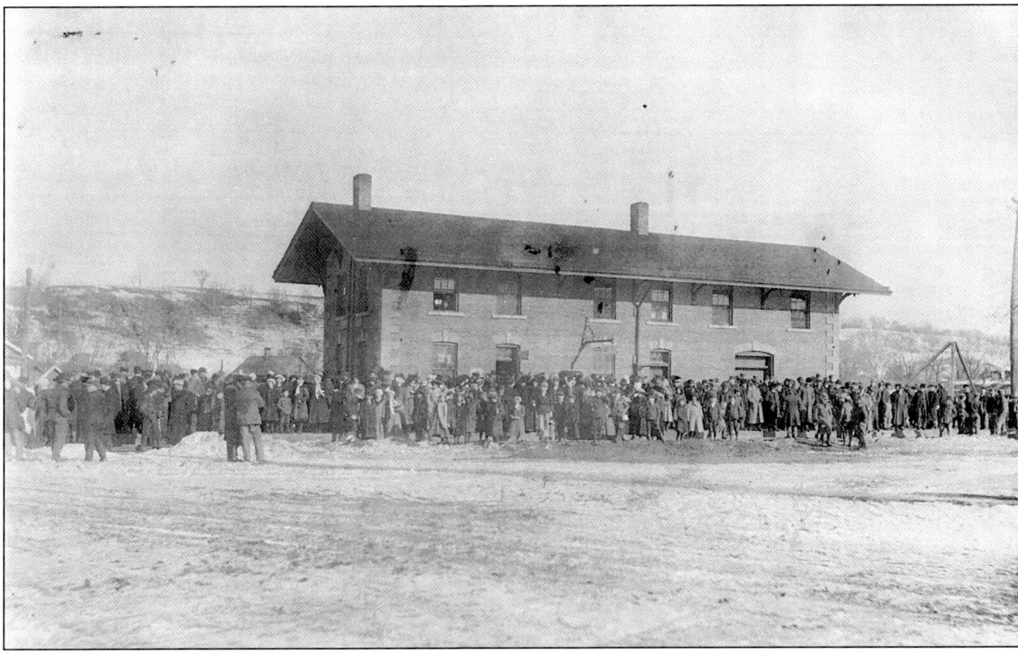

AN EARLY VIEW OF THE RAILROAD DEPOT ENTITLED "WAITING FOR THE DAIRY TRAIN AT CLERMONT." The photograph is probably dated around 1890. After 1870 Clermont saw a significant growth in its economic development due to improved agricultural technology and the rail access.

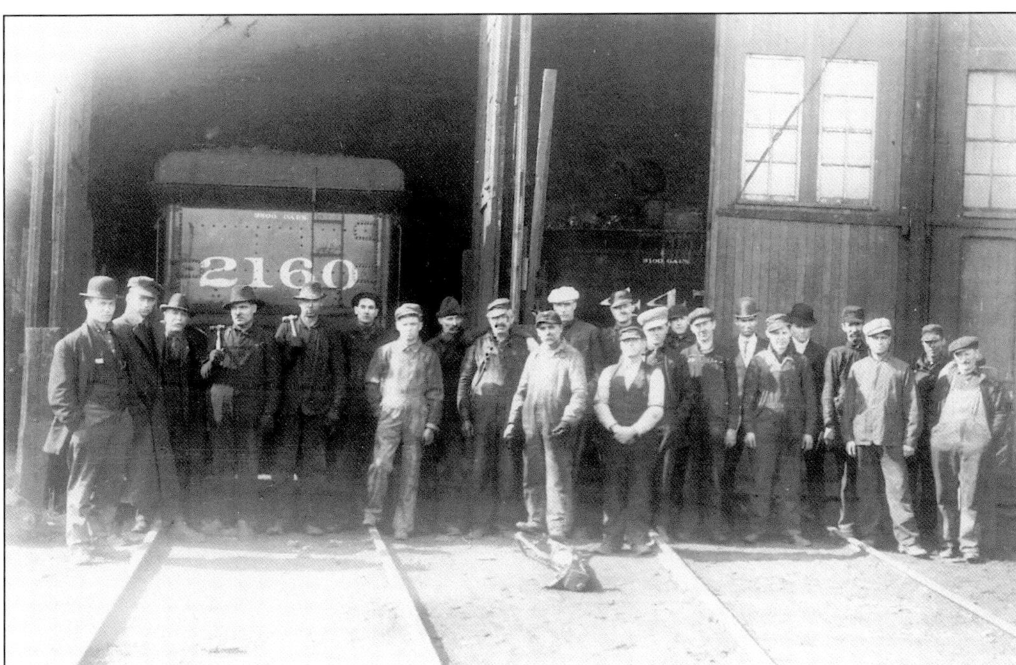

UNIDENTIFIED WORKERS AT THE RAILROAD YARD.

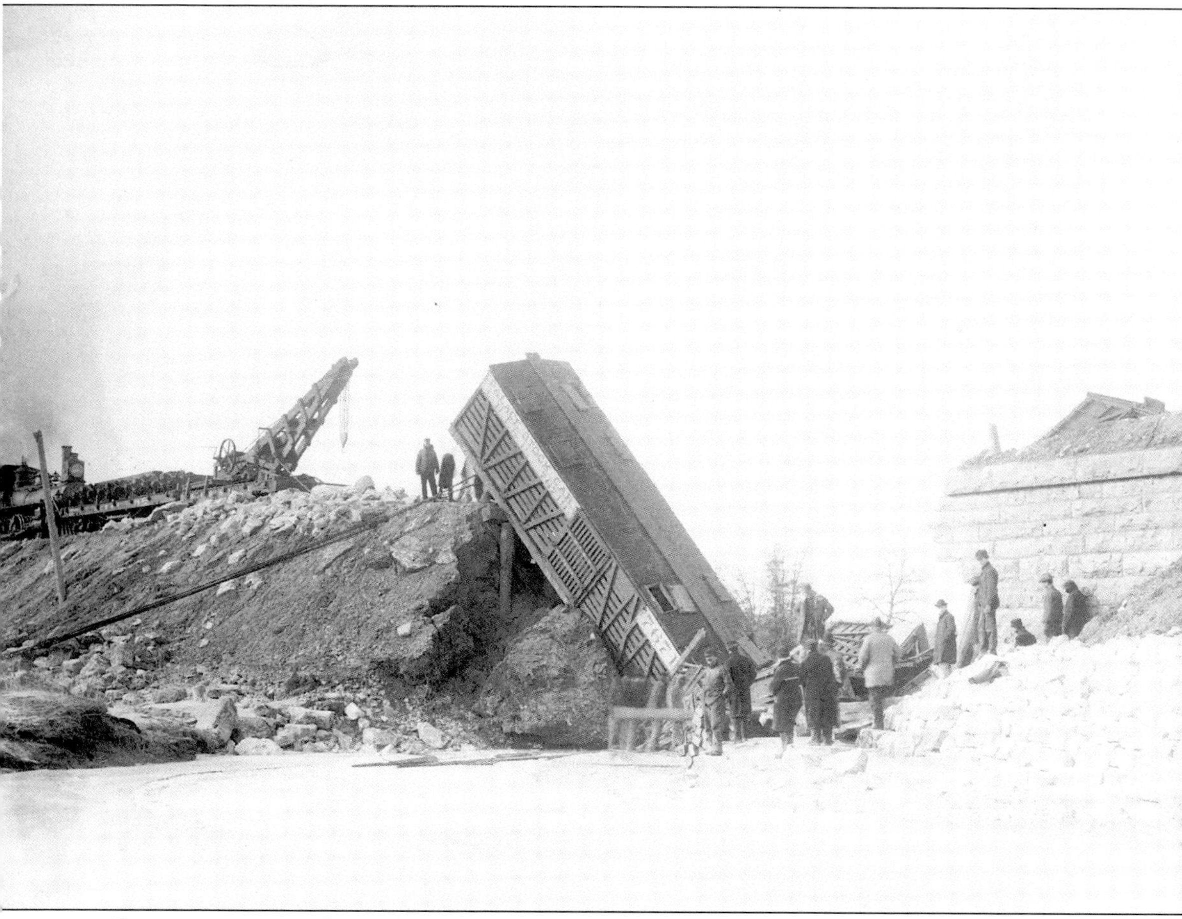

Flood across the Sand Creek, c. 1901. A dramatic shot of a derailment. The exact location of the accident cannot be identified.

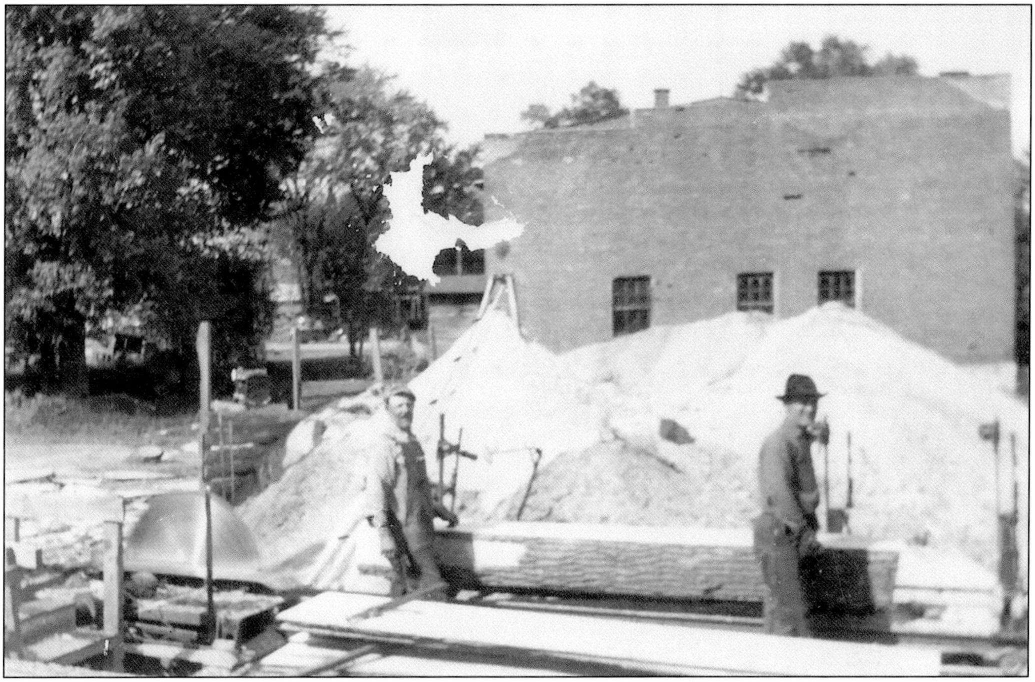

Will Nelson's Sawmill at Clermont, c. late 1920s. The men in the photo are John Sampson (left) and George Durcher (right). Johnson's garage and Pauhpakeena Hall (a community meeting place) are in the background.

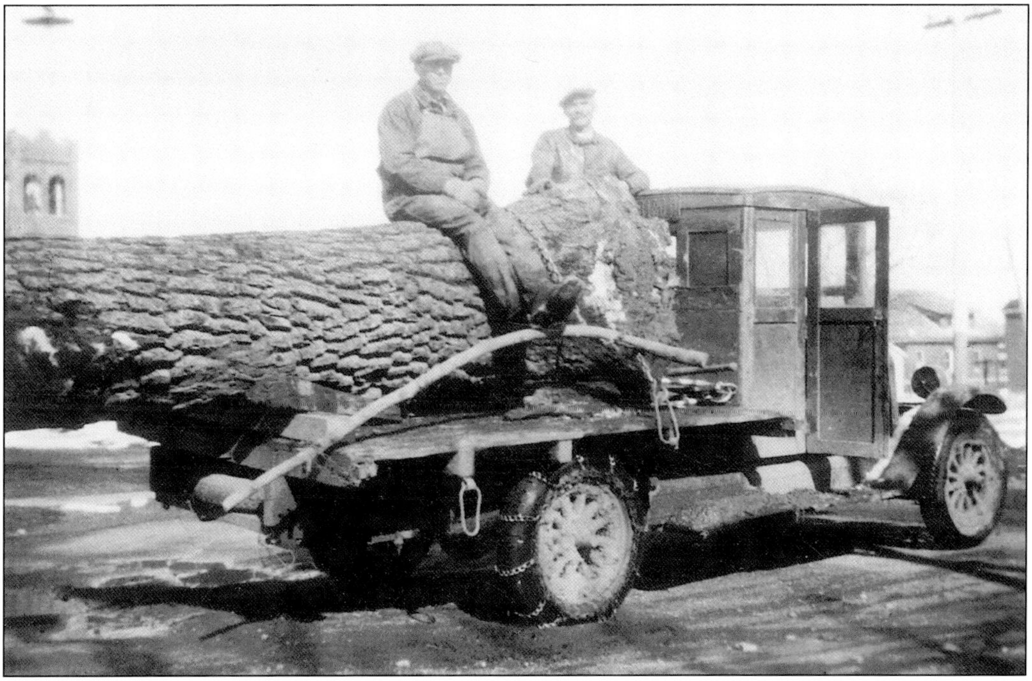

Hauling Lumber by Truck, c. 1930s. The steeple of the Episcopal church is seen in the upper left corner.

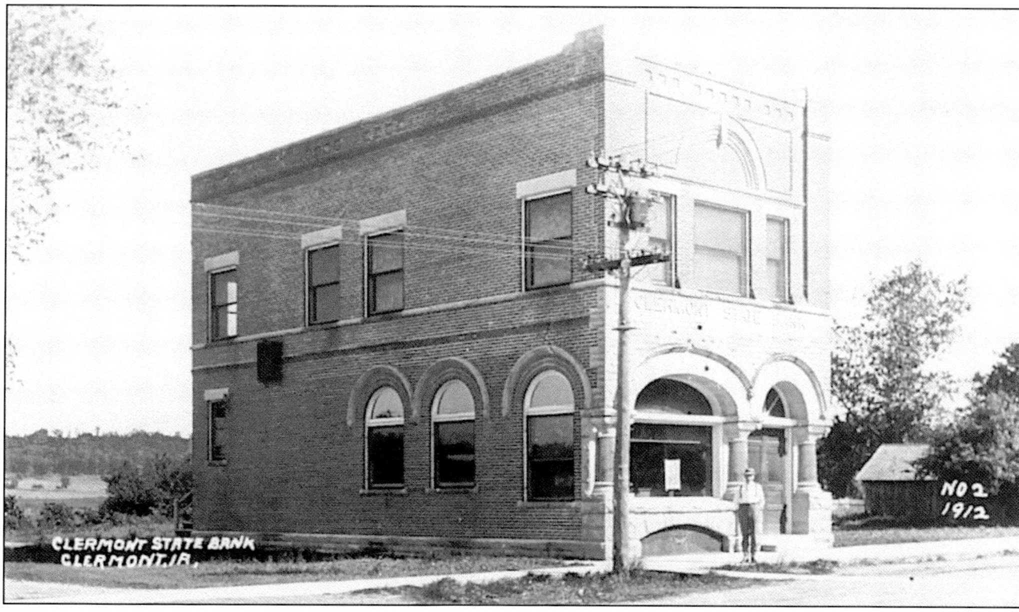

Clermont State Bank, 1912. Although not the first bank in town, the Clermont State Bank is probably the first "real" bank building in town. It was completed in 1909 with Ben Gruver as cashier. It is now the Clermont Museum.

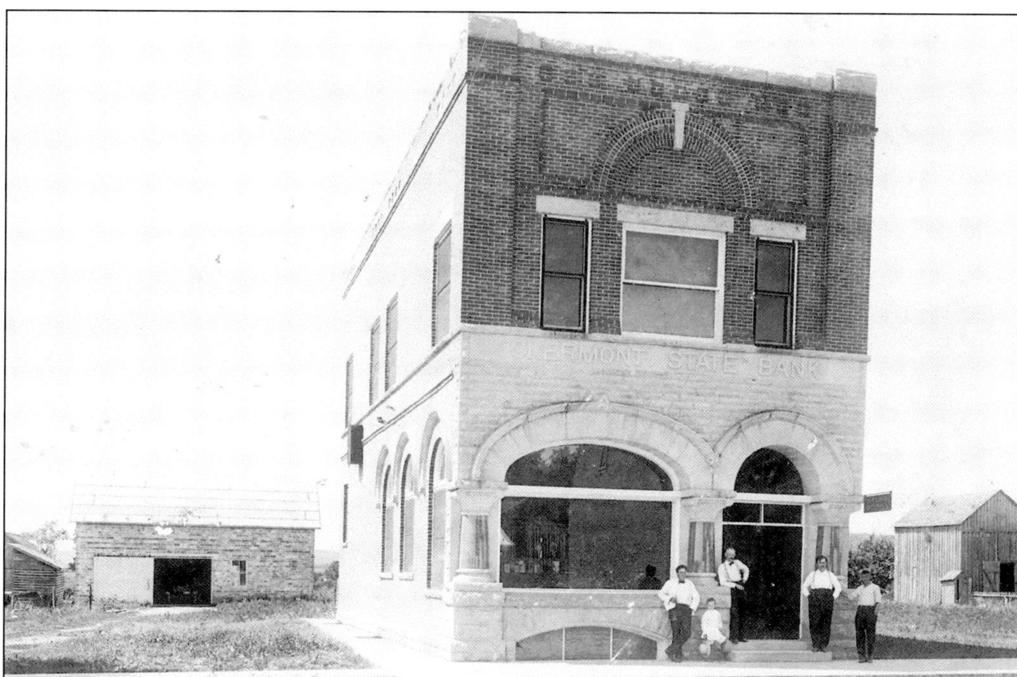

Clermont State Bank, c. 1912. The people are identified (from left to right) as: William Larrabee Jr., William Larrabee III, Ben Gruver (cashier), Dr. Berry (who had an office upstairs), and an unknown man. Note the old barn to the left that is still standing today.

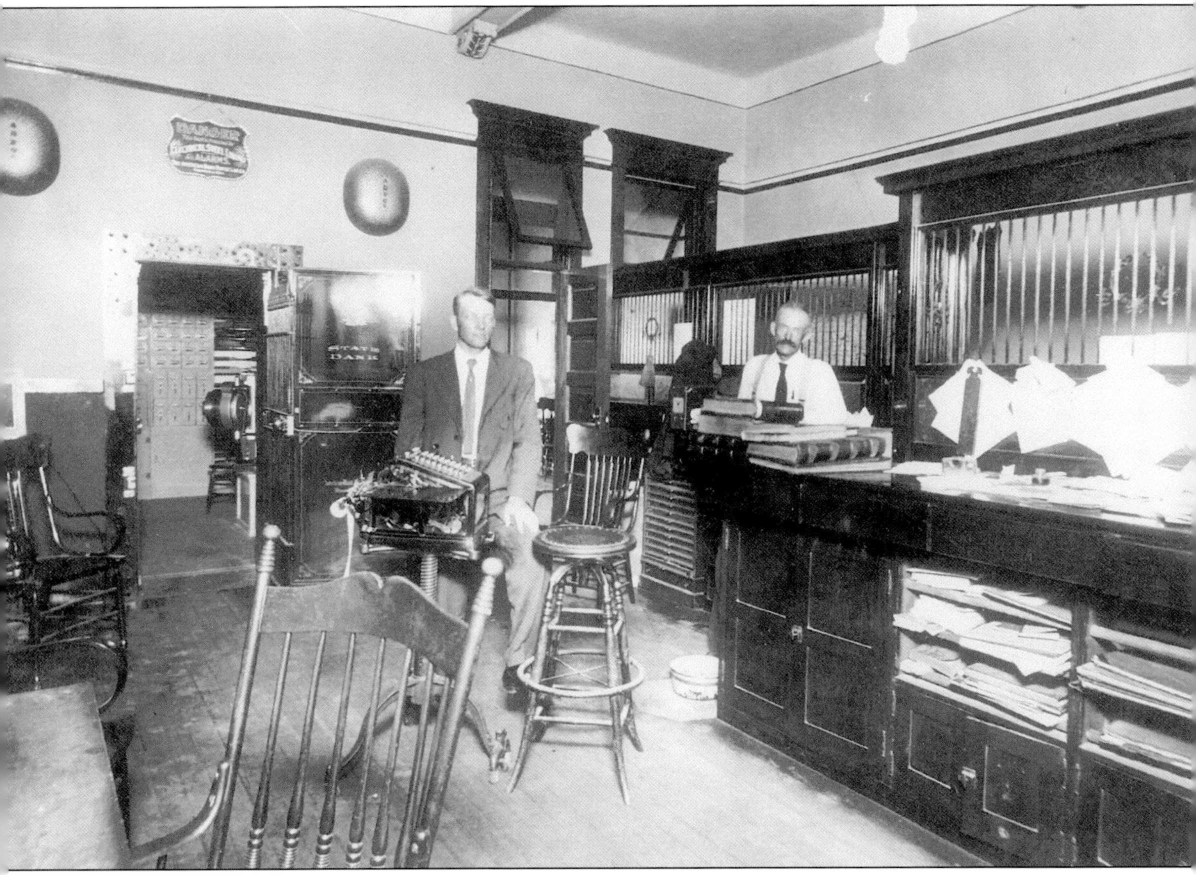

INTERIOR OF CLERMONT STATE BANK. Probably the back offices. The individuals have been identified as Ben Gruver (?) on the left and Alfred Olson on the right.

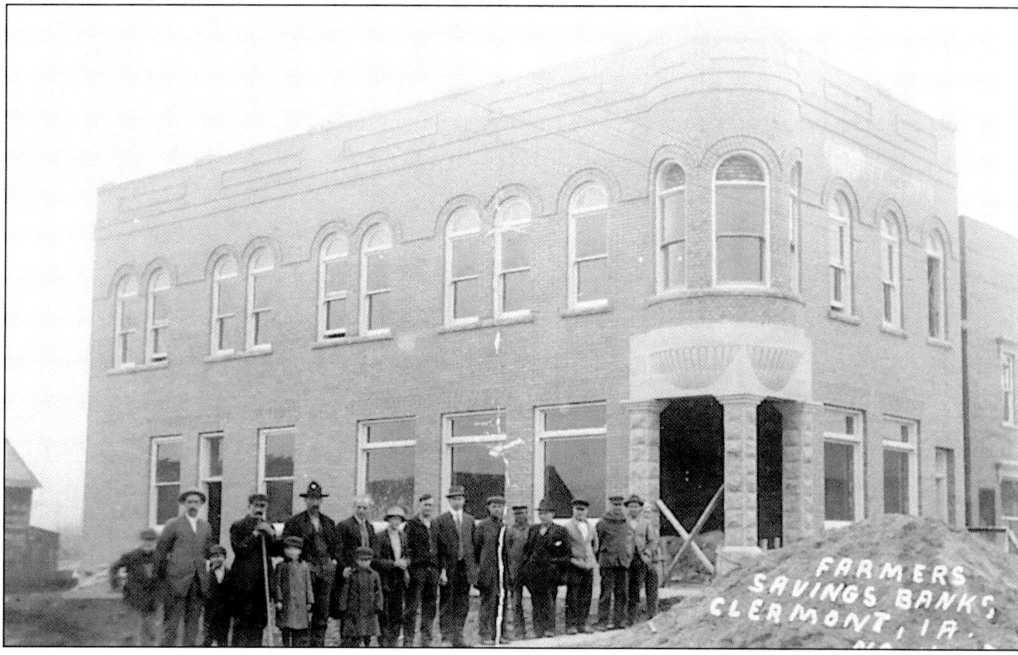

Farmer's Savings, 1912. This bank was completed at the cost of $10,000 and opened for business in March 1914. In this photograph, workers appear to be posing for a final photograph.

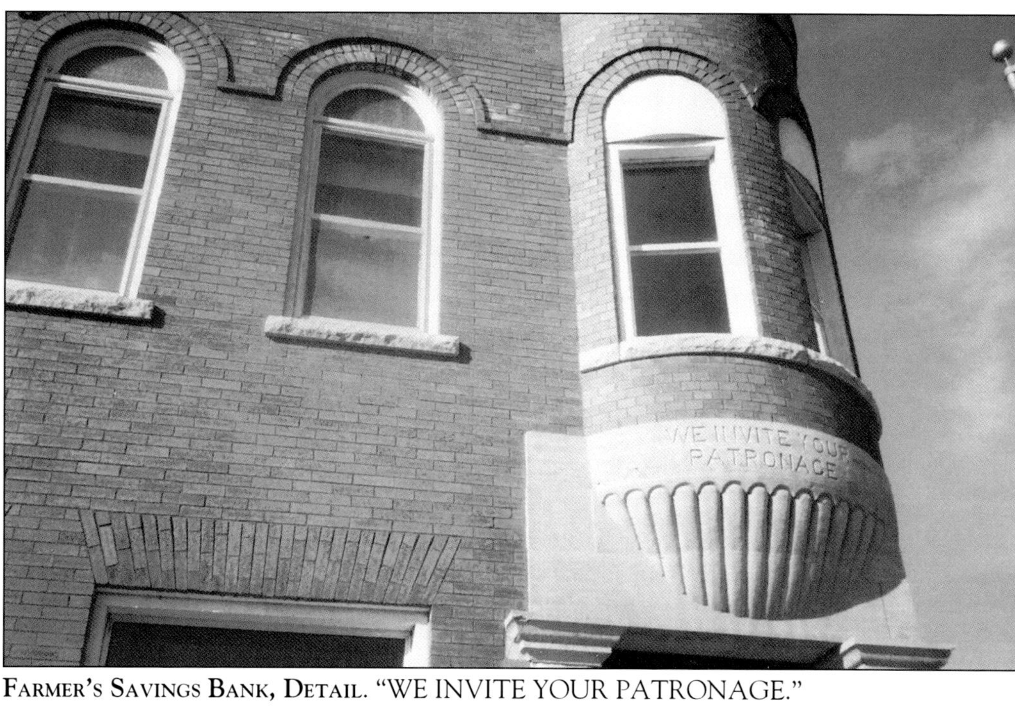

Farmer's Savings Bank, Detail. "WE INVITE YOUR PATRONAGE."

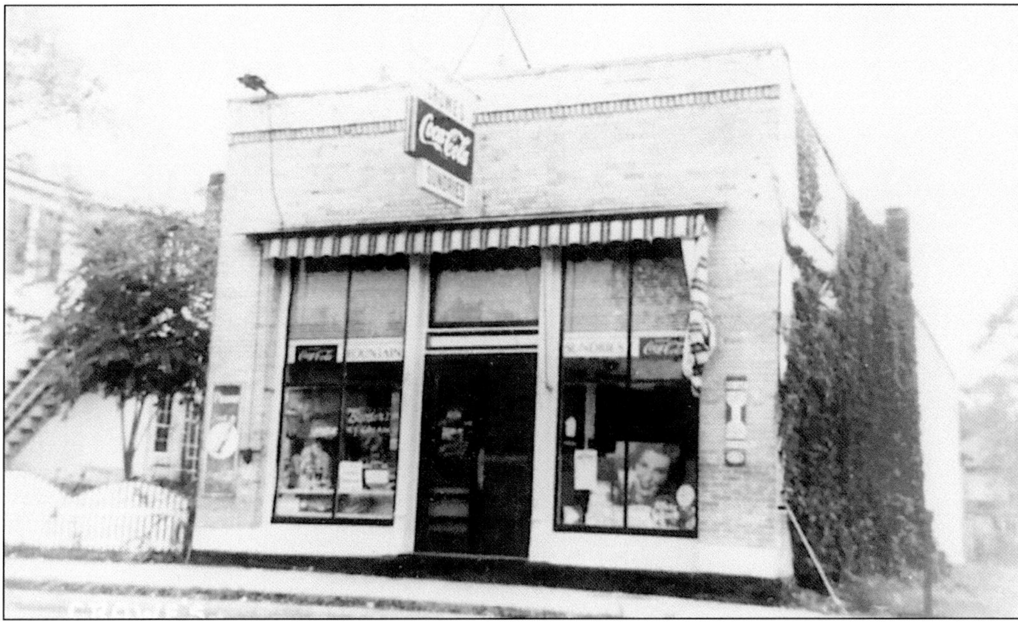

Crowe's Drugstore on Main Street. The store was owned and operated by William and Lillian Crowe in the early 1900s. Will, a pharmacist, filled prescriptions, sold schoolbooks, and other supplies. He later added a soda fountain. The site of the drugstore is now the Brick City Mercantile.

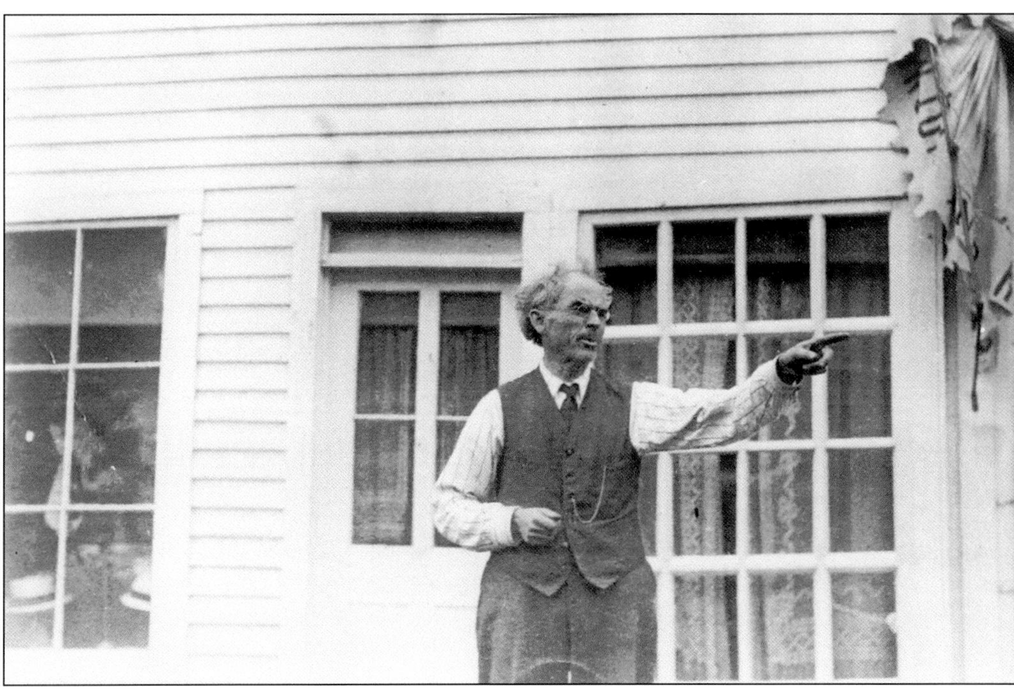

Will Crowe Standing outside the Drugstore.

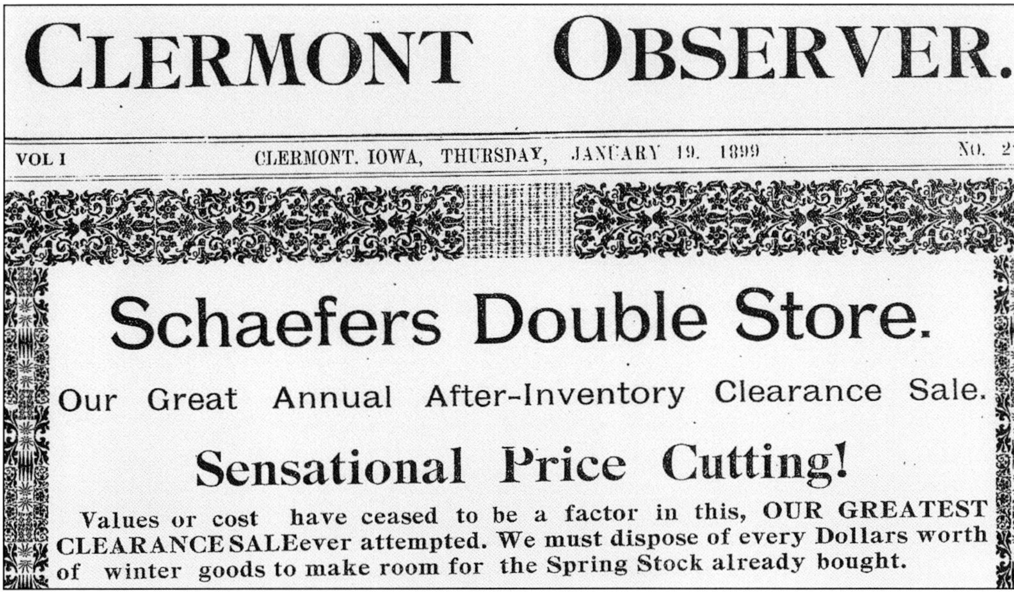

CLERMONT OBSERVER.

VOL I CLERMONT, IOWA, THURSDAY, JANUARY 19, 1899 NO. 22.

Schaefers Double Store.

Our Great Annual After-Inventory Clearance Sale.

Sensational Price Cutting!

Values or cost have ceased to be a factor in this, OUR GREATEST CLEARANCE SALEever attempted. We must dispose of every Dollars worth of winter goods to make room for the Spring Stock already bought.

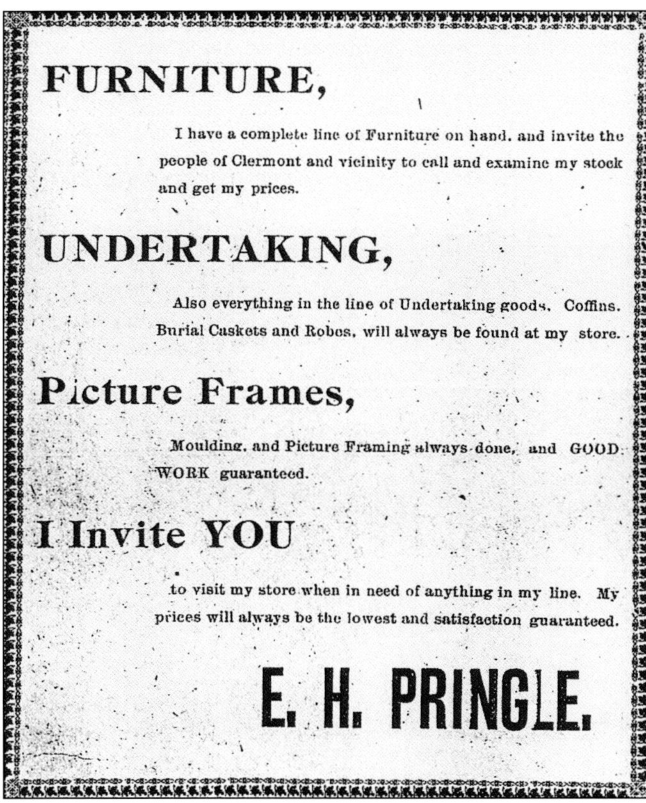

FURNITURE,

I have a complete line of Furniture on hand, and invite the people of Clermont and vicinity to call and examine my stock and get my prices.

UNDERTAKING,

Also everything in the line of Undertaking goods. Coffins, Burial Caskets and Robes, will always be found at my store.

Picture Frames,

Moulding, and Picture Framing always done, and GOOD WORK guaranteed.

I Invite YOU

to visit my store when in need of anything in my line. My prices will always be the lowest and satisfaction guaranteed.

E. H. PRINGLE.

EARLY ADVERTISEMENTS. These appeared in the *Clermont Observer*, January 19, 1899, and feature "Schaefers Double Store" and "E.H. Pringle."

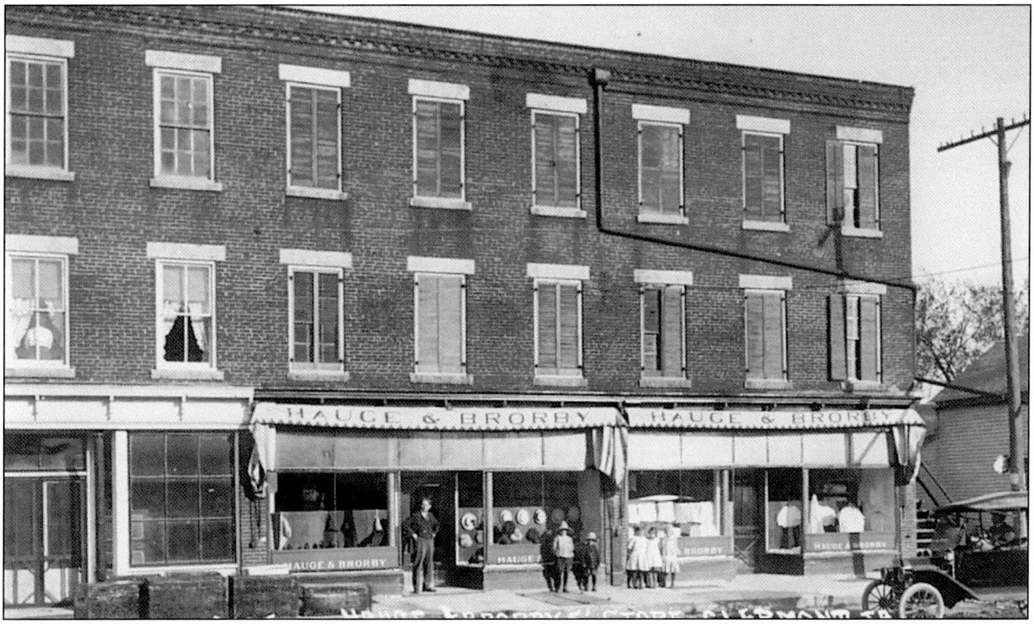

HAUGE & BROPHY'S DOUBLE STORE. The store was formally Schaefers on Main Street, and featured dry goods and farm goods. Joe Brophy is probably standing out in front with several Clermont residents.

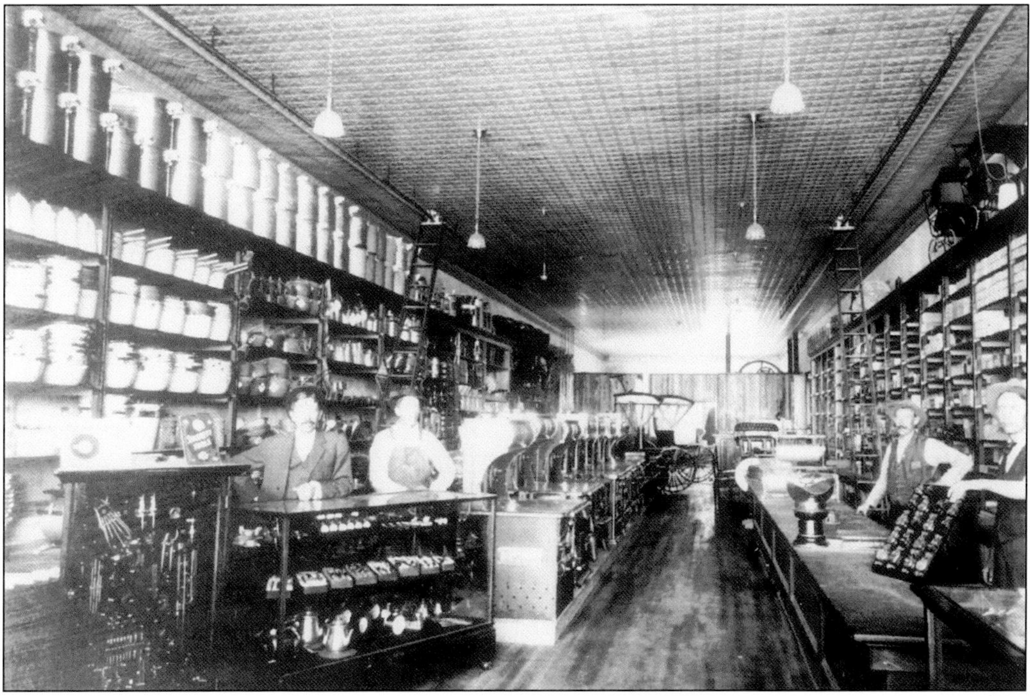

INTERIOR OF THE "DOUBLE STORE" IN CLERMONT. The employees cannot be identified.

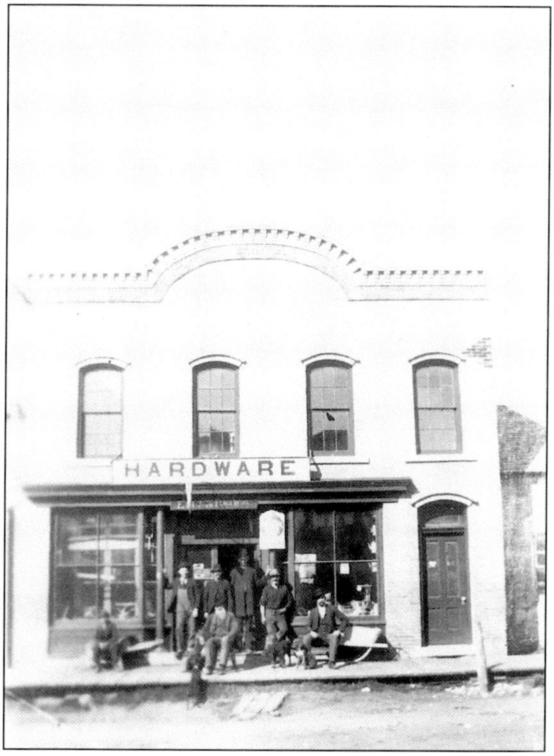

VERY OLD HARDWARE STORE, C. 1890S. Although the men in the photograph have not been identified, note the old gentleman with the beard. Also note the tin coffeepots in the window.

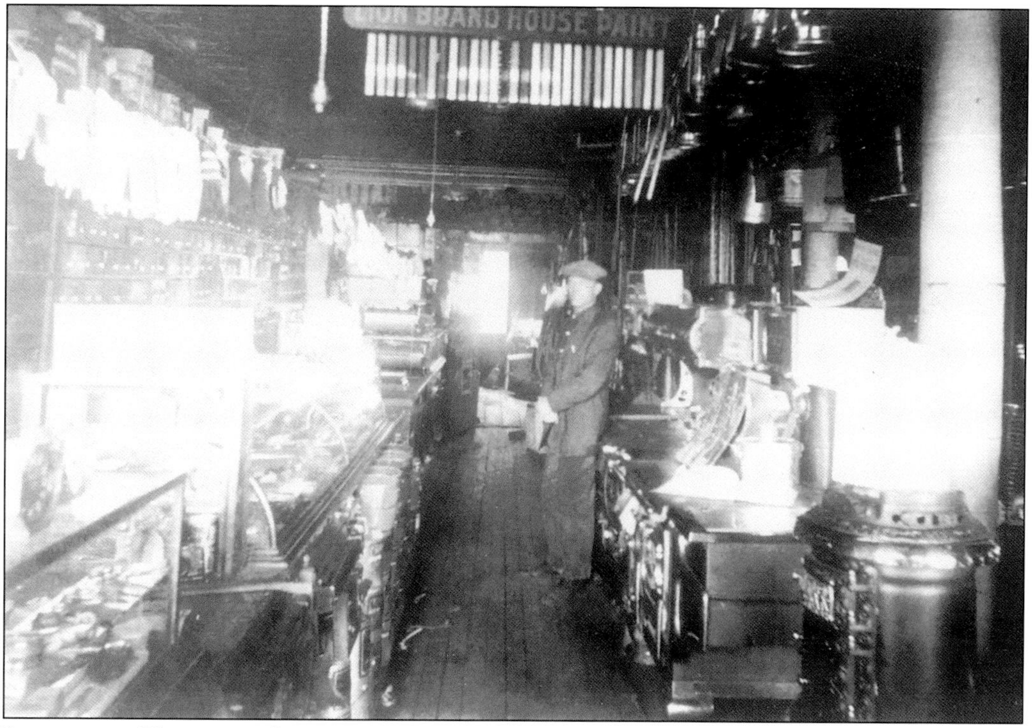

INTERIOR OF HARDWARE STORE, C. 1913.

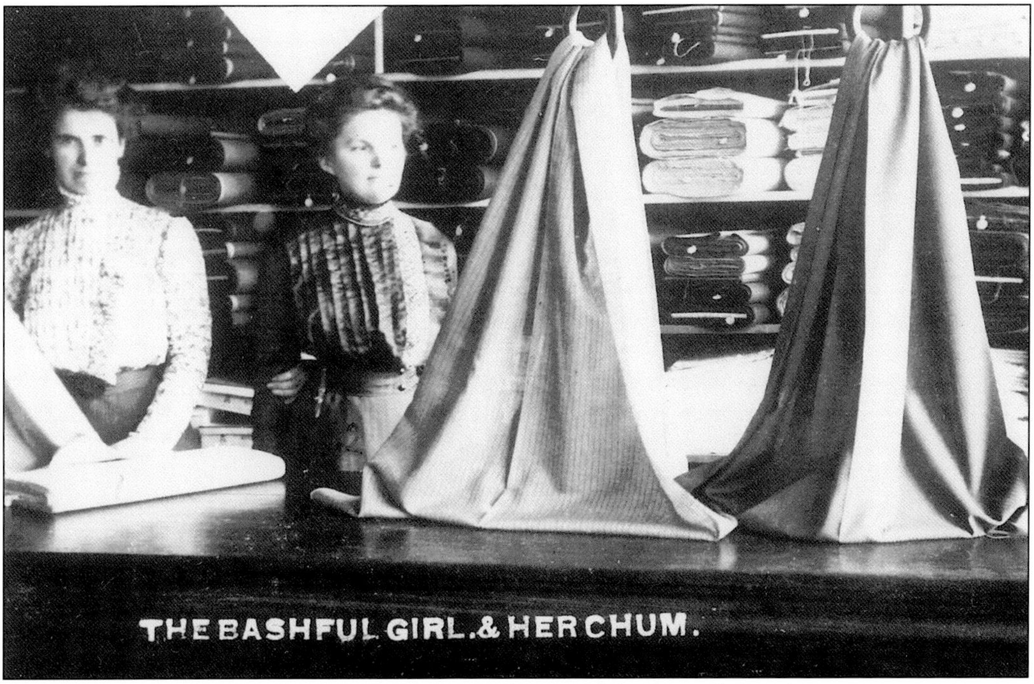

ROUNDS BROTHERS STORE, INTERIOR. The employees of the Rounds Brothers store are Margaret "Midge" Sheehy on the left and Mayme Sheehan Burke on the right.

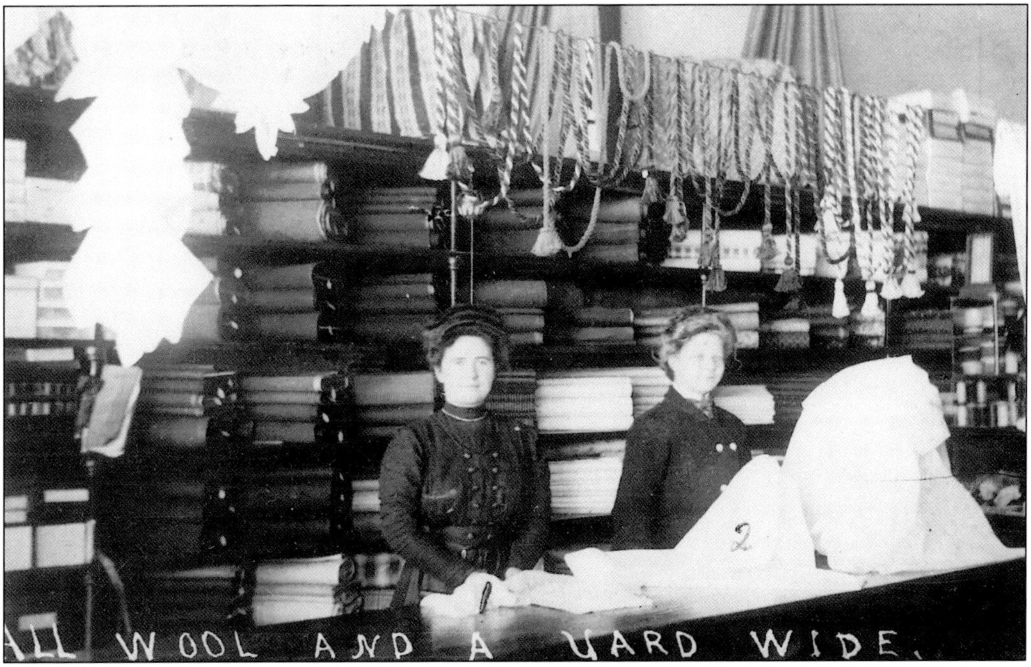

ROUNDS BROTHERS STORE, INTERIOR. The employees are Nell Burke Rounds and Hannah Paulson.

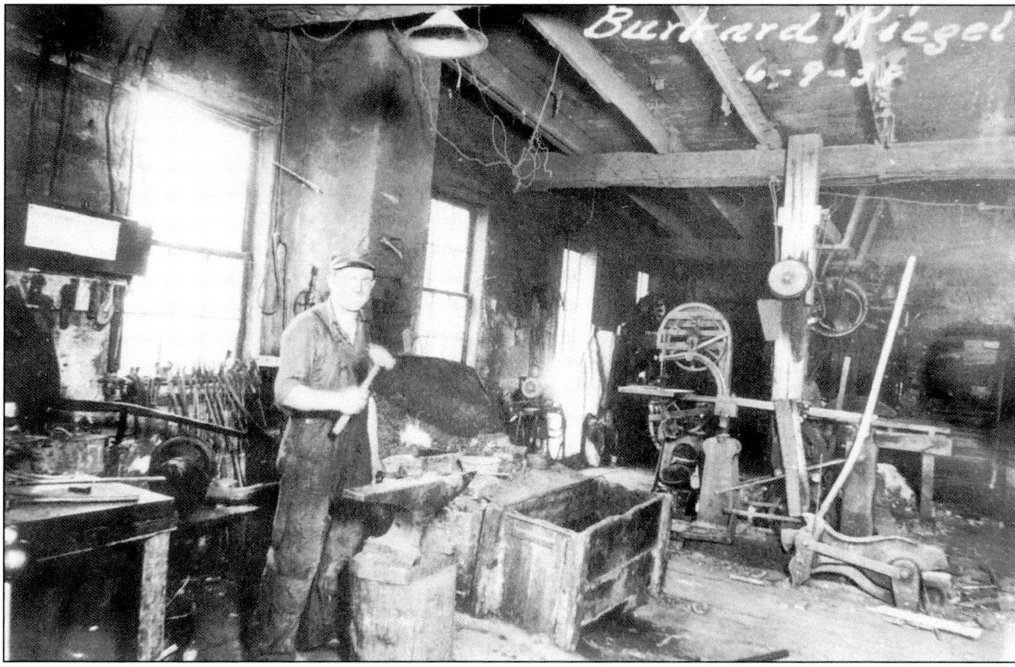

Burkhard Riegel's Blacksmith Shop, c. **1930s.** Burkhard Riegel was the last blacksmith, in a succession of blacksmiths in Clermont, to use the building as a forge and shop.

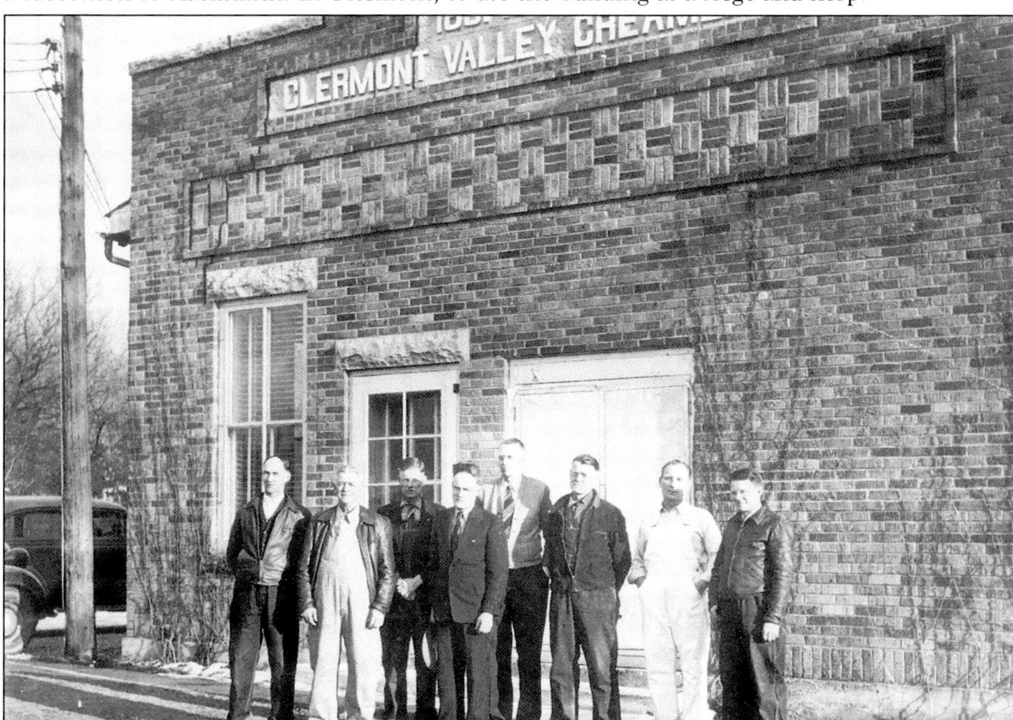

Clermont Valley Creamery. The creamery was a thriving industry in Clermont for many years.

Seven

Public Spaces and Private Places

Clermont has two cemeteries, St. Peter's Catholic Cemetery and God's Acres (Protestant cemetery), located at opposite ends of the town. If you explore the headstones in St.Peter's, you will discover the names of some of the old Irish families, sometimes with the name of the town in Ireland where the individual was born. In God's Acres cemetery, members of the Larrabee family are buried and you can see the impressive marble headstone of William Larrabee Sr. The old Clermont Opera House (1912) is still very much a part of town life and is used as a community center. Rocky Dell is only now vaguely remembered by a few older residents of Clermont, but it was once a popular picnic and hiking area. Two of the oldest structures are the former Clermont House, or Brown's Hotel, and the old jail house, a very private, or public, space depending upon how you look at it!

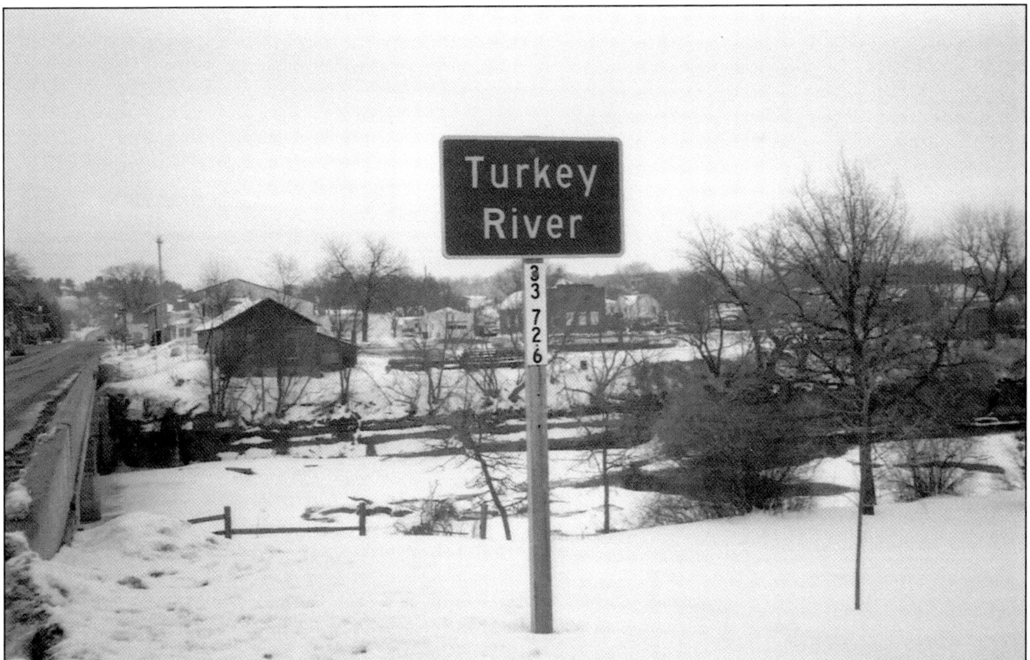

Turkey River. The Turkey River was the key to Clermont's success as an agricultural center. Residents also fished and went swimming in the river.

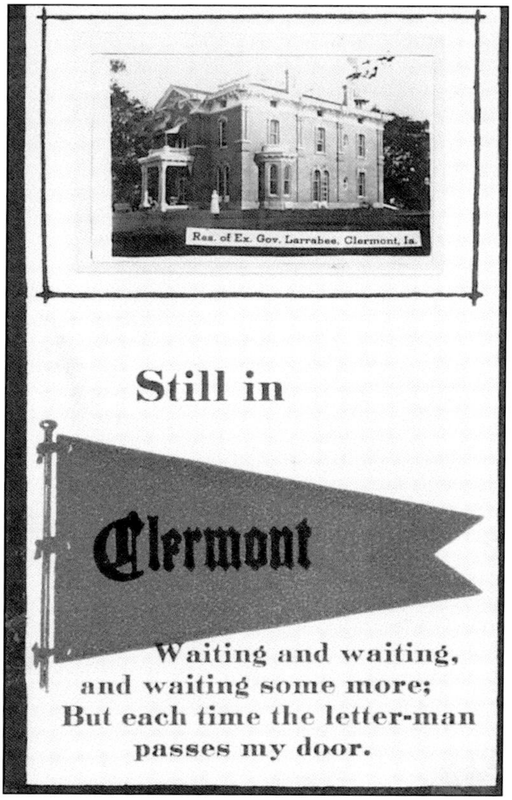

SPECIAL POSTCARDS FROM CLERMONT. These postcards were probably produced in the late 1920s. They feature Montauk, the residence of Iowa's former governor William Larrabee.

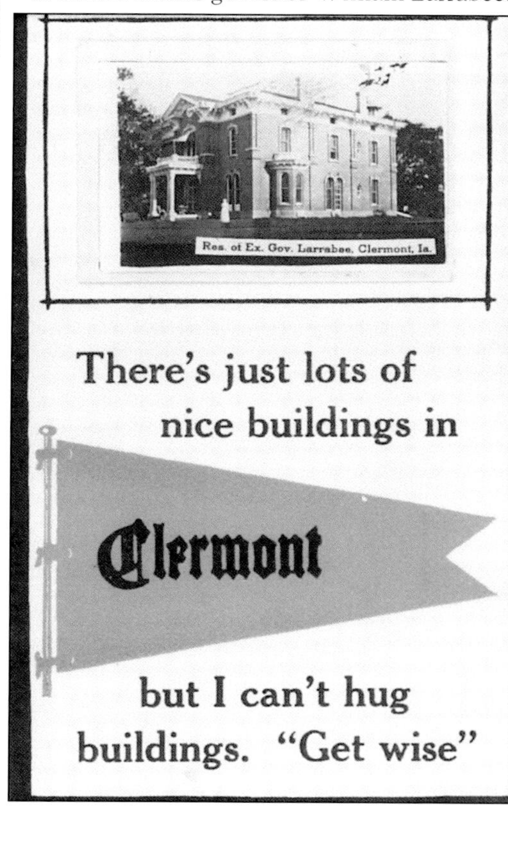

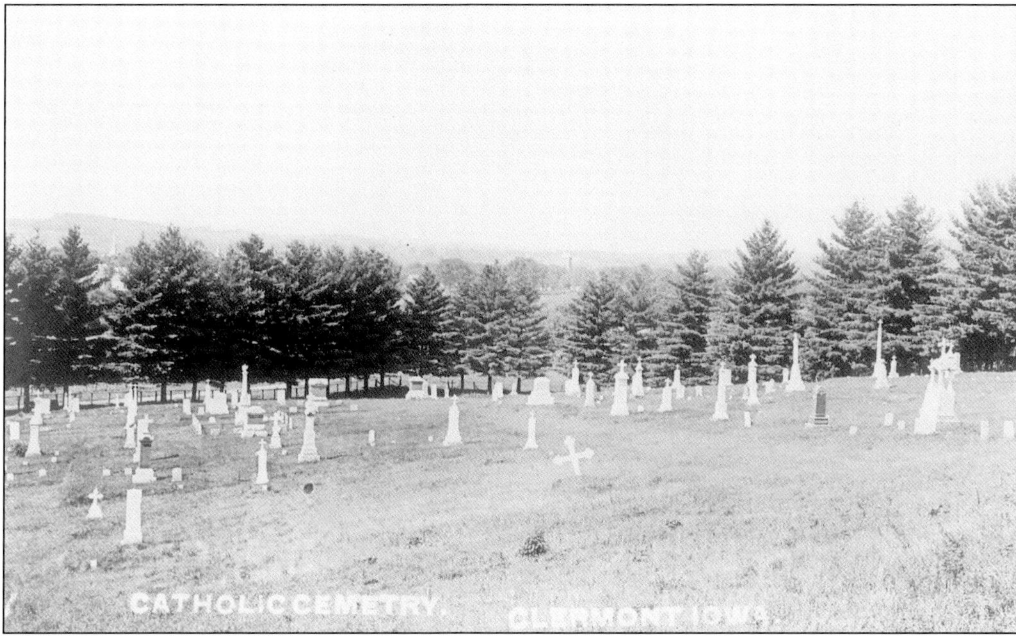

CATHOLIC CEMETERY, C. 1912. The cemetery is located on the northeast side of Clermont. The land for the cemetery was purchased from William Larrabee in 1874. Many members of the old Irish families are buried here.

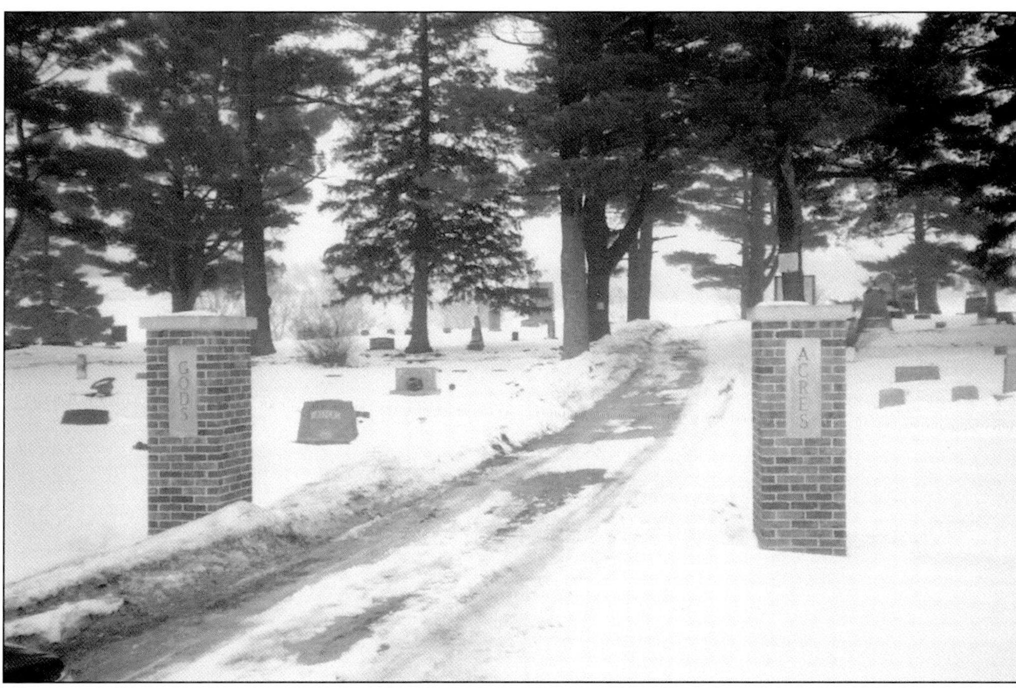

ENTRANCE TO GOD'S ACRE CEMETERY (PROTESTANT CEMETERY). Members of the Larrabee family are buried here.

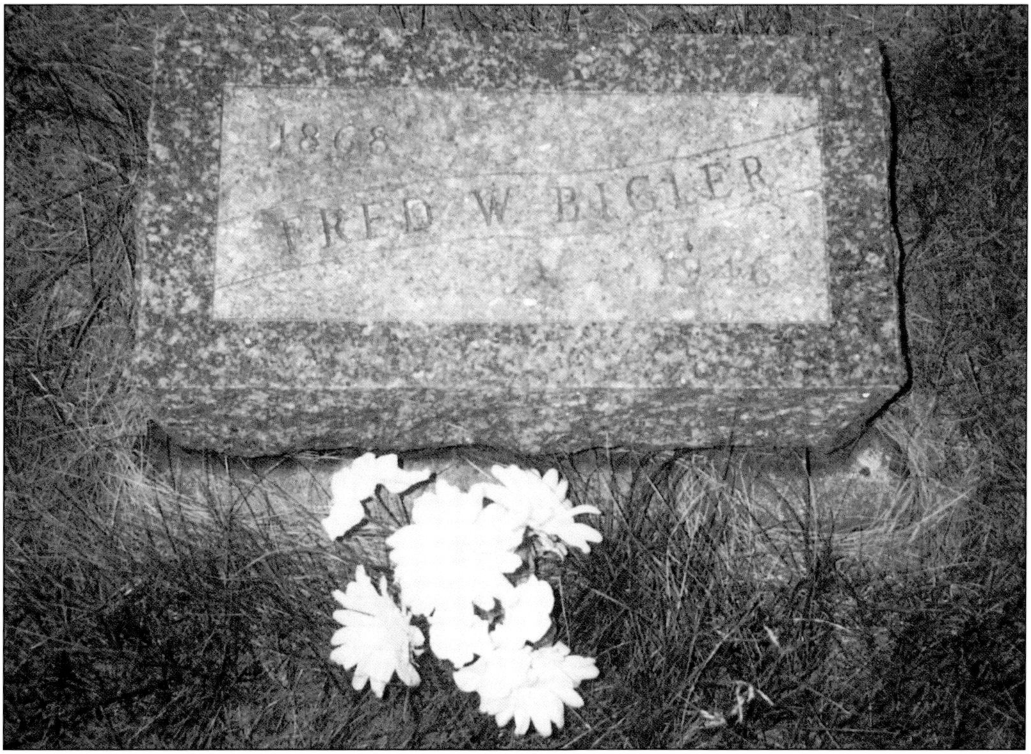

CATHOLIC CEMETERY, DETAIL OF GRAVES. Fred Bigler was a resident of Clermont, as well as Kate Bigler.

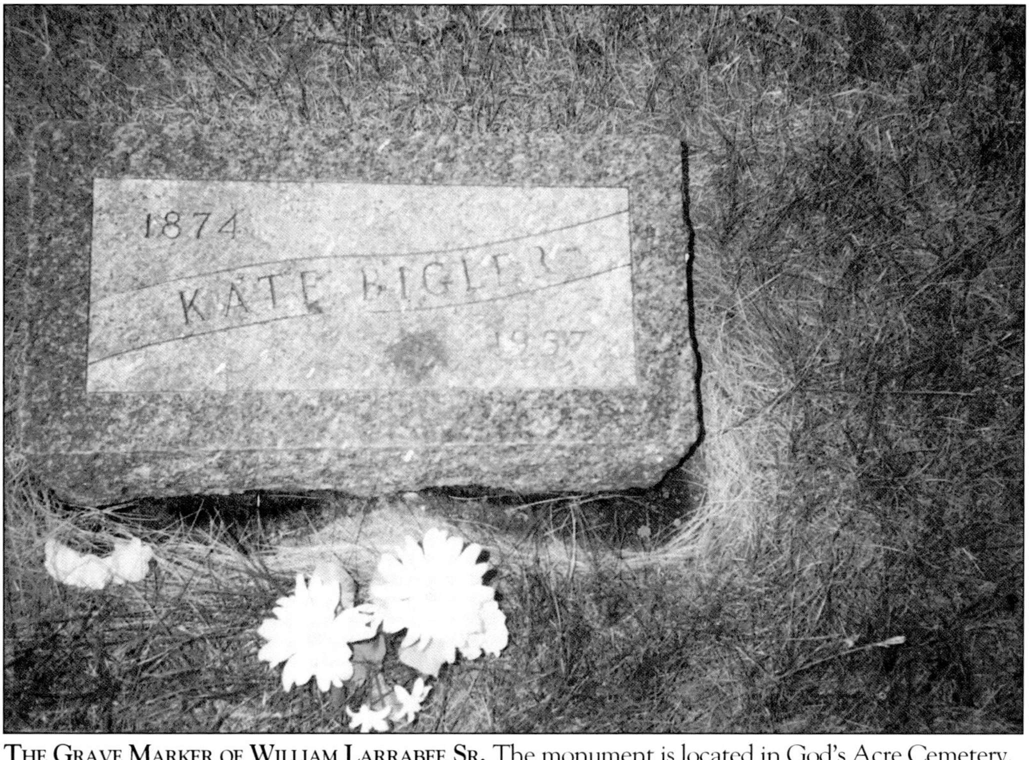

THE GRAVE MARKER OF WILLIAM LARRABEE SR. The monument is located in God's Acre Cemetery.

The Grave Marker of Anna Matilda Larrabee. Her monument is also located in God's Acre Cemetery.

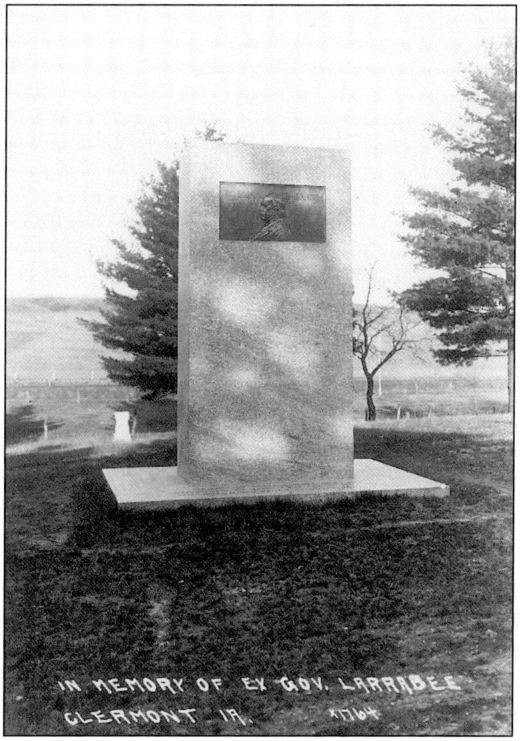

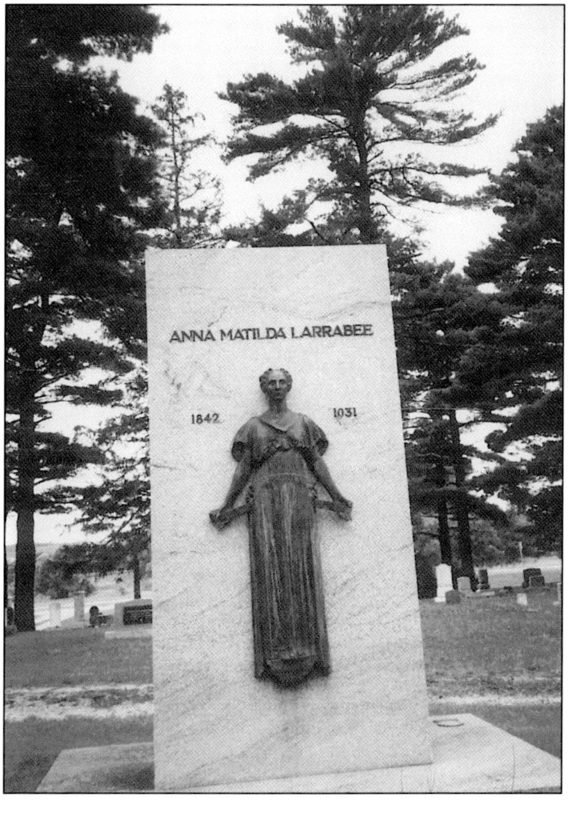

The Grave Marker of Augusta Larrabee Dolliver in God's Acre Cemetery.

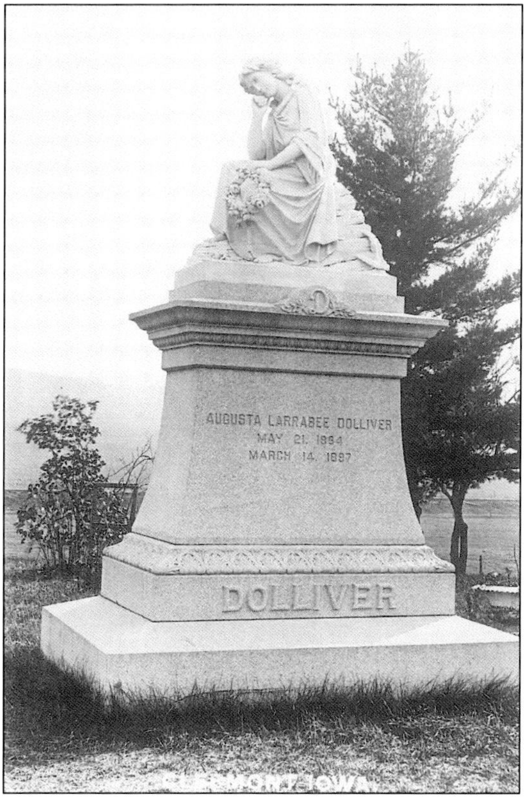

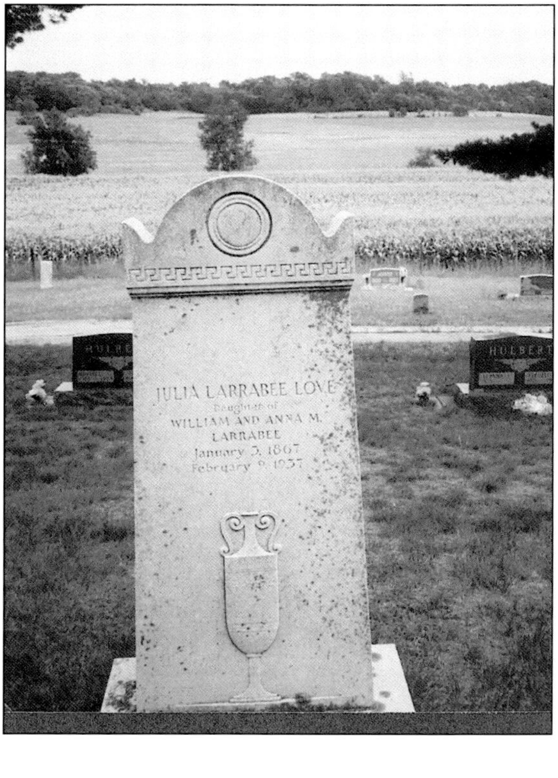

THE GRAVE MARKER OF JULIA LARRABEE LOVE IN GOD'S ACRE CEMETERY.

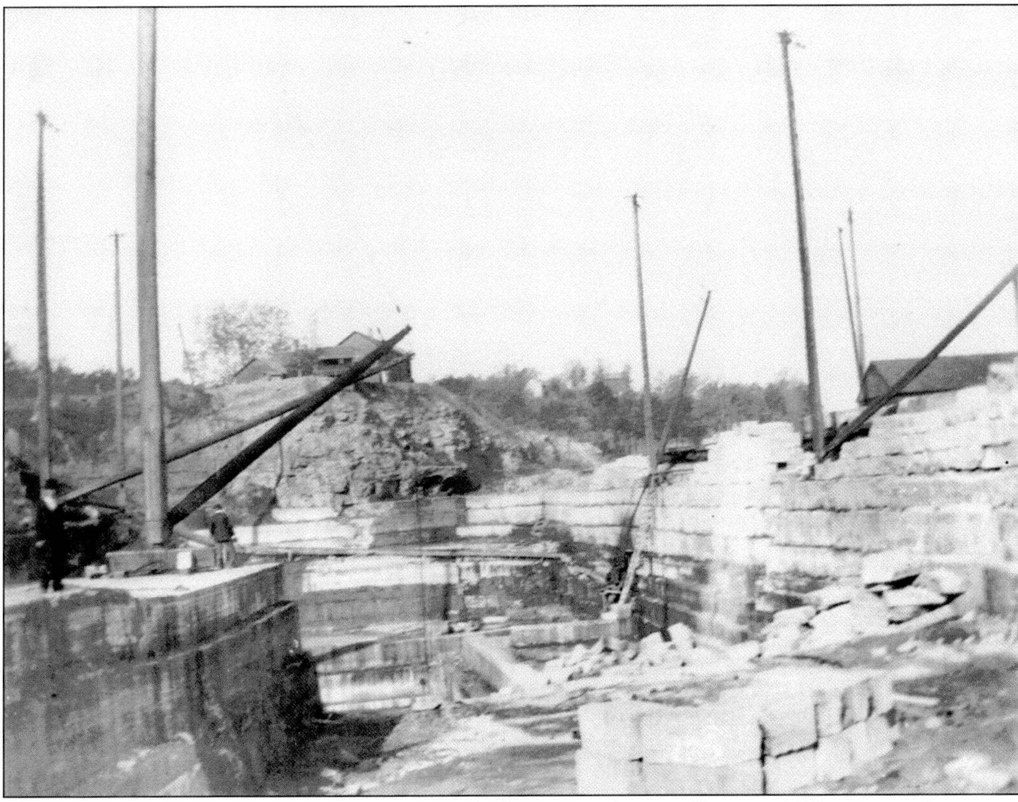

Views of the Williams Quarry. Located about 3 miles northeast of Clermont, the quarry provided stone for the trim on doors and windows for many buildings in Clermont and other towns in northeast Iowa. Most notable examples in Clermont are the trim on the Episcopal church, at Montauk, and blocks used in the Larrabee School.

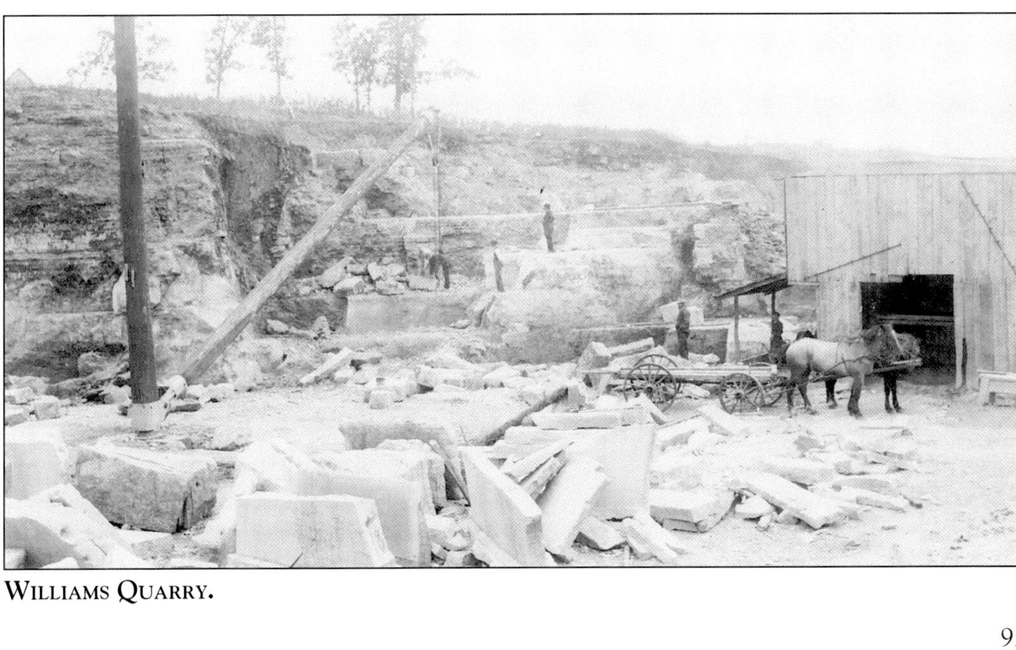

Williams Quarry.

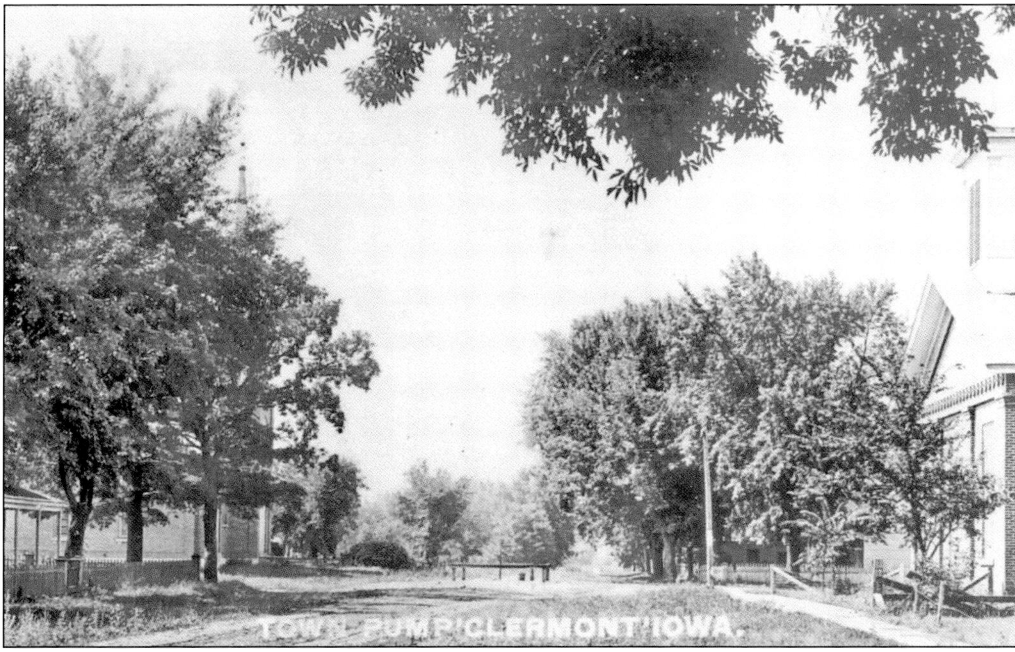

Site of the Town Pump in Clermont. The town pump was located at the intersection between the Union Sunday School and the Methodist church (now the Masonic temple). The building to the right with the white steeple is the Methodist church. The house with the porch in the left foreground was once owned by Elizabeth Sullivan. The steeple of the Lutheran church can be seen through the trees.

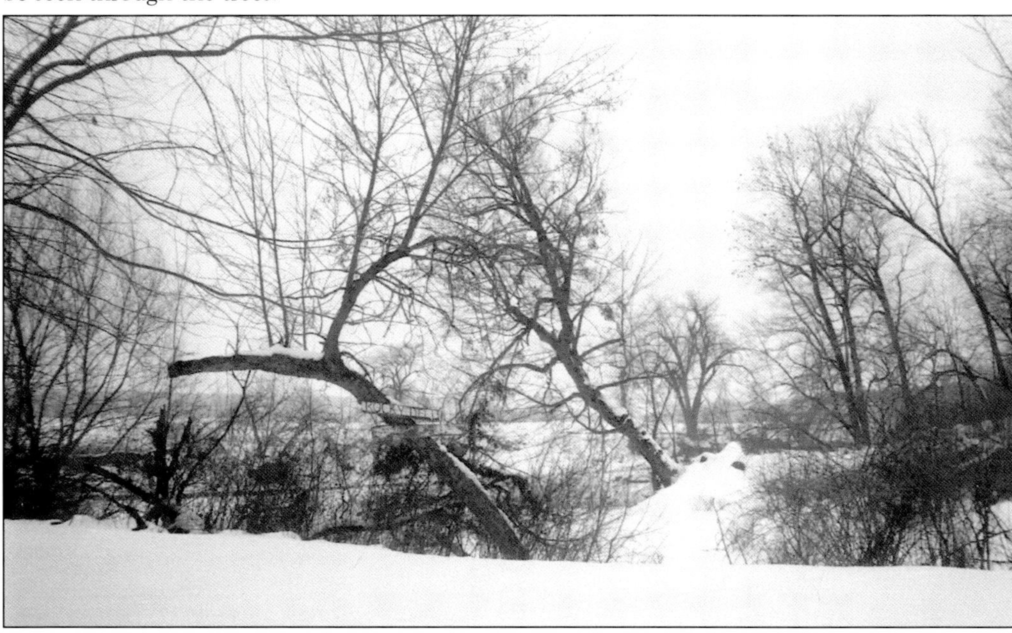

Rocky Dell. Rocky Dell is located south of Clermont across the Turkey River. In the early 1900s, it was a favorite spot for campers and picnic-goers. Along the creek, which ran into the river, children found Indian arrowheads and other treasures. They may also have found hepaticas, trilliums, and pink lady slippers on "Hepatica Hill."

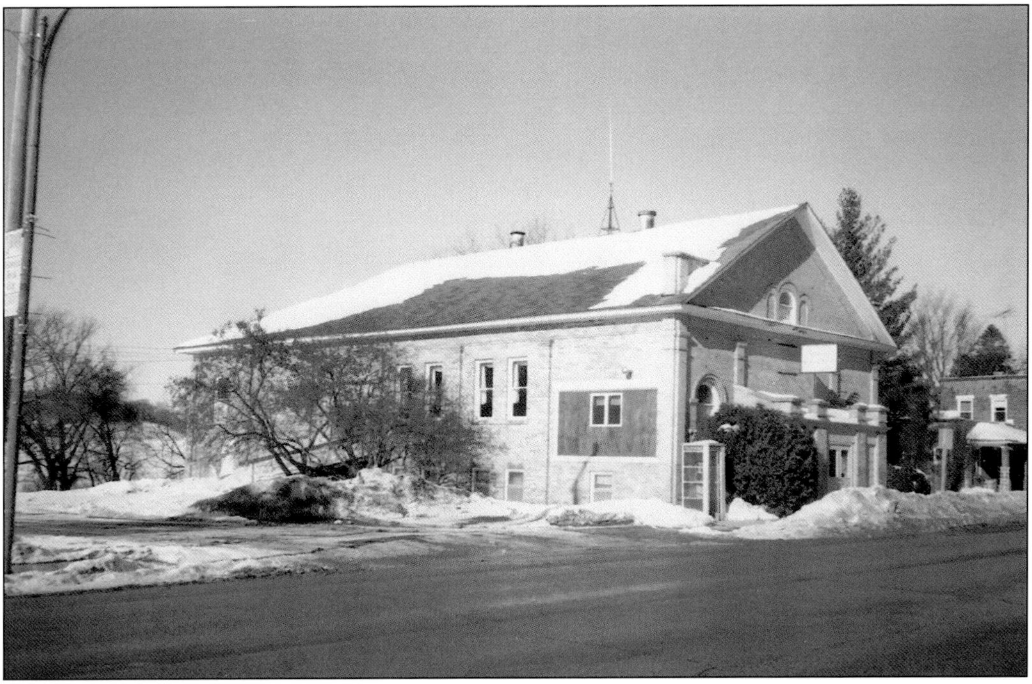

The Opera House. The Opera House was completed in 1912 with Harry E. Netcott as architect. It had a seating capacity of 500 with a balcony. The House became the center of town activities at least until 1930, and featured stage plays, movies, and dances.

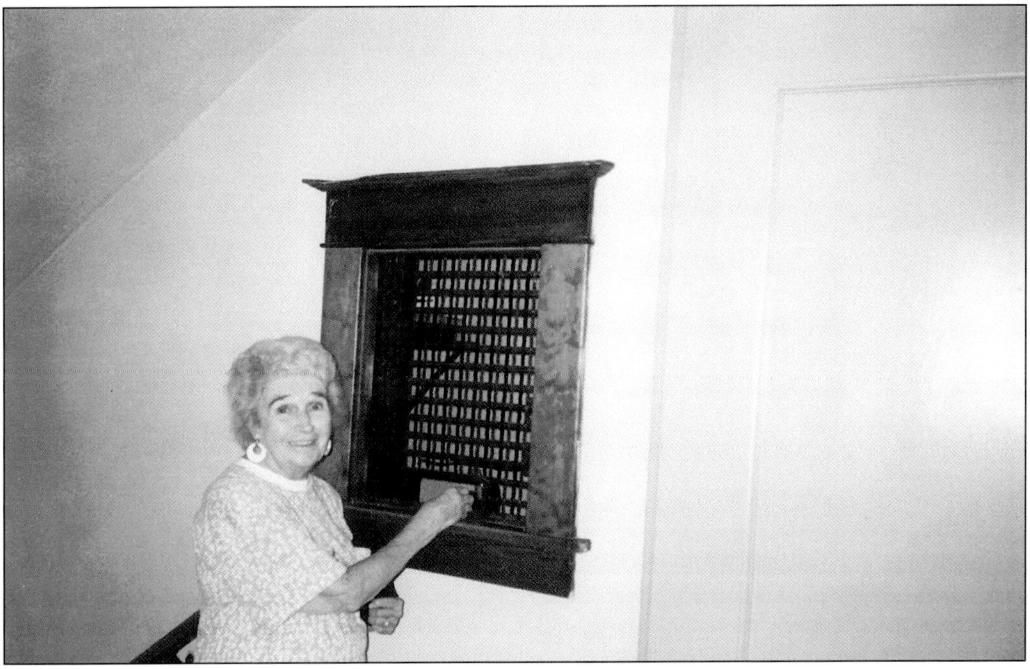

Interior of the Opera House. View of a ticket window in the opera house.

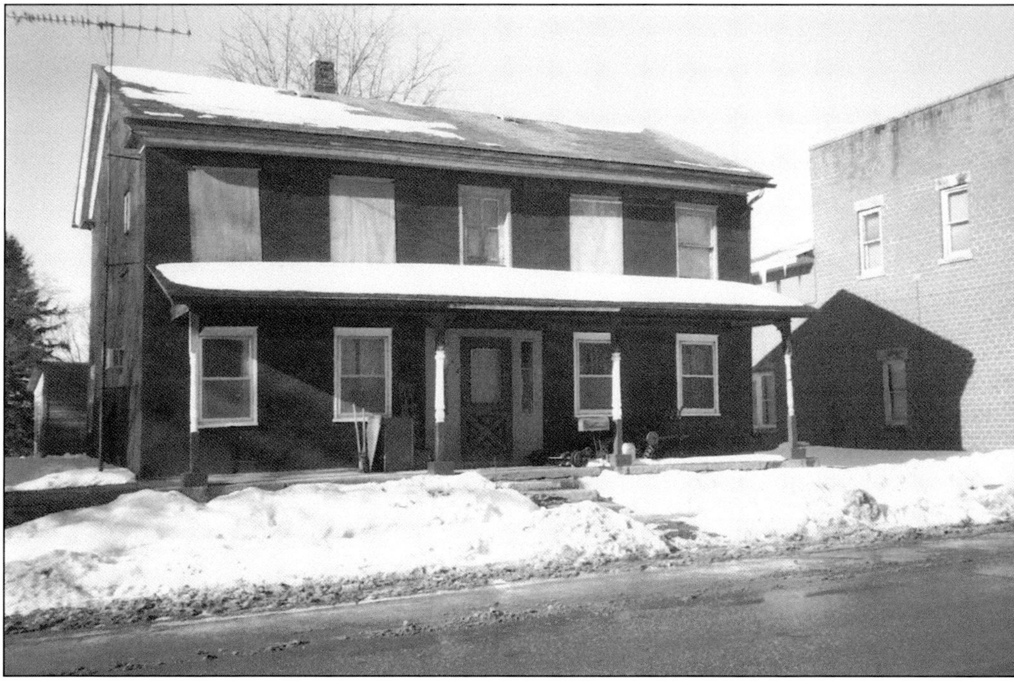

Brown's Hotel/Clermont House Hotel, Current Photograph. Mr. Brunson probably began construction on "Brown's Hotel," or "Clermont House Hotel," in 1850 or 1851. Mr. C.D. Carlton, the owner of the mill, completed the hotel in 1852. Mr. Edwin Brown may have purchased the hotel from P.J. Wright and renamed it the "Brown's Hotel." It is probably one of the oldest structures in town. Ulysses S. Grant may have slept here.

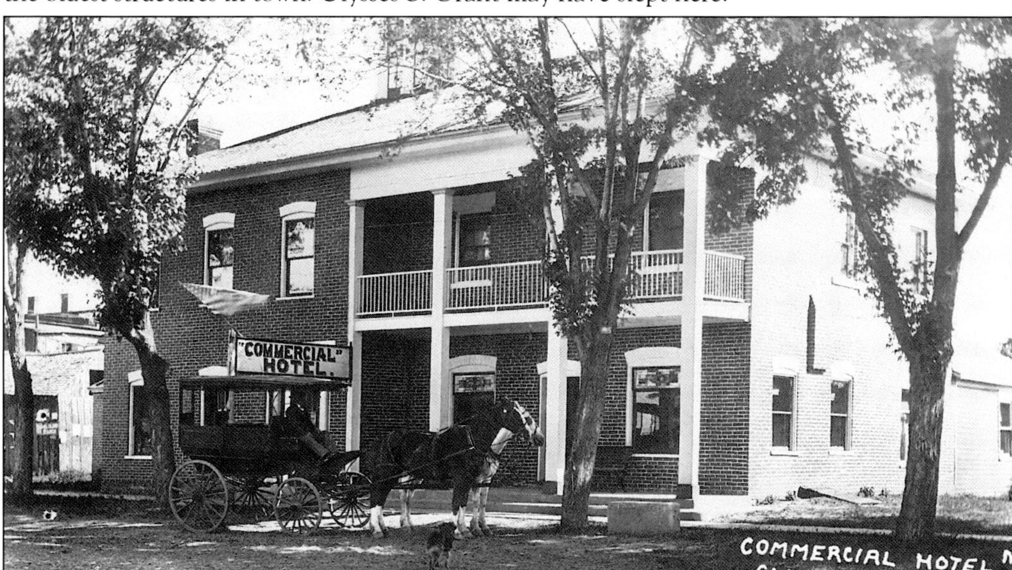

Commercial Hotel, 1912. The new hotel, constructed by Captain G.A. Appelman, was located on what is now Union Street. Mr. and Mrs. Martin Van Dibble ran the hotel for a time. Martin's sister Mrs. Jessie Triem also worked in the hotel. M.V. Dibble ran a "bus" (horse and buggy) service from the railroad depot to the hotel.

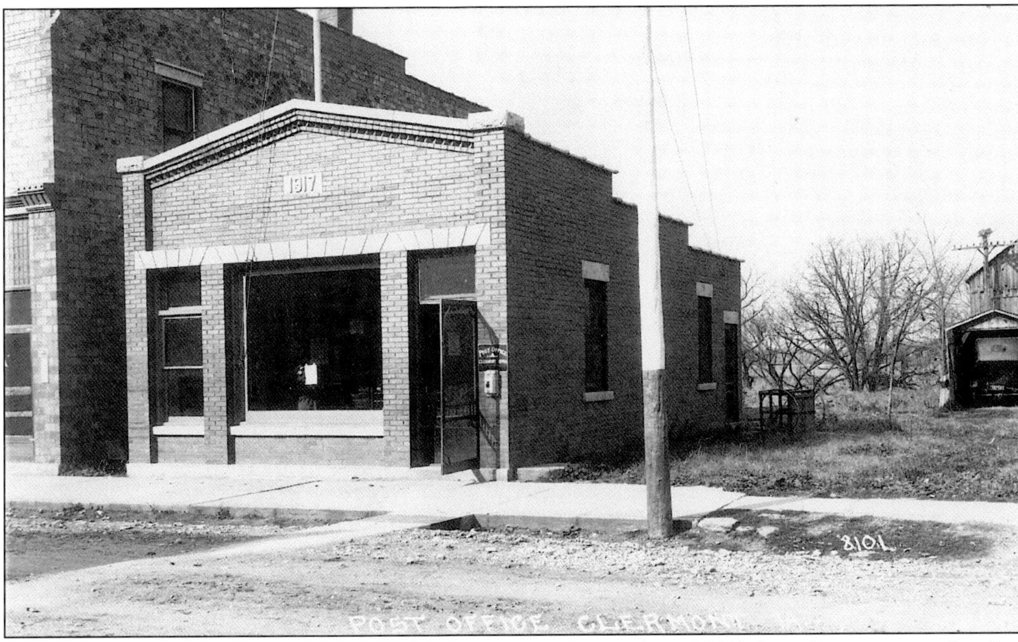

Post Office at Clermont. The building was constructed in 1917, but this was not the first post office. The first postcard was delivered on May 22, 1873, to Dr. Hinckley.

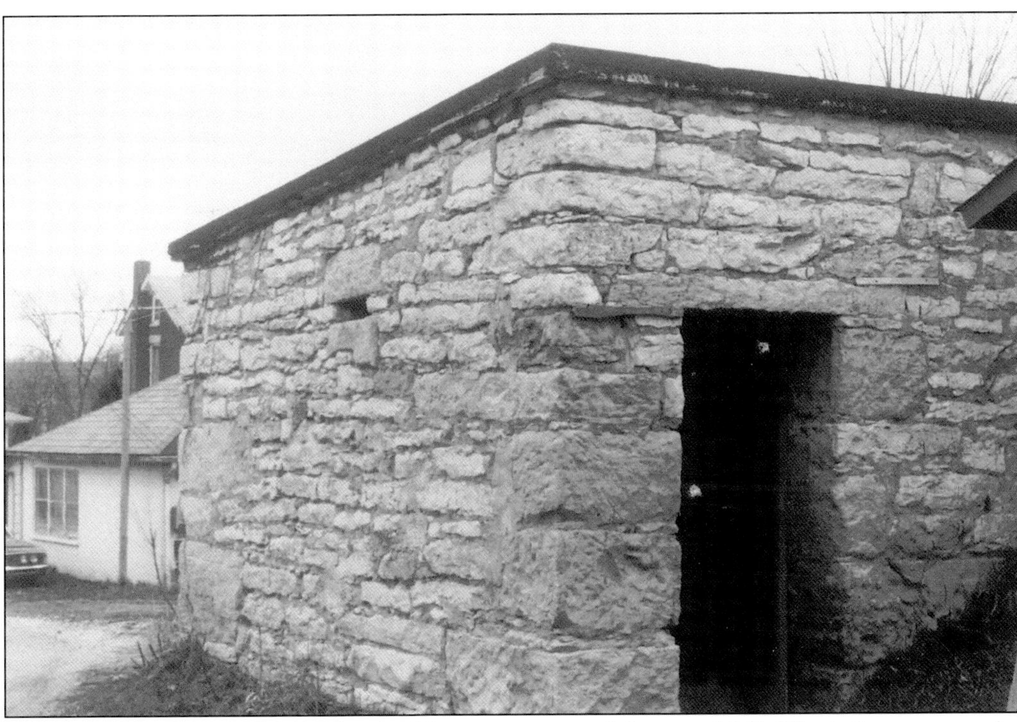

Old Jail. This is one of the oldest buildings in town and dates to 1852. The jail, constructed of limestone, had only one cell with 4-inch slits for light. It was most likely (and probably often) used to offer "shelter" to the inebriated for a night or two.

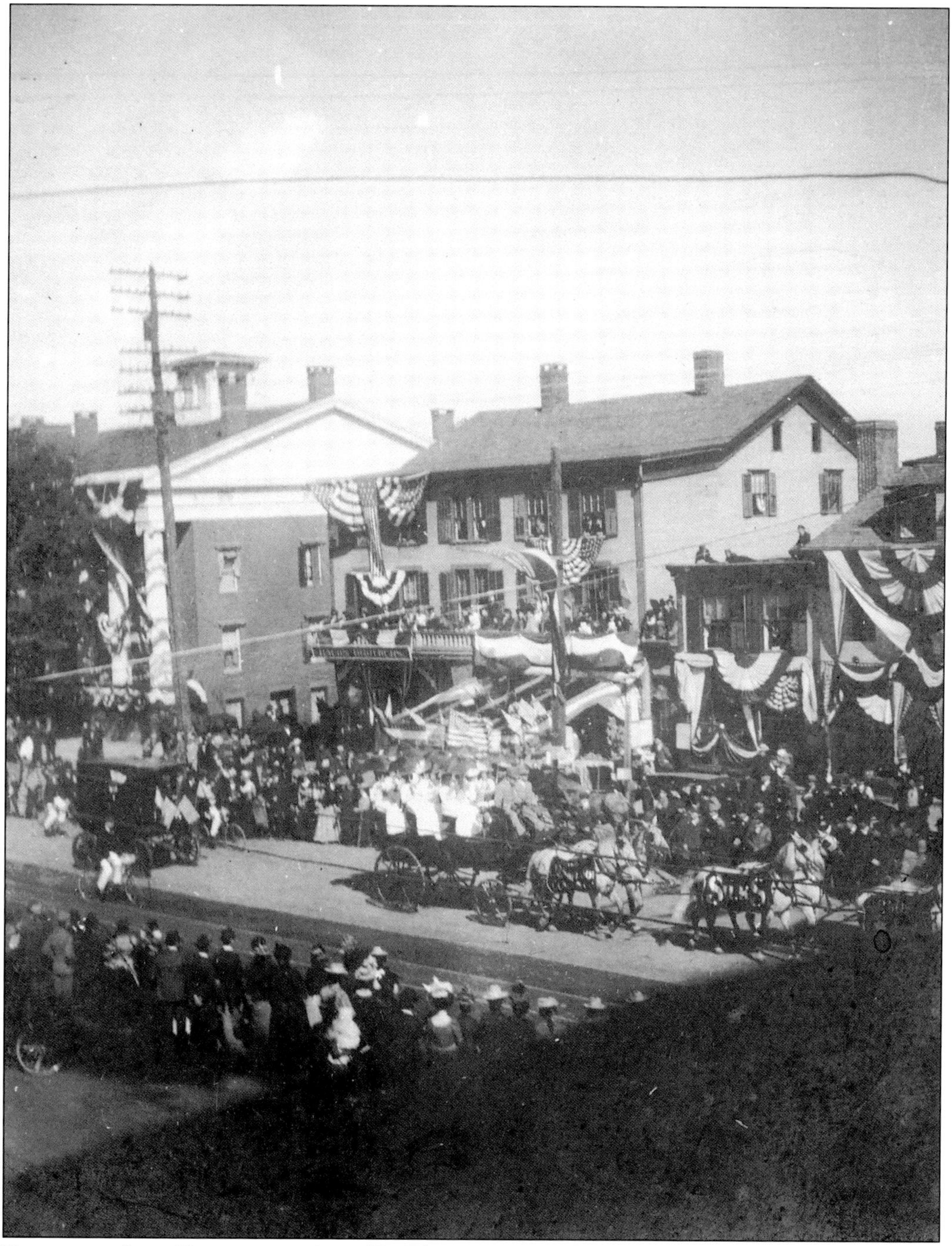

Fourth of July Parade, c. 1900 (?). The Commercial Hotel with its distinctive cupola is on the left. The prosperity of this period is evident in the buildings. The parade appears to be proceeding along the road to Elgin.

Eight

MONUMENTS AND DEDICATIONS

The dedication of the statues of Abraham Lincoln and David B. Henderson on June 19, 1903, represented something of a milestone in Clermont's history, as this was the first time the town made an effort to acknowledge a heroic past. The presentation ceremonies were presided over by the Twelfth Iowa Infantry, Henderson's old Civil War regiment, while the West Union High School Band and the Clermont Chorus supplied the music. Those present included 250 veterans of the Civil War, the guest of honor, David Henderson, and other notaries. According to the late Frances Cline, one of the town historians, the soldiers were housed at Montauk, at Pahpukkeena Hall (an early community meeting place), and at the Union Sunday School. B.C. Gruver, H.B. Rogers, and John Miller were responsible for the free meals, water, and ice. The following photos are views of the monuments as well as the ceremonies surrounding the dedication.

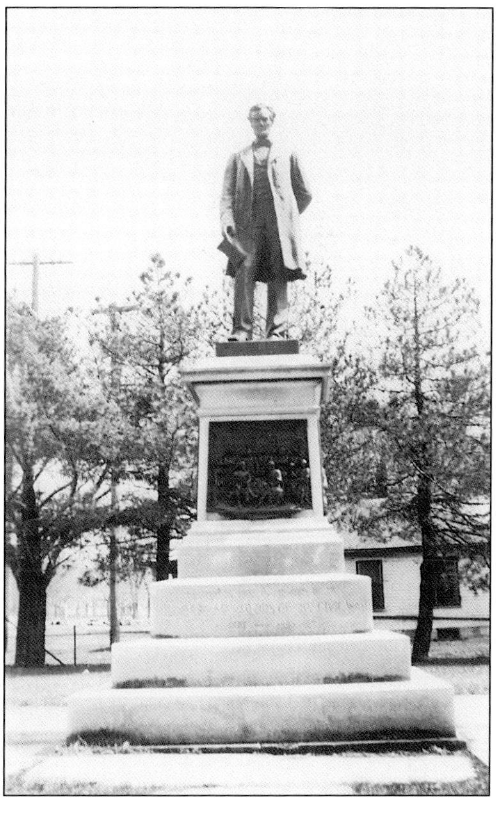

LINCOLN STATUE. This remarkable bronze likeness of Abraham Lincoln was originally cast from a life mask. It remains a town treasure.

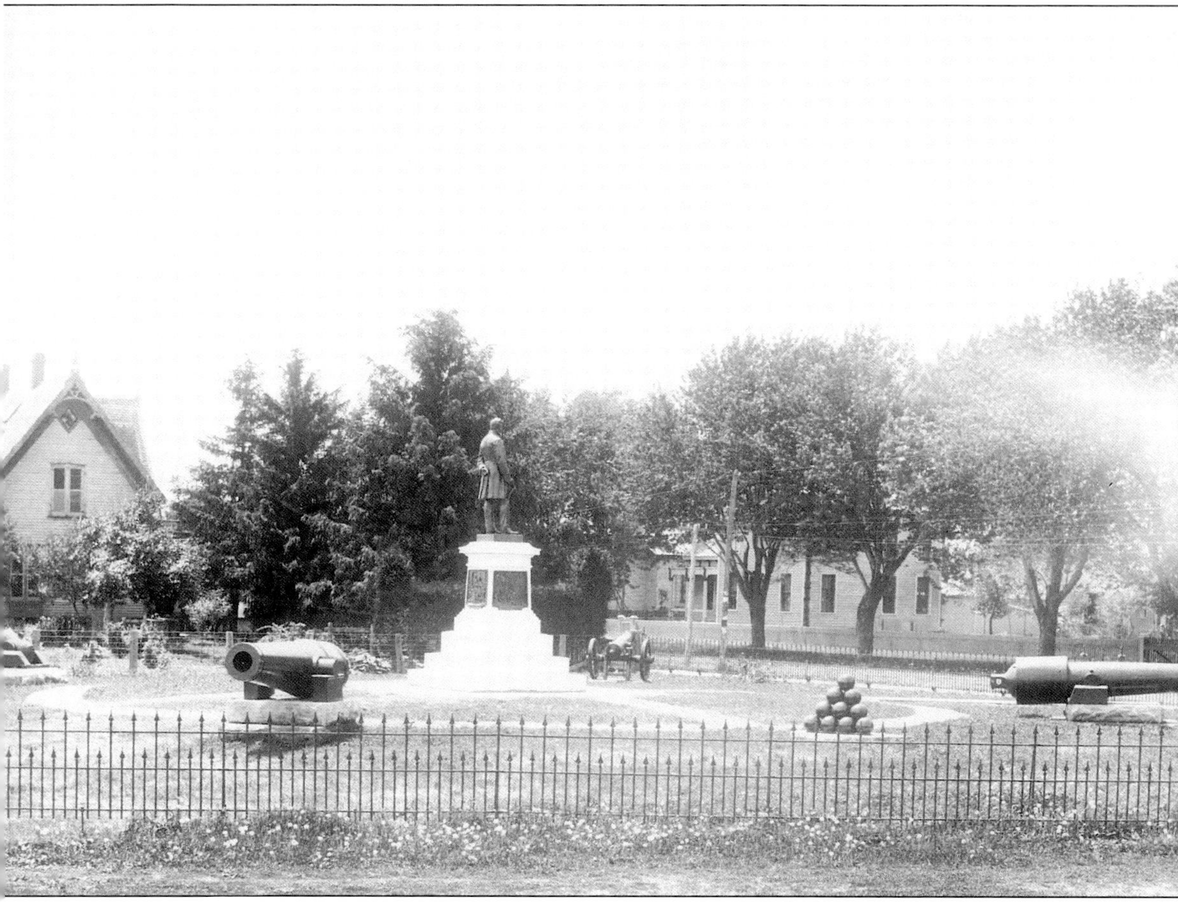

Lincoln Monument and View of Park. William Larrabee commissioned this statue in 1912. The view of the monument shows the four Civil War cannons and assorted cannon balls that once guarded the park. Balls and cannons were melted down for scrap during World War II. The monument was raised with block and tackle and a four-horse team. The citizens of Clermont paid for the park at 25¢ a share.

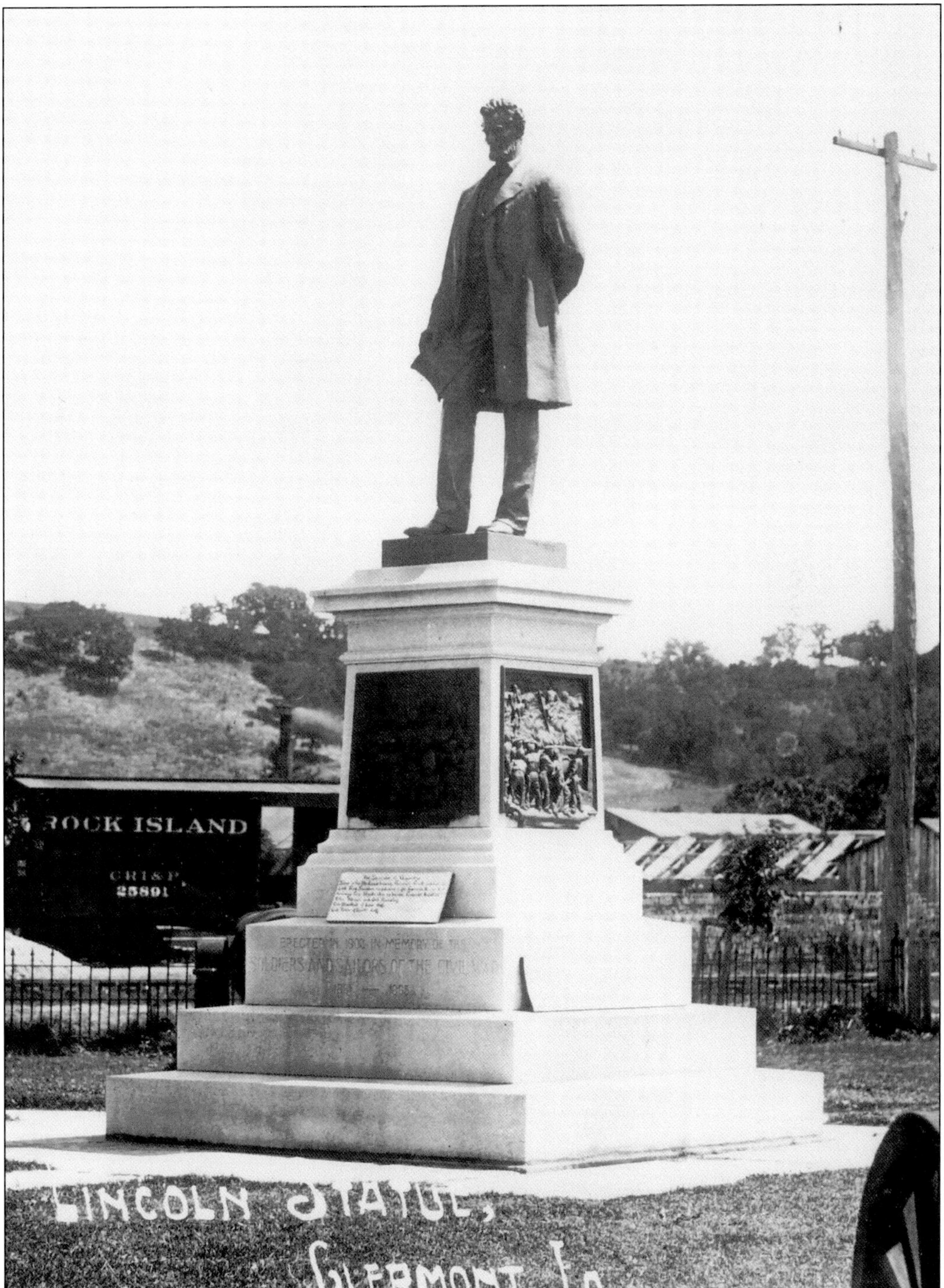

VIEW OF LINCOLN MONUMENT. This scene of the Lincoln monument provides a view of the brickyard in the background. The monument was sculpted by George Bissell of Mount Vernon, N.Y., and depicts Lincoln holding the Emancipation Proclamation. The likeness of Lincoln was taken from a life mask and is considered to be an accurate portrait of the president.

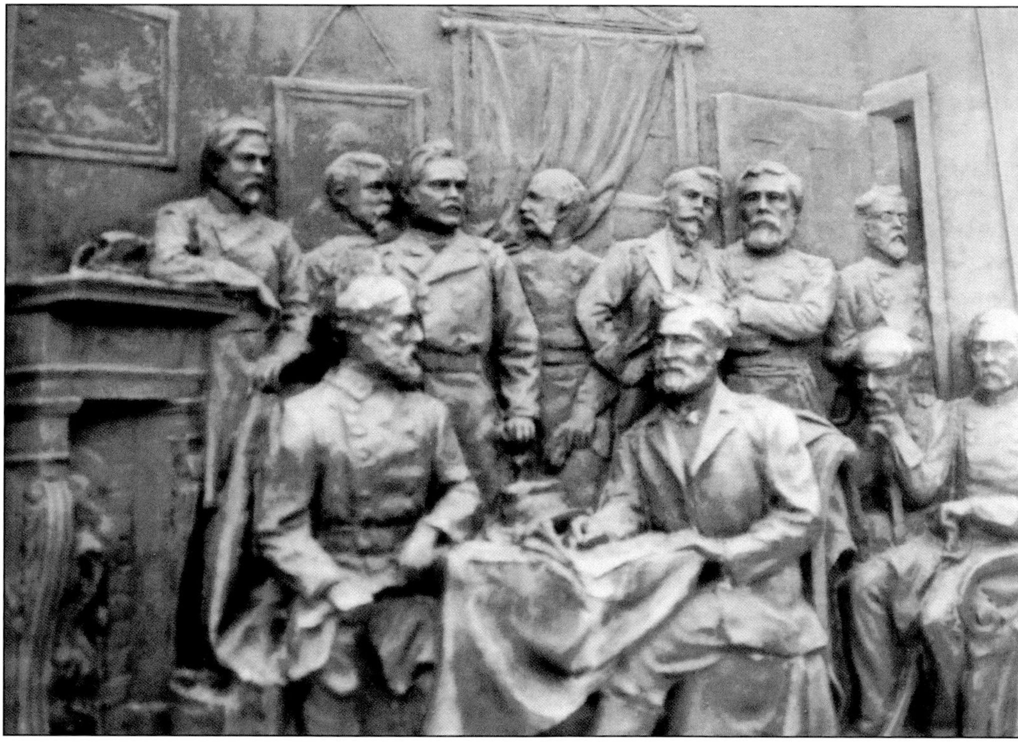

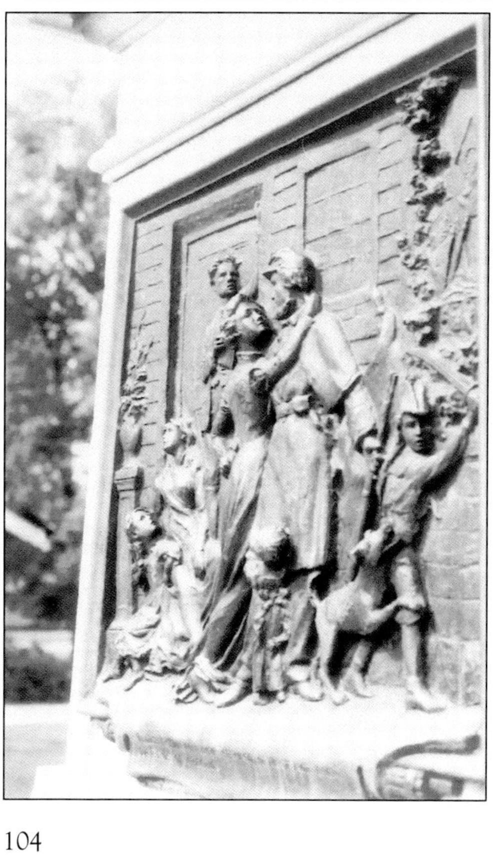

These four bas relief plaques were also sculpted by George Bissell. They depict the following:

"APPOMATOX COURTHOUSE"-WEST. The scene depicts General Robert E. Lee's surrender to General Ulysses S. Grant at the Appomatox Courthouse.

"TOM HENDERSON LEAVING HOME"-EAST SIDE. Tom Henderson, the brother of David Henderson, lost his life in the Civil War. He lived on a farm north of Clermont. Here we see him bidding his wife and children farewell as he departs with Company C of the 12th Iowa regiment.

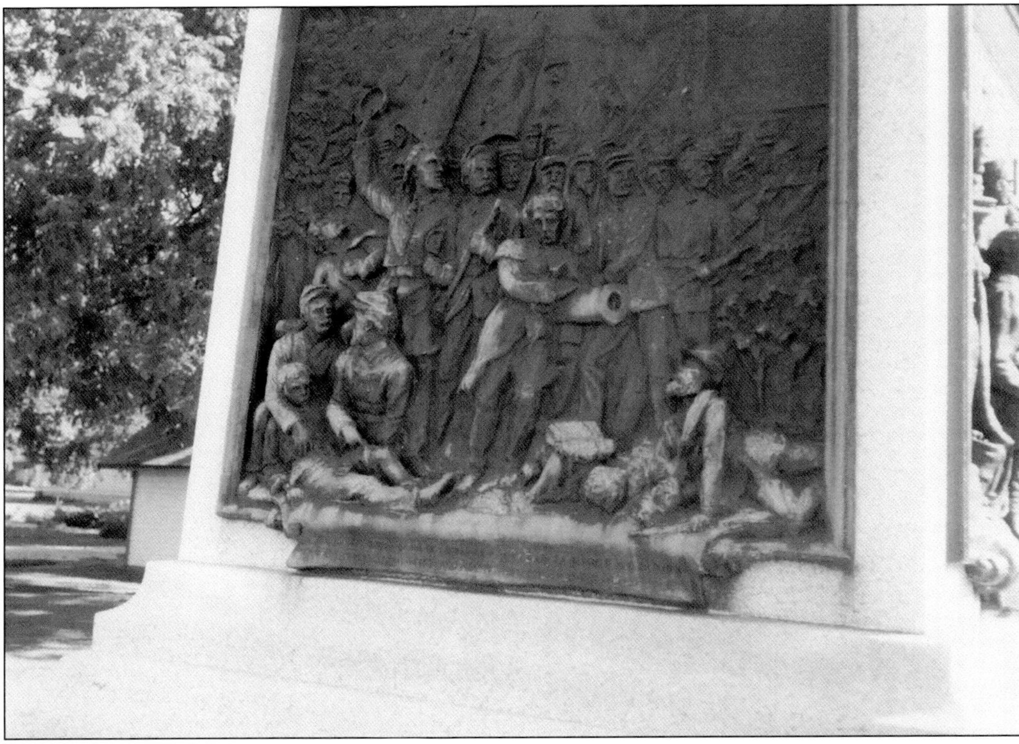

"THE BATTLE OF SHILOH"-NORTH SIDE. The scene depicts Clermont soldiers fighting at Shiloh during the Civil War.

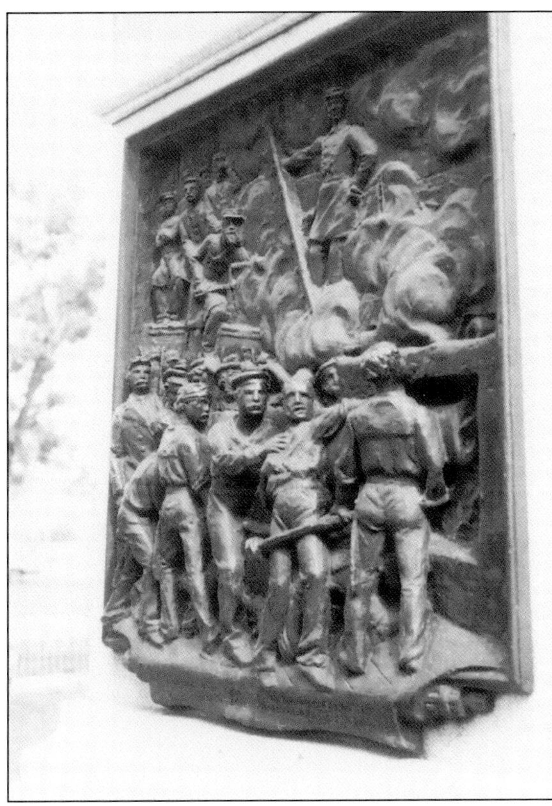

"THE BATTLE OF MOBILE BAY"-SOUTH SIDE. Admiral David Glasgow Farragut is strapped to the rigging of his flagship, *Mississippi*, while George Dewey is standing on the deck below.

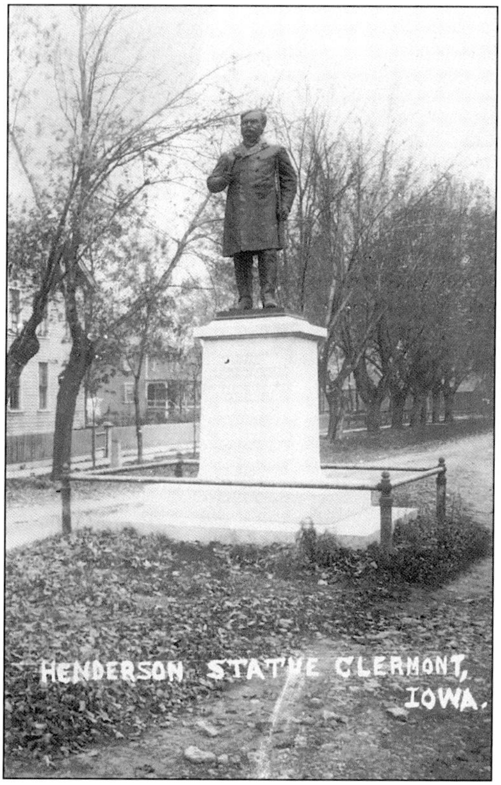

HENDERSON MONUMENT. The statue of David Bremner Henderson (1840–1906) stands a heroic 7 feet, 6 inches high. Erected by Gov. William Larrabee, the bronze giant, once commanding a central location on Mill Street, now stands in the front yard of the Episcopal church. Henderson, avid supporter and friend of Larrabee, was a popular political figure and legislator who served as a member of Congress from the third district in Iowa for ten consecutive terms and as the Speaker of the House in 1899 and in 1901. The statue was sculpted by George Massey Rhind.

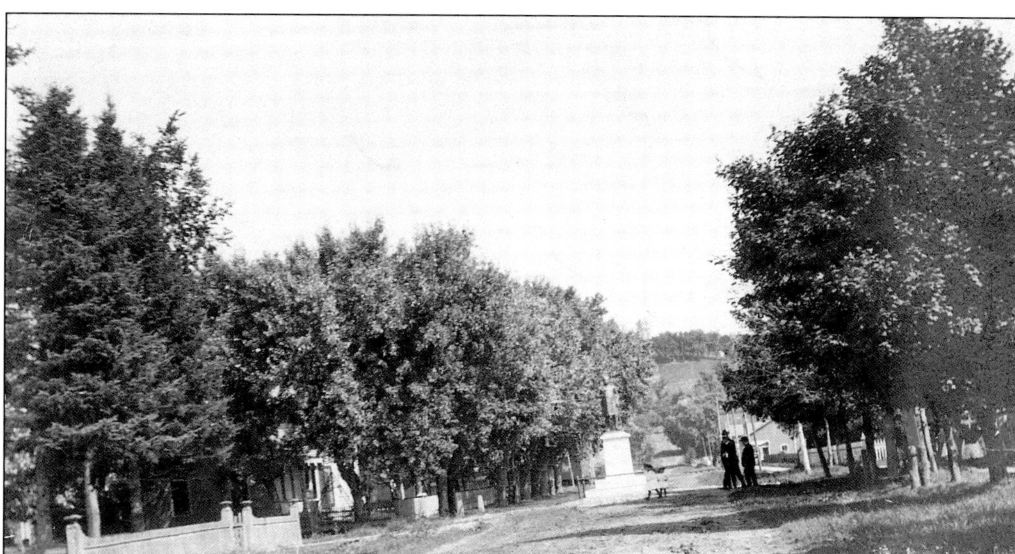

HENDERSON MONUMENT IN THE MIDDLE OF MAIN STREET.

GRAND DEDICATION AT CLERMONT

FRIDAY, JUNE 19, 1903

PROGRAM

Assemble at Lincoln Monument at 2:00 P. M.

Music........................ West Union H. S. Band
Invocation........................... Rev. M. S. Rice
Music.............................. Clermont Chorus
Presentation of Lincoln Monument.............
.... Hon. Wm. Larrabee
Response....................... Mayor J. H. Sheehan
Music........................ West Union H. S. Band

Assemble at Henderson Statue.

Music................................ Clermont Chorus
Unveiling of Statue.......... Miss Helen Larrabee
Music......................... West Union H. S. Band

PRESENTATION OF STATUE.

Dedication Ceremonies by 12th Iowa Infantry.
Music......................... West Union H. S. Band

Assemble at Pavillion.

Vocal Music---
Address .... Col. D. B. Henderson
Music........................ West Union H. S. Band
Address .... Hon. J. P. Dolliver
Music.............................. Band with Chorus

REUNION PROGRAM.

Friday, June 19.

Sunset Salute—Lowering the Flag.
Martial Music.
7:00 P. M.—Assemble in Pavillion.
Music.

Invocation .... Dr. T. J. Bassett

Assemble at Henderson Statue.

Music................................ Clermont Chorus
Unveiling of Statue.......... Miss Helen Larrabee
Music......................... West Union H. S. Band

PRESENTATION OF STATUE.

Dedication Ceremonies by 12th Iowa Infantry.
Music......................... West Union H. S. Band

Assemble at Pavillion.

Vocal Music---
Address .... Col. D. B. Henderson
Music........................ West Union H. S. Band
Address .... Hon. J. P. Dolliver
Music.............................. Band with Chorus

REUNION PROGRAM.

Friday, June 19.

Sunset Salute—Lowering the Flag.
Martial Music.
7:00 P. M.—Assemble in Pavillion.
Music.

Invocation .... Dr. T. J. Bassett

Vocal Music.

Address of Welcome to the "Twelfth" .... A. H. Loomis
Response .... Major D. W. Reed

Music.

Address .... Hon. W. B. Allison

Music.

Reading—"The Man Without a Country" .... Miss Beulah Wright, U. I. U.
Love Feast.—Opened by Col. Jack Stibbs, Hon. R. W. Tirrell, Capt. E. B. Soper
Reading Letters from Absent Comrades.
12:00 P. M.—Midnight Tattoo.

Saturday, June 20th.

Sunrise Salute—6:00 O'clock Reveille.
8:00 A. M.—Assemble at Headquarters.
Music
Business Meeting.
Singing Songs, Telling Stories, Visiting, Love Feast and Good Time For All.
12:00 M. Adjourn. Good Bye.

THE Rock Island and C., M. & St. P. will issue tickets at reduced rates; also furnish special trains for the occasion. All are invited to attend and take part in these exercises

GRAND DEDICATION AT CLERMONT. This is the original program printed for the dedication ceremonies of the Lincoln and Henderson statues.

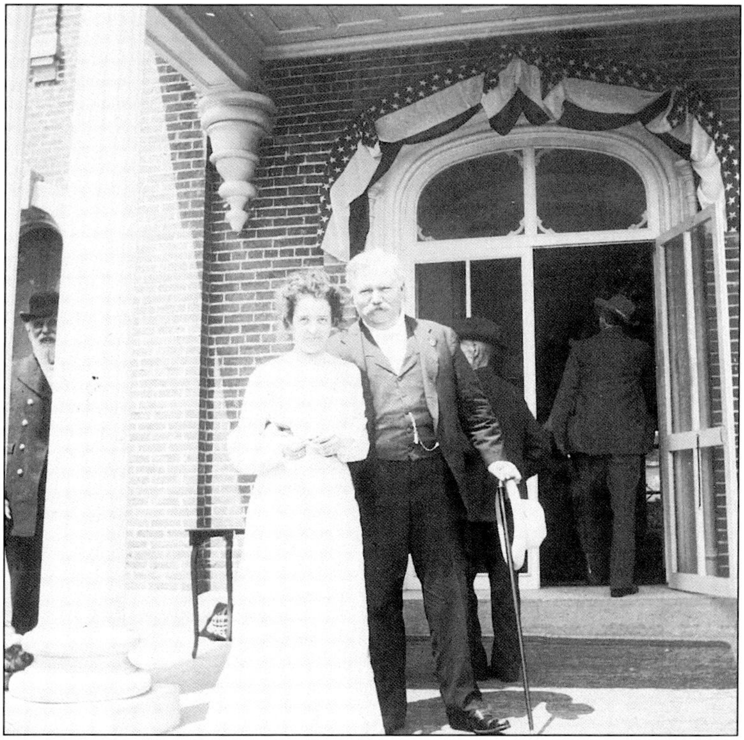

VIEWS FROM MONTAUK DURING THE CEREMONY. Helen Larrabee with David Henderson in front of Montauk.

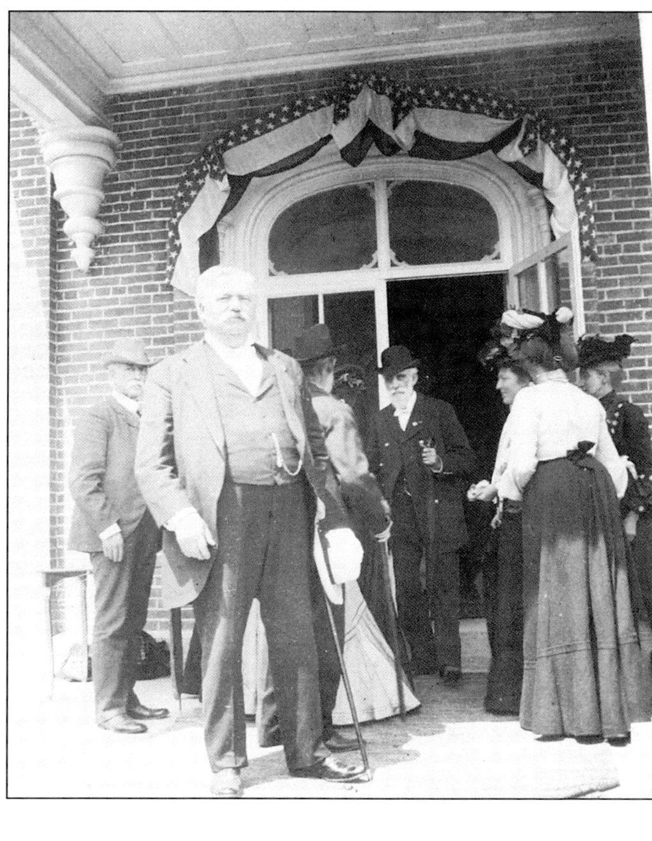

DAVID HENDERSON ON THE LAWN AT MONTAUK DURING THE DEDICATION CEREMONIES.

Mrs. William Larrabee Sr. Mrs. Larrabee is pictured here greeting dignitaries during the dedication ceremonies festivities.

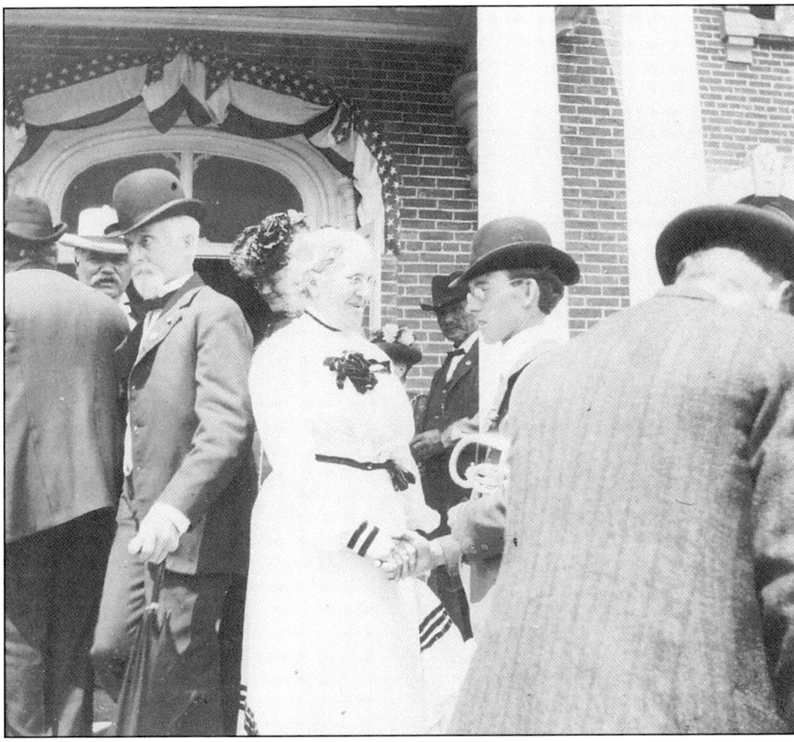

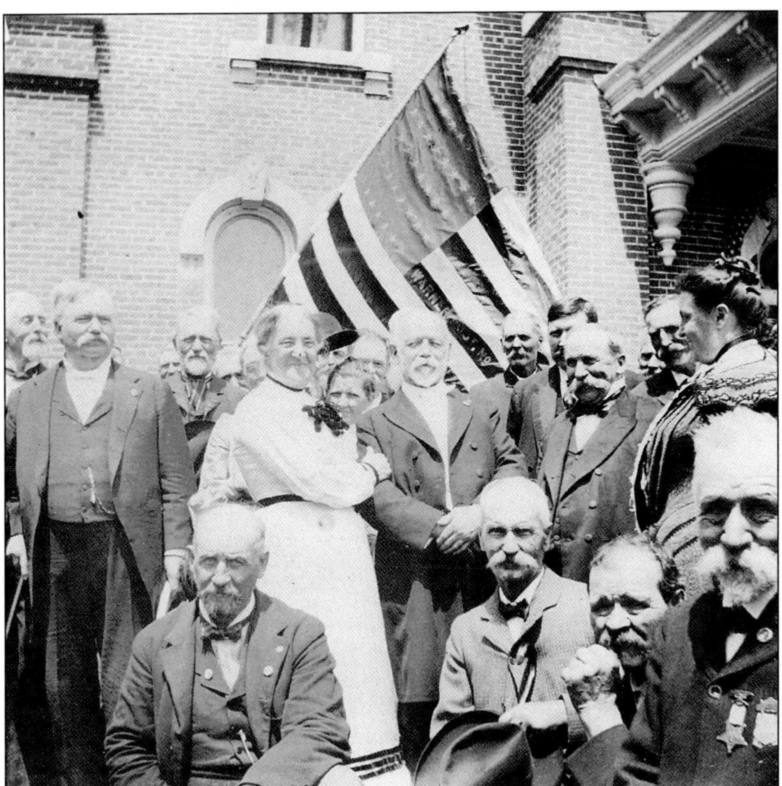

Mrs. William Larrabee Sr. Mrs. Larrabee is shown here with members of the 12th Iowa Infantry at Montauk. David Henderson is on the far left.

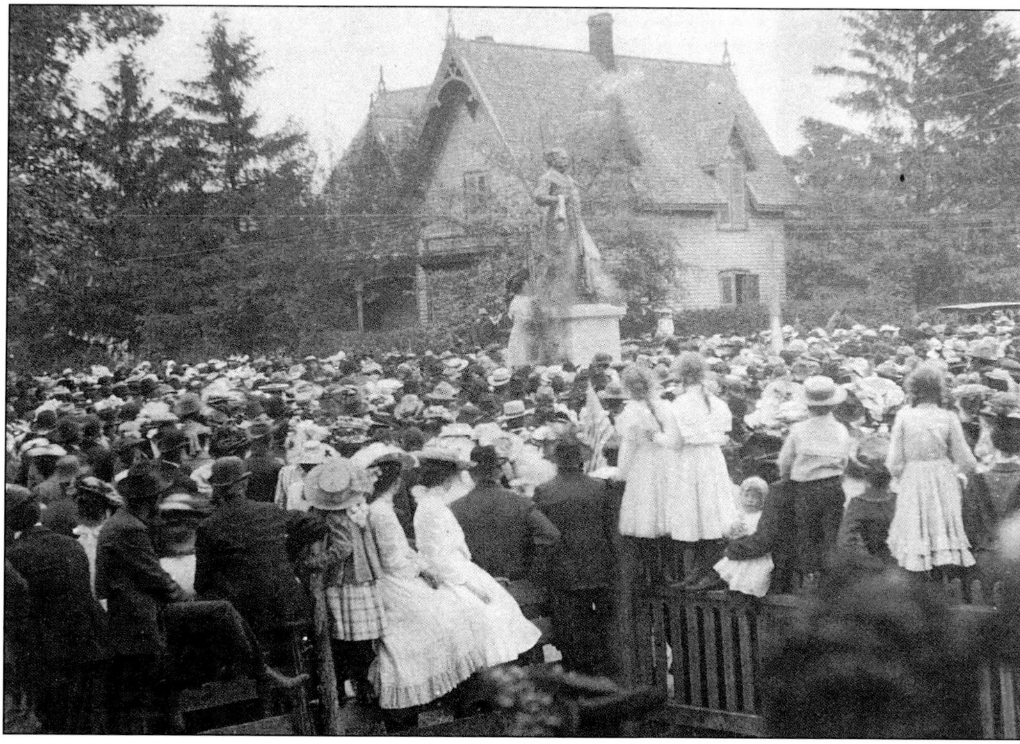

VIEW OF STREET DURING DEDICATION CEREMONY.

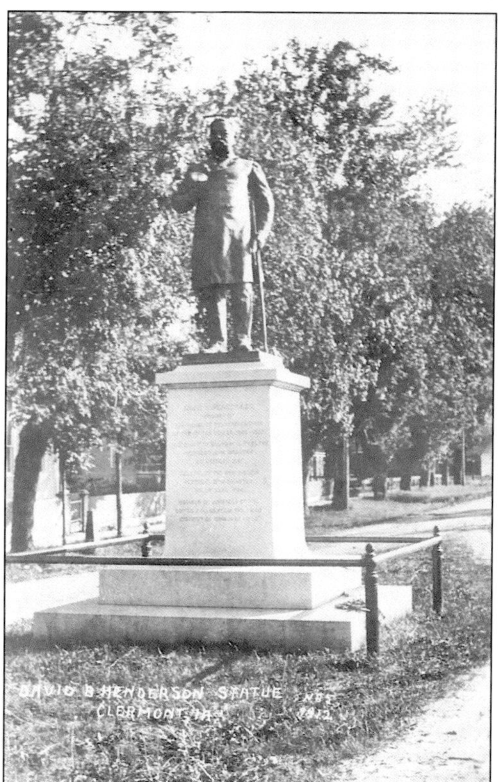

HENDERSON MONUMENT ON MAIN STREET.

Nine

People and Families

Some family names are well known in Clermont while others are not, their stories being only fragile memories. Clermont does remember and honor the founders and early settlers of the town with an impressive bronze plaque with the names of these families clearly inscribed. The plaque is located in the park at the north end of town. These names include Appleman, Baker, Blackett, Calvin, Carlton, Dibble, Dixon, Hendershott, Hinkley, Larrabee, Lewis, Payne, Pringle, Sawyer, Stedman, Thompson, and Weck. The following photos represent only a small fraction of the many people who have lived in Clermont.

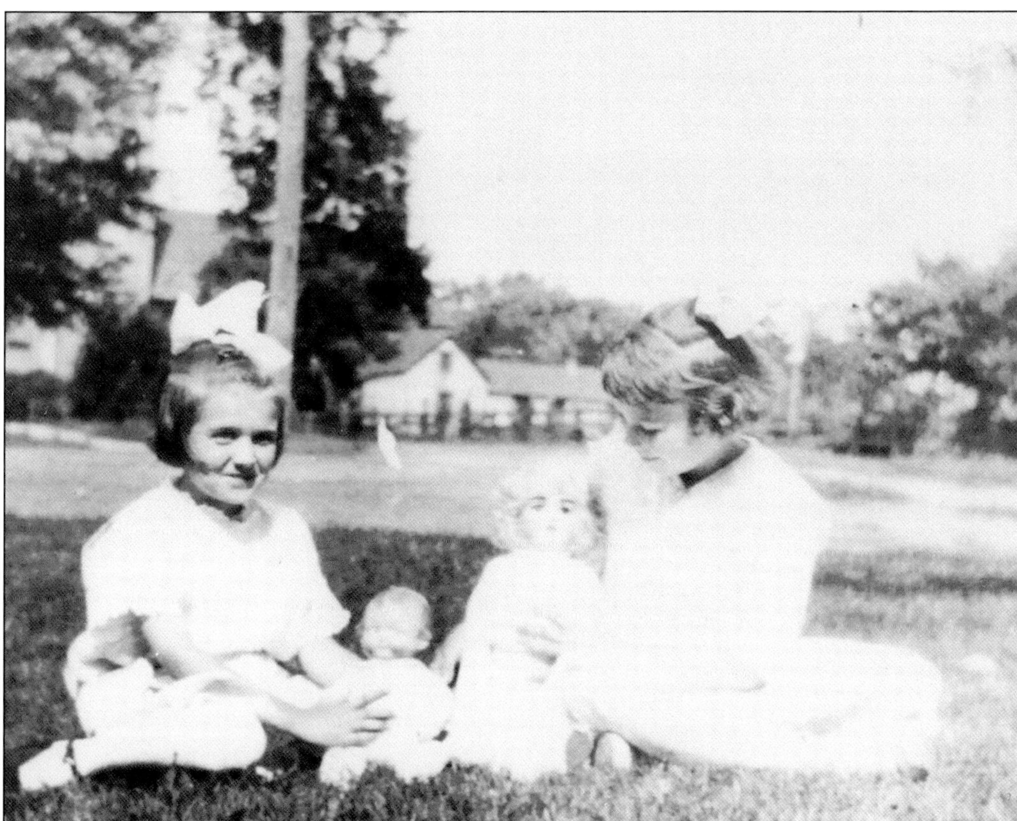

Anna Bigler and Ruby Robbins with "Billie" and "Flora Dora."

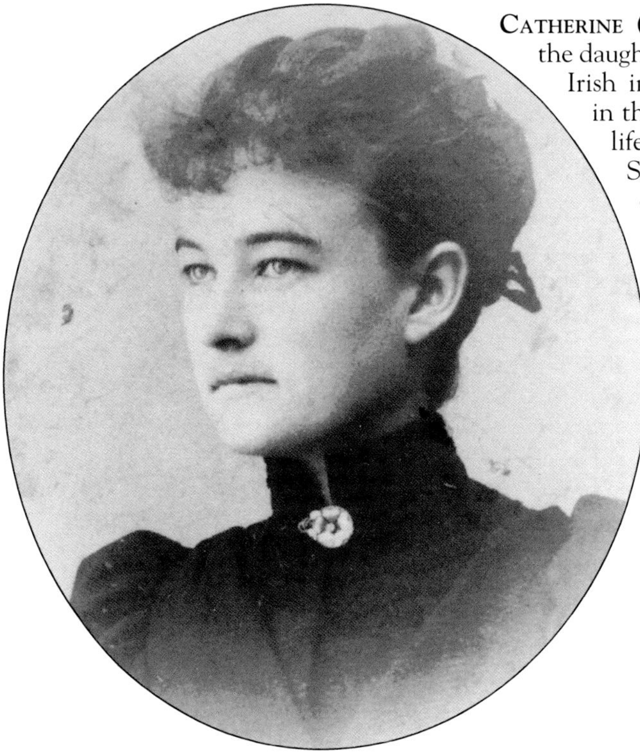

CATHERINE ("KATE") (1874–1957). Kate was the daughter of Cornelius and Mary Sullivan, Irish immigrants who came to Clermont in the mid-1850s. She lived most of her life on the corner house on Larrabee Street across from the Lutheran church. She raised three children in Clermont, Floyd, Charles (Chuck), and Anna.

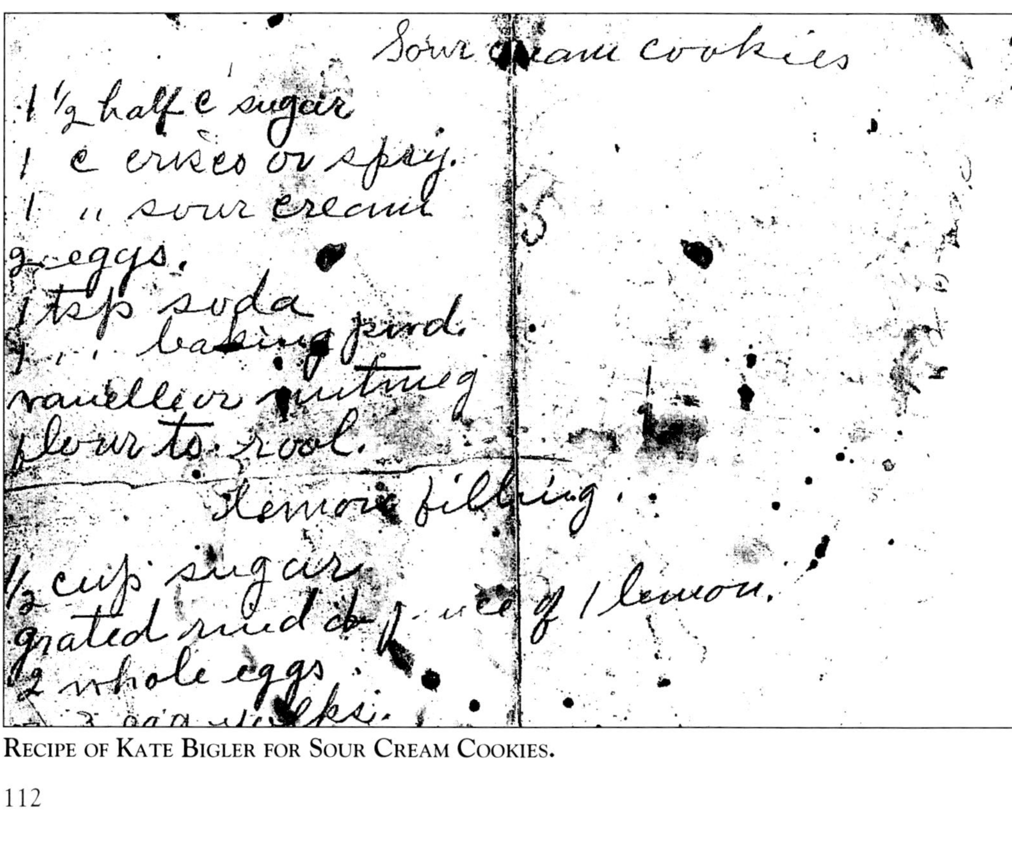

Sour cream cookies

1 1/2 half c sugar
1 c crisco or spry.
1 " sour cream
2 eggs.
1 tsp soda
1 " baking powd.
vanilla or nutmeg
flour to rool.

Lemon filling

1/2 cup sugar
grated rind & juice of 1 lemon.
2 whole eggs
2 egg yolks.

RECIPE OF KATE BIGLER FOR SOUR CREAM COOKIES.

FRED BIGLER (1879–1946). He was the son of Frederick Bigler Sr. and Susan Bigler (Wenger). He owned a harness shop on Main Street and married Kate Sullivan in 1897. He built the house on Larrabee Street across from the Lutheran church.

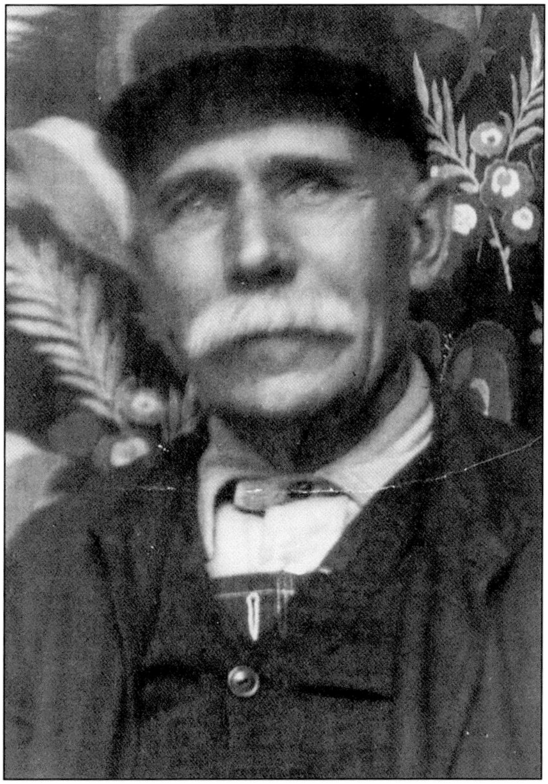

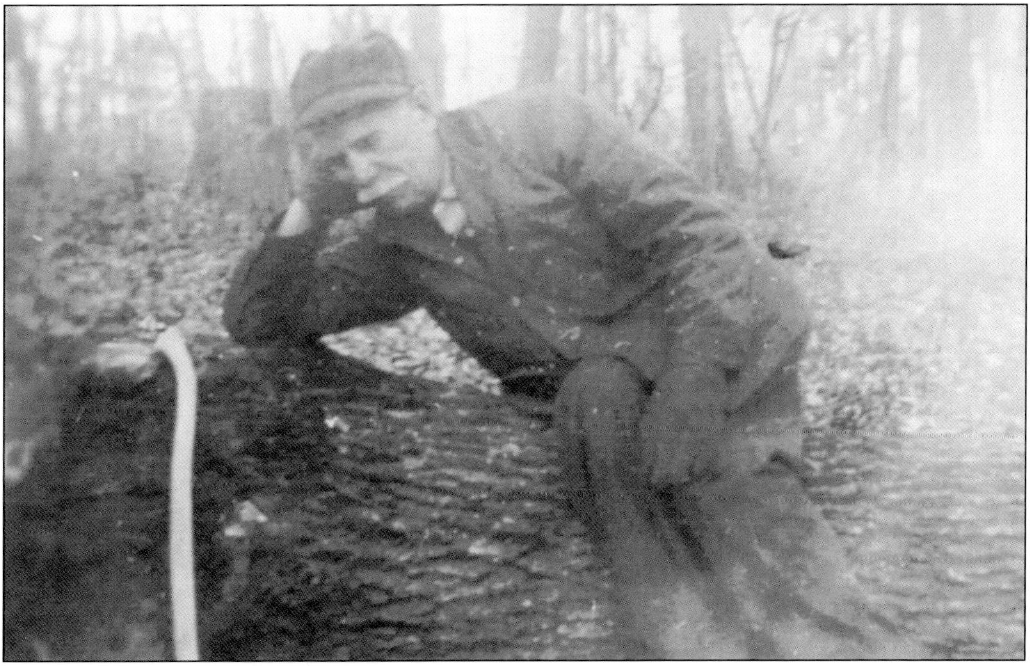

Fred Bigler, in repose, also owned a sawmill at the back of his harness shop. His specialty was walnut logs that he processed and sold. From this beautiful wood, bowls and furniture were created. The walnut trees he planted are still in front of the house he built on Larrabee Street.

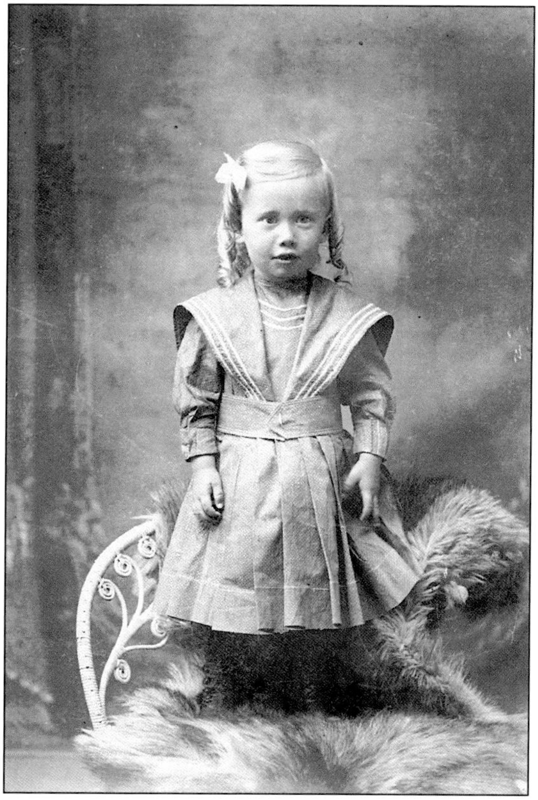

FLOYD BIGLER (1899–1959), C. 1902. Floyd was the eldest son of Fred and Kate Bigler. He worked in the Double Store in Clermont. He married Irene LeValley and moved to Cedar Falls where he remained for the rest of his life.

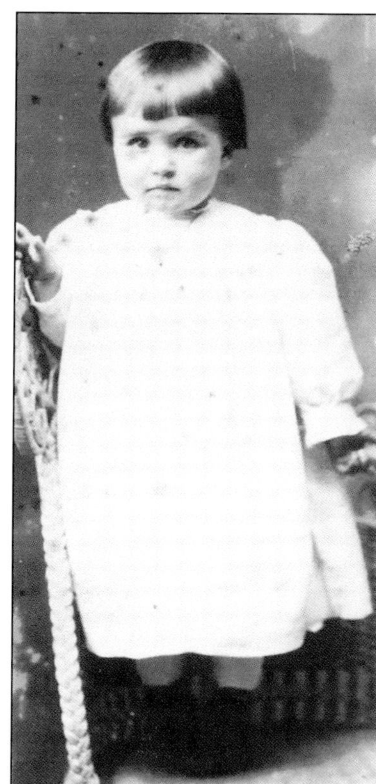

ANNA BIGLER, C. 1908–1909. Anna Bigler was the youngest child of Fred and Kate Bigler. She attended the University of Northern Iowa and returned to teach school in the Larrabee building. She married Nicolay Jurgens in 1930 and moved to Minneapolis where she raised six children.

KATE BIGLER WITH DAUGHTER ANNA AT THE BACK DOOR OF HOUSE, C. 1918.

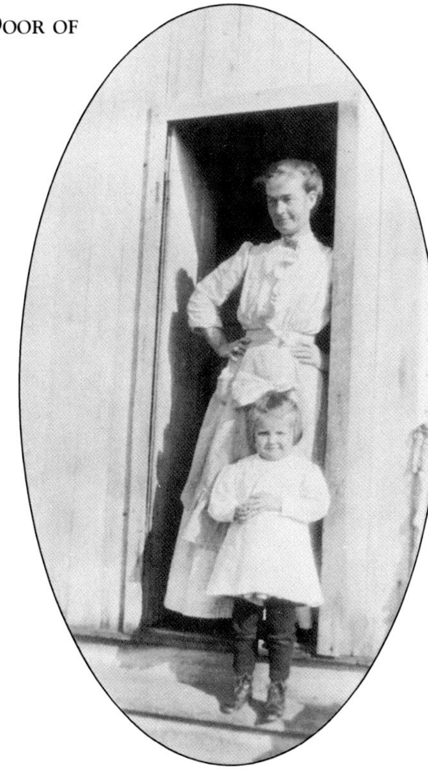

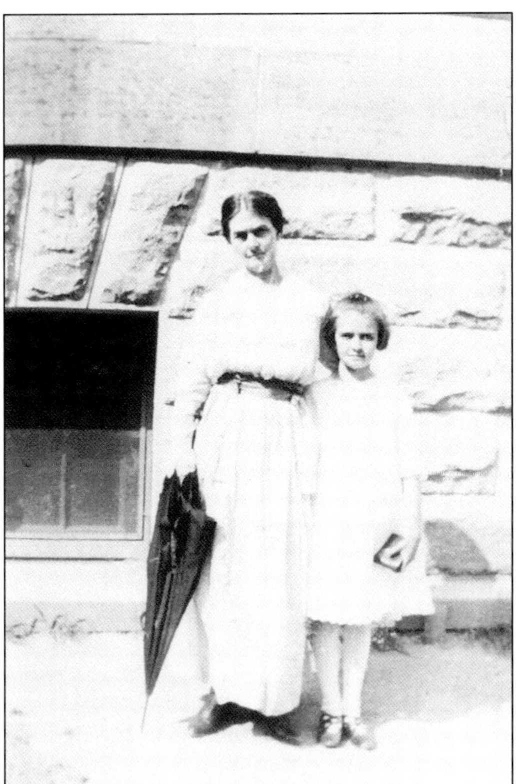

KATE BIGLER (NEE SULLIVAN) WITH DAUGHTER ANNA BIGLER, C. 1910.

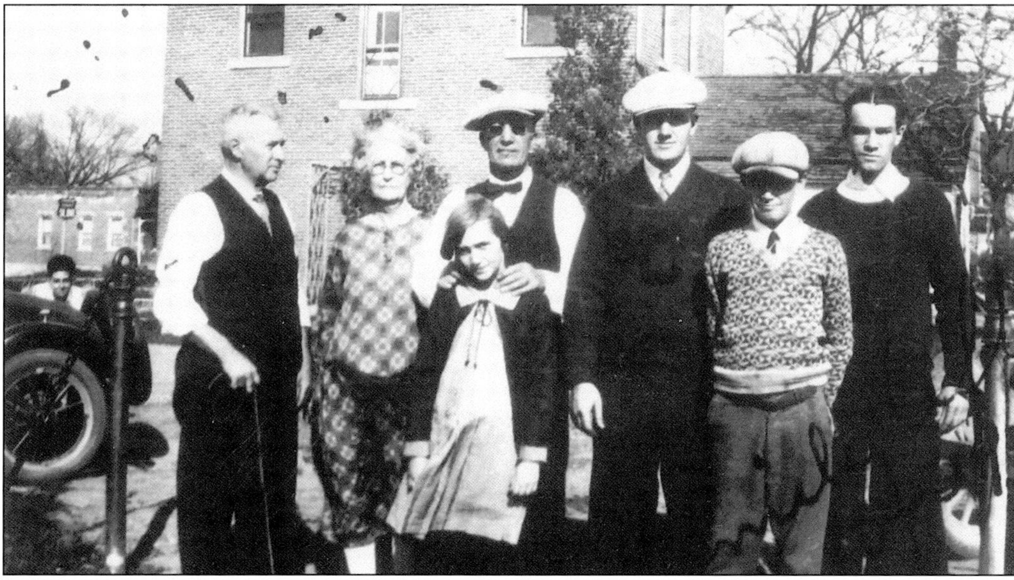

SIMPSON FAMILY, C. 1926. Pictured here are Grandpa and Grandma Still, Art Simpson (father), Buster, Rossiter, Dean, and Lenore in front. Art Simpson fell to his death in a mill accident.

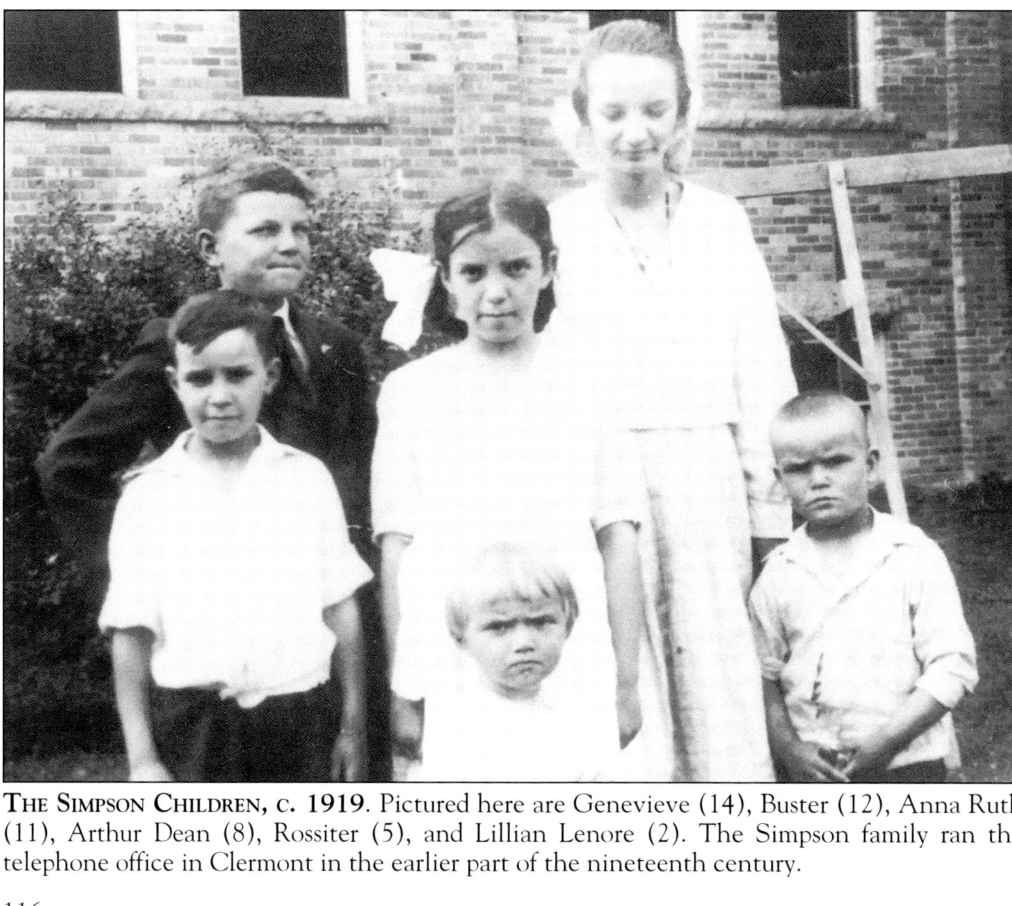

THE SIMPSON CHILDREN, C. 1919. Pictured here are Genevieve (14), Buster (12), Anna Ruth (11), Arthur Dean (8), Rossiter (5), and Lillian Lenore (2). The Simpson family ran the telephone office in Clermont in the earlier part of the nineteenth century.

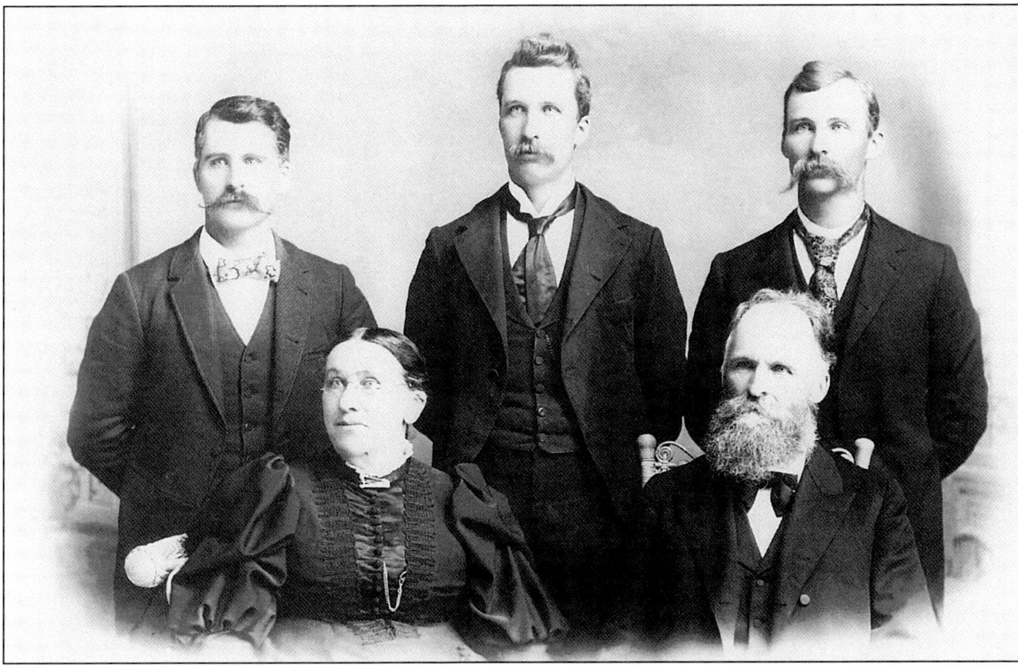

The Becker Family. Frederick ("Doc") Becker practiced medicine in Clermont from 1875 until the late 1890s. Born in Gutenberg, Germany, in 1838, Becker received his medical training at a medical college in Cleveland, Ohio, and at the Homeopathic Medical College in St. Louis, Missouri. He held a number of positions of honor including president of the state board of medical examiners in 1889 and president of the state board of health for several years. He married Sophia Miller in 1859. Pictured here from left to right are (top row) Carl F., George A., and Frederick J.

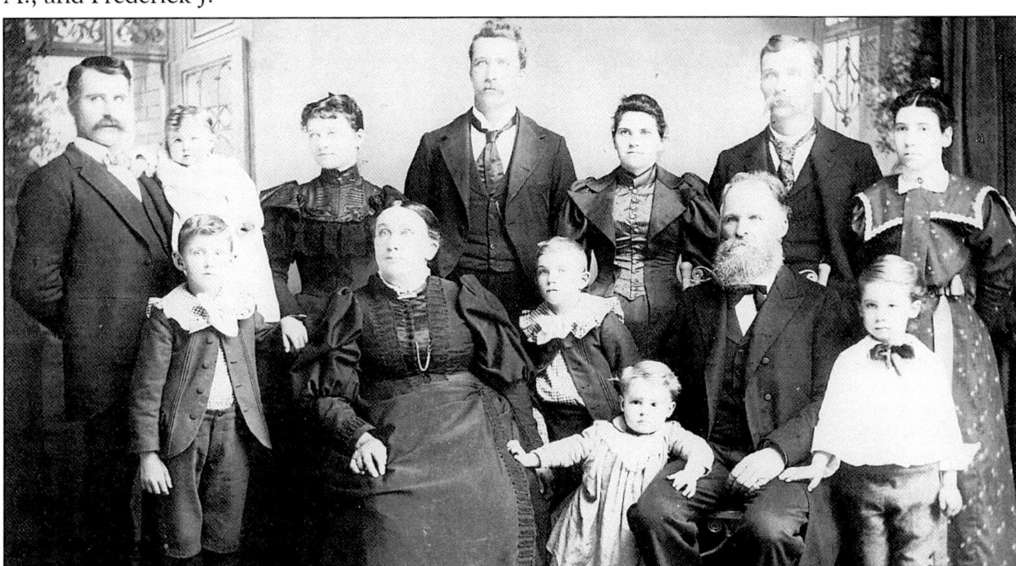

The Extended Becker Family. Sophie and Frederick Becker are shown here with their sons, with their wives and children. Alice Ford Becker, the great aunt of the author, is the second adult from the left in the top row.

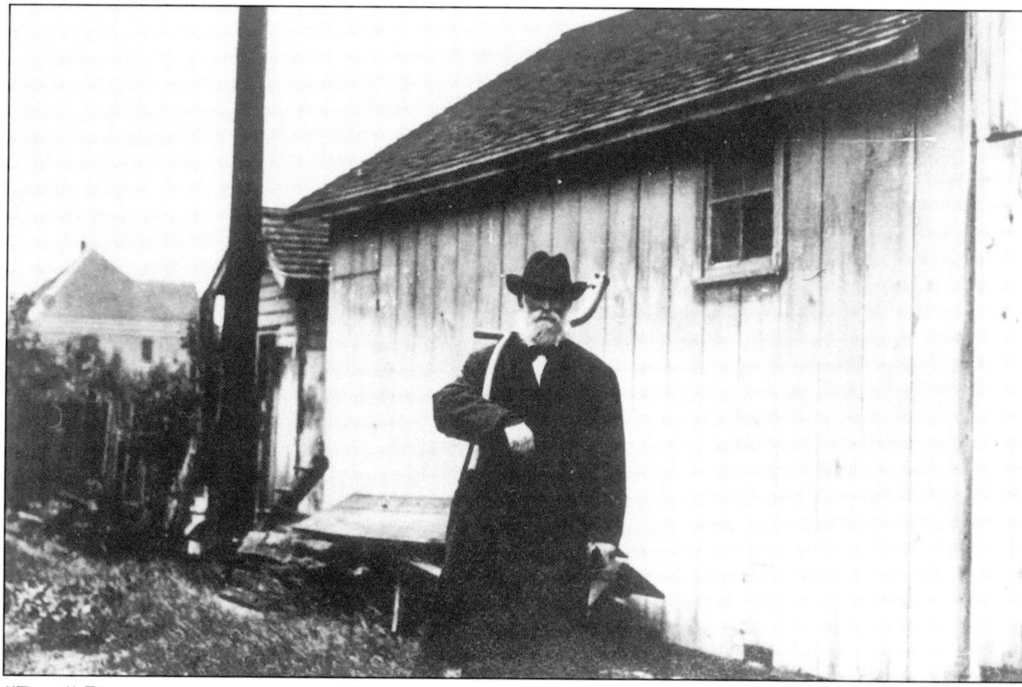

"Doc" Becker on the run in Clermont.

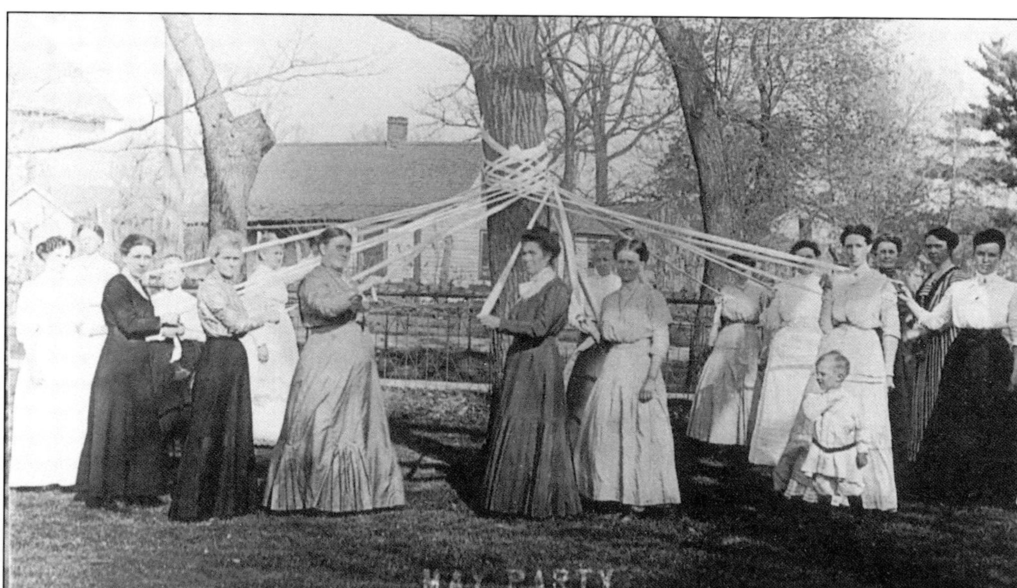

May Party in Clermont, c. 1913. Mrs. William Larrabee Jr. is the second from the left. Lena Gerber is fourth from the left.

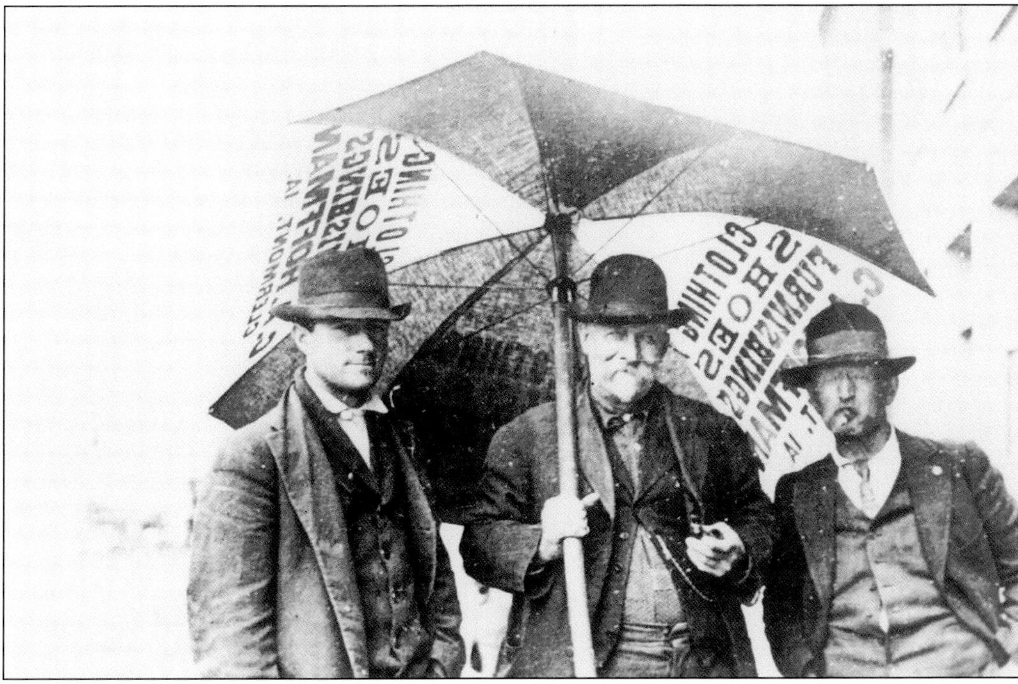

FROM LEFT TO RIGHT, DAN BURKE, JOHN SHEEHY, CHARLES OLSON. Dan Burke was married to Mame Sheehan and owned a store in town; John Sheehy, who carries an umbrella advertising "Clothing, Shoes, Furnishings, C.A. Hoffman, Clermont, IA," was married to Johanna Sullivan and raised 13 children on a farm near Clermont.

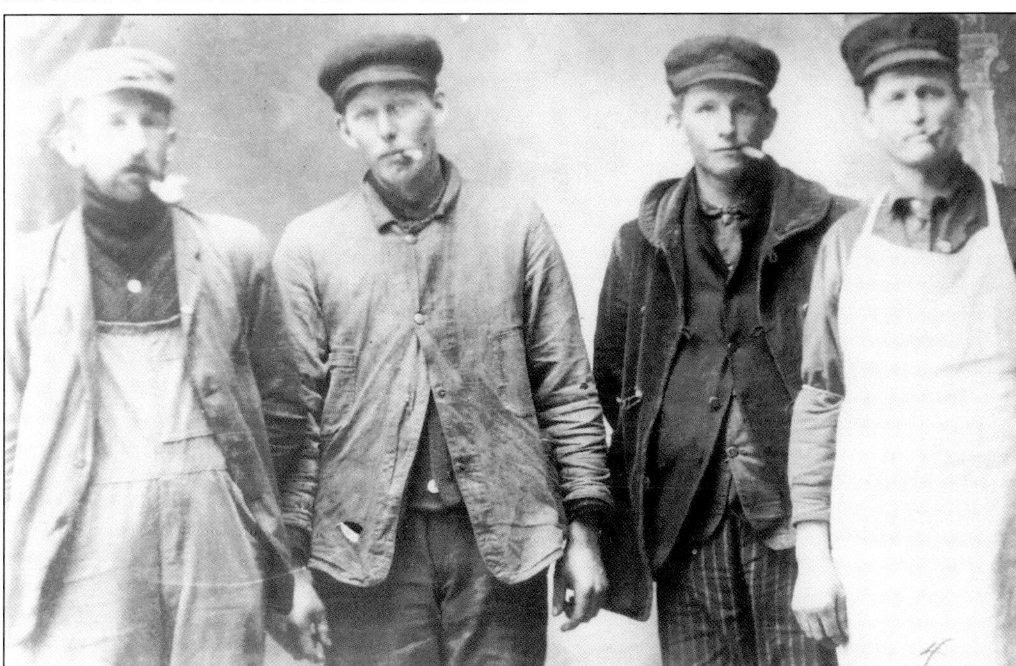

FROM LEFT TO RIGHT, JOHN ROLF, NELS OLSON, GEORGE SCHAVE, FRANK PRINGLE. Pringle owned an ice cream parlor on Main Street.

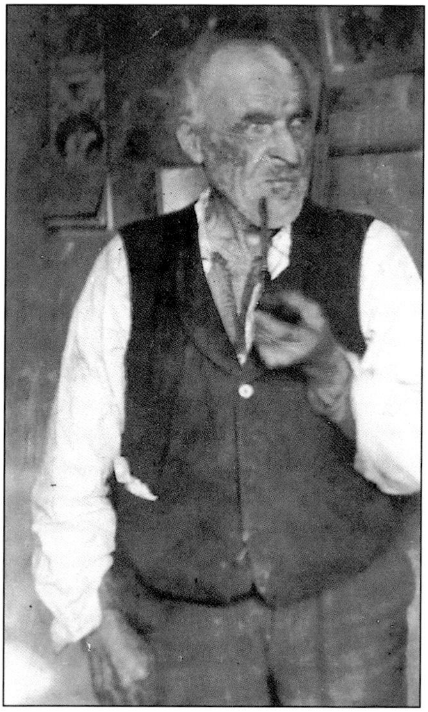

PADDY RILEY (DATES UNKNOWN). Not a great deal is known about the background of Paddy Riley ("Ratty Paddy") except that he was an eccentric Irishman who lived a simple life about a mile from the town of Clermont at the top of Dibble Hill. Paddy tried his hand at gold prospecting but was (of course) unsuccessful. His claim to fame was his gift for storytelling (with occasional accurate predictions of the future) and his remarkable fiddle playing. Paddy may still haunt the environs of Clermont.

PADDY RILEY WITH HELEN LARRABEE (?). Paddy was very popular with the Larrabees and was often invited to play his fiddle on different occasions. The location and occasion of this photograph is unknown. Paddy, of course, is holding his trusty fiddle.

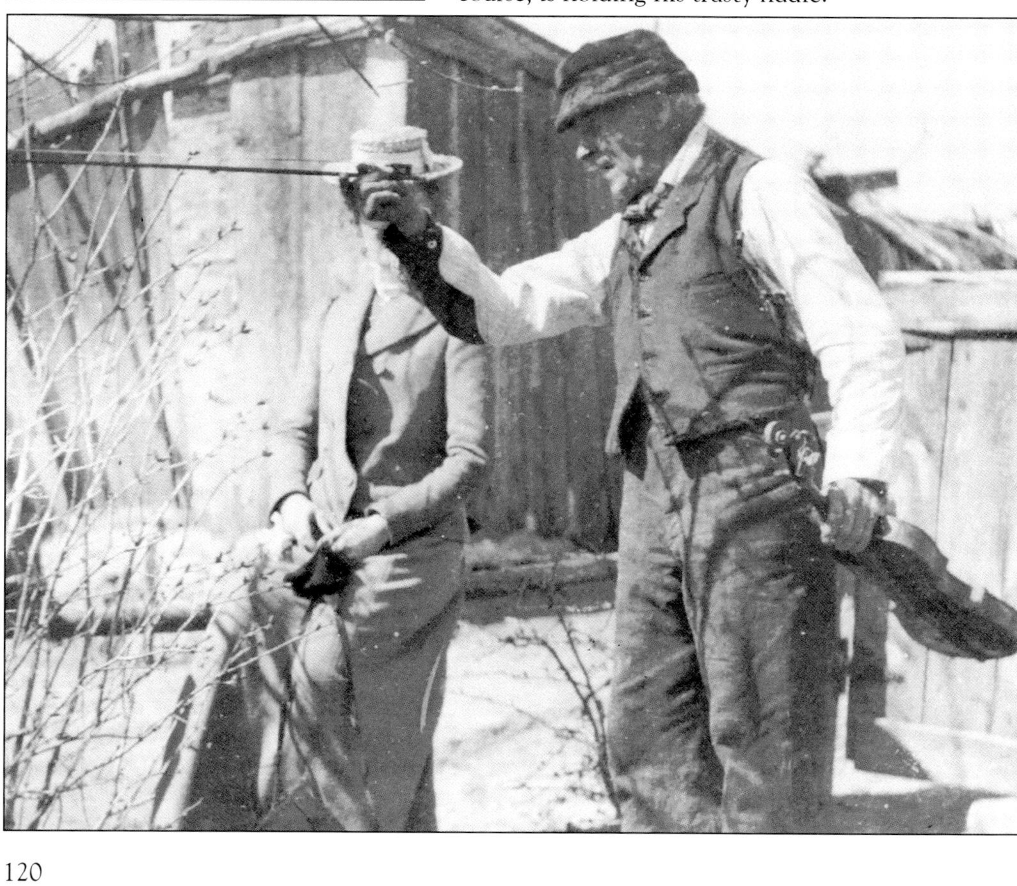

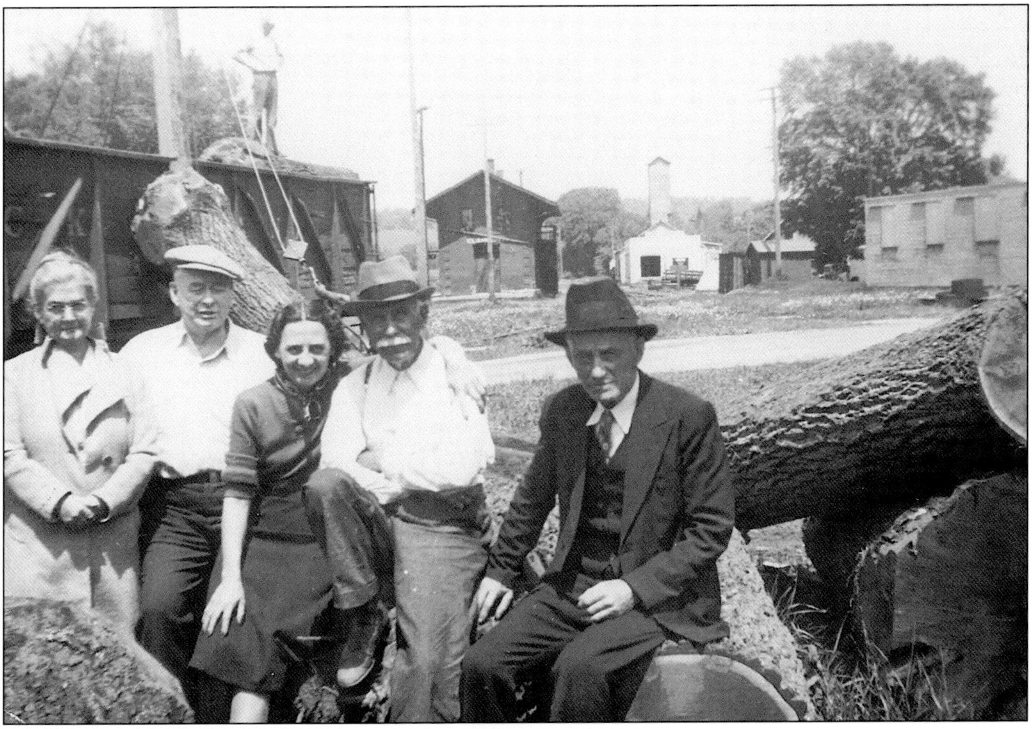

From left to right: Kate Bigler, Mr. and Mrs. Ole Marsh, Fred Bigler, Maurice Callahan. They are seated on walnut logs about to be loaded on a railroad car. Note the Railroad Depot in the distance.

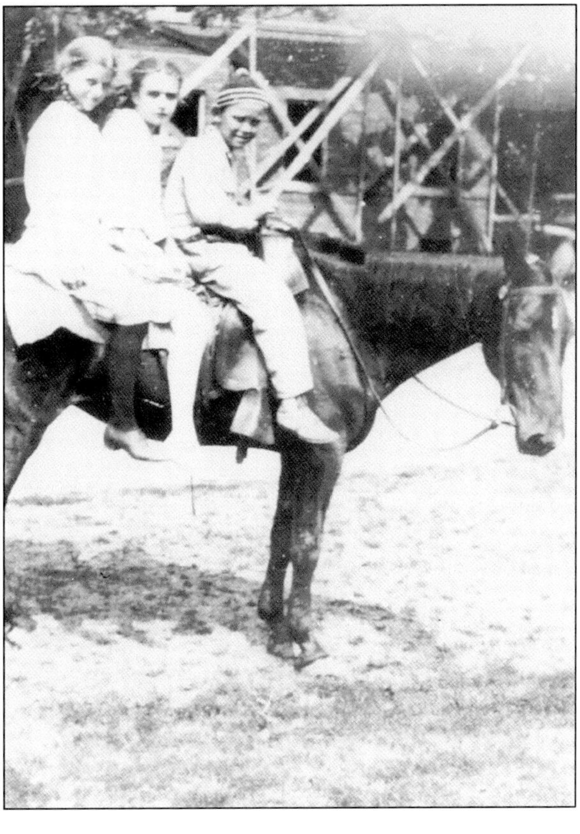

June West, Anna Bigler, Tom Schmitz, c. 1918. The children are pictured on the back of "Sally." Note the house of Christian Miller in the background. It appears that the house is under construction.

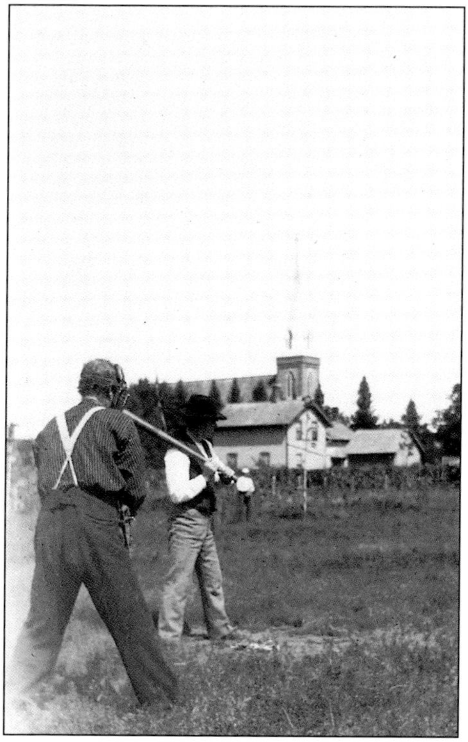

Take Me Out to the Old Ball Game. The following four photographs are views of an afternoon baseball game in Clermont. Baseball was a popular pastime and games were regularly played. "Town teams" were formed and often competed against one another. The man at bat in the first photograph to the left is probably William Larrabee Jr. The precise date of this game is unknown, although it is certainly pre-1913, as the original steeple of the Catholic church is still present.

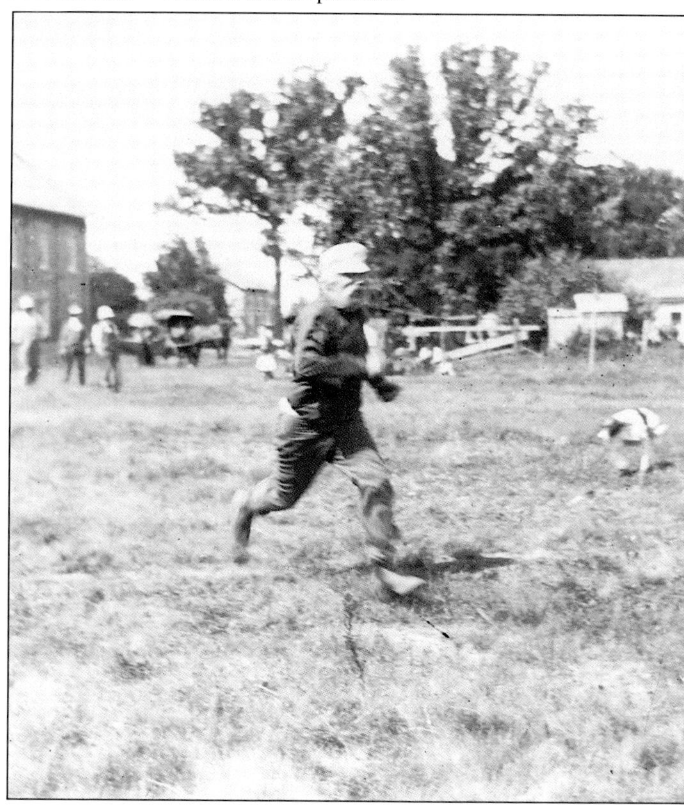

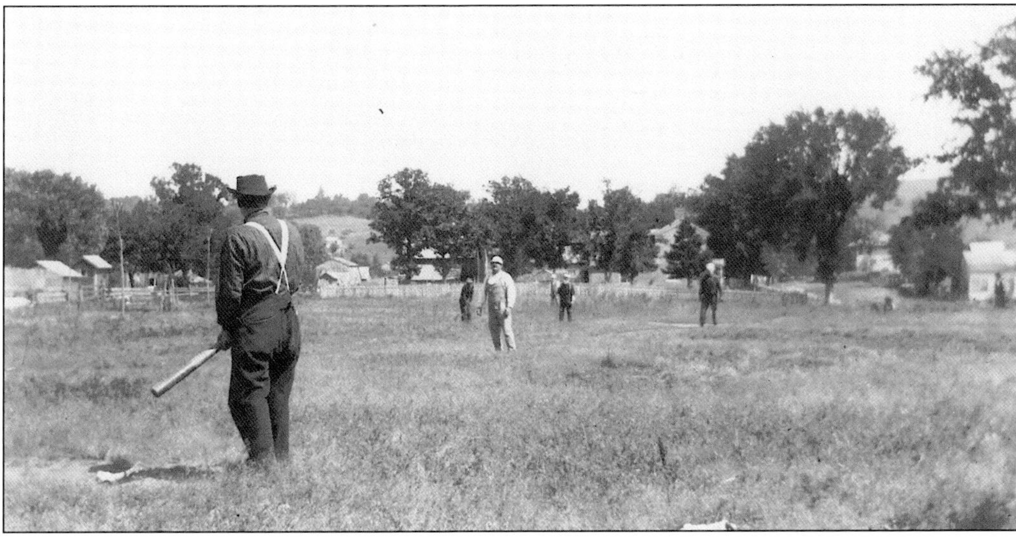

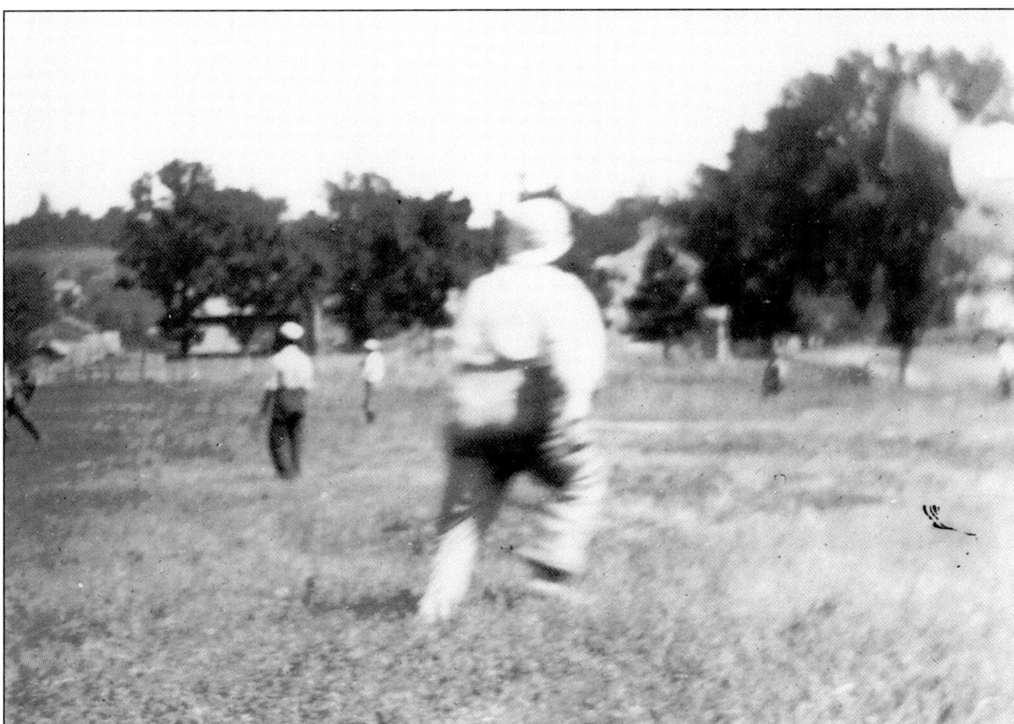

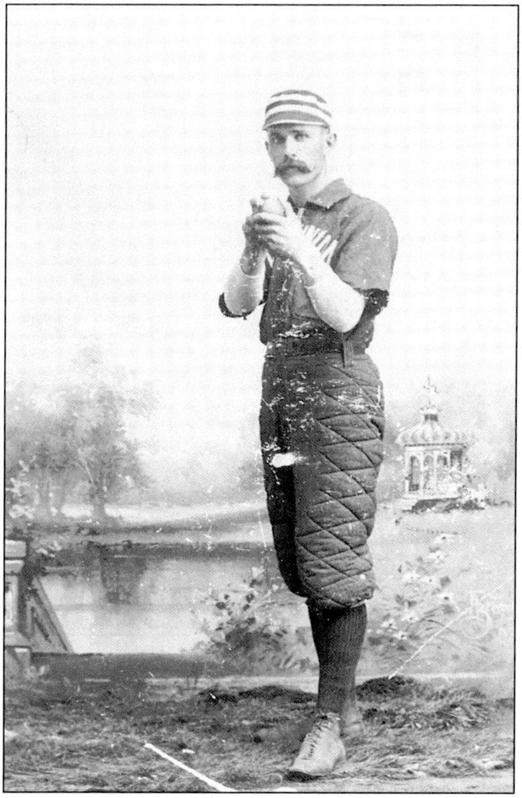

"OLD FRITZ." Fred Bigler, often referred to as "Old Fritz," was a member of the Clermont baseball town team and often scored the winning point in more than one game.

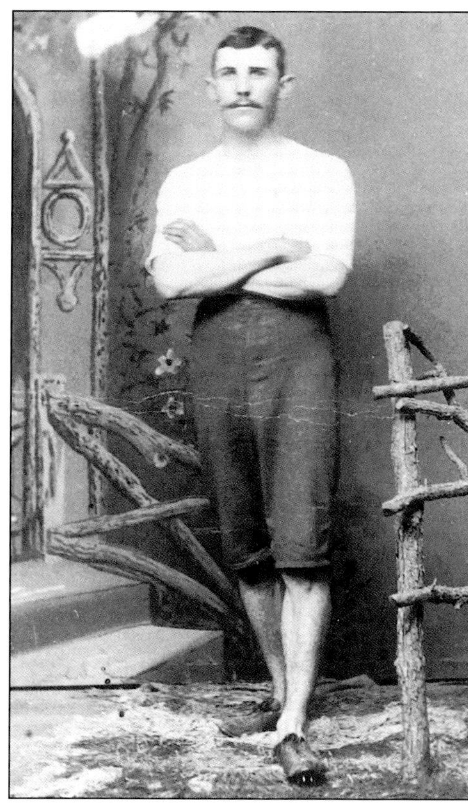

FRED BIGLER. Bigler also ran for the track team at Upper Iowa University in Fayette.

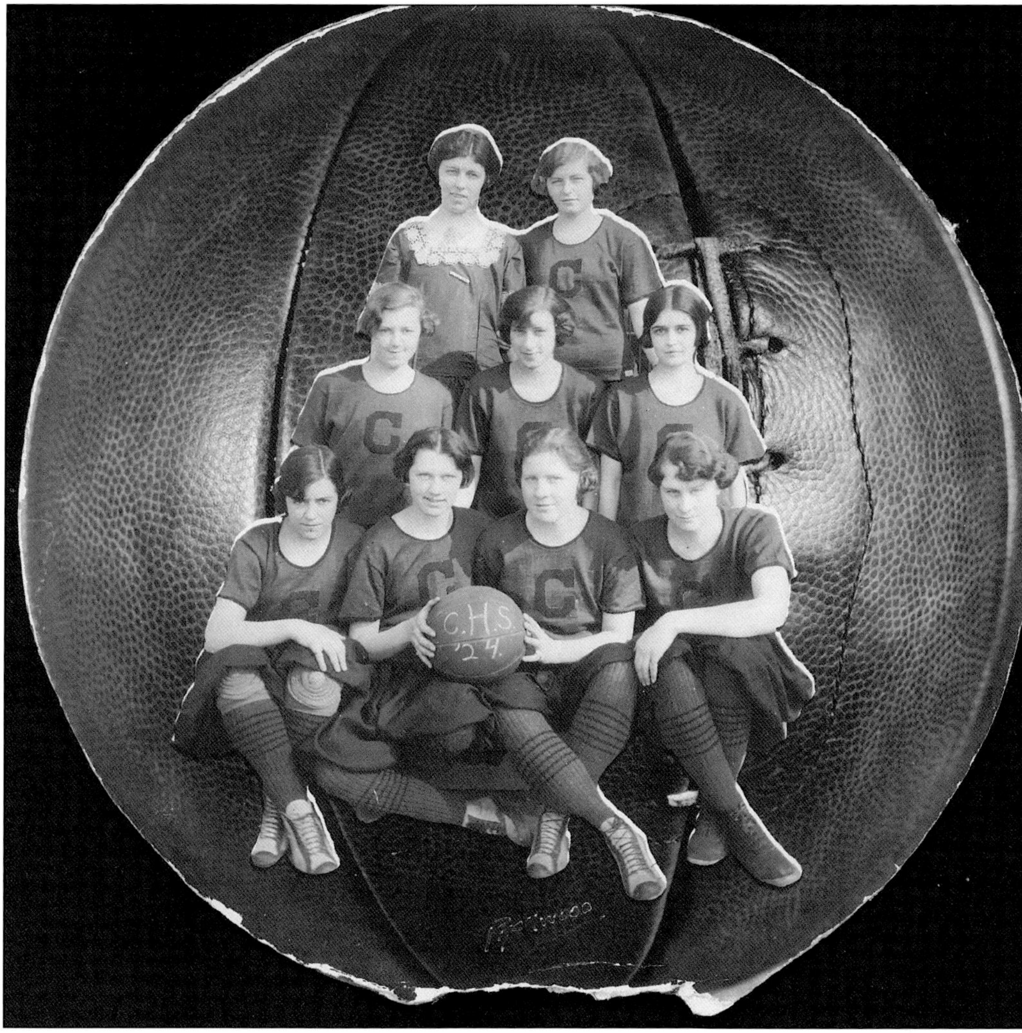

Basketball Team, 1924. Members of the team from left to right are (front row) Birde Shipton, Thelma Scott, Irene Opperid, and Agnes Nordhus; (middle row) Grace Miller, Ada Miller, and Anna Bigler; (top row) Margaret Greeter Green (coach) and June West.

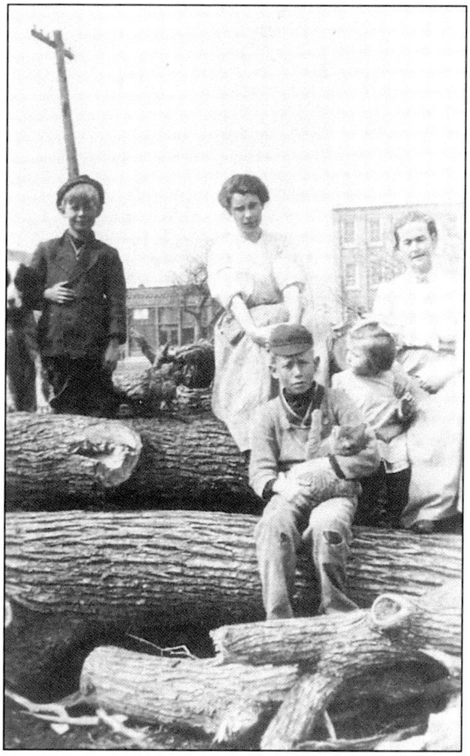

Out on a Limb. From left to right are Chuck Bigler, Midge Sheehy, Floyd Bigler (with cat), Anna Bigler (little girl), and Kate Bigler, *c.* 1903.

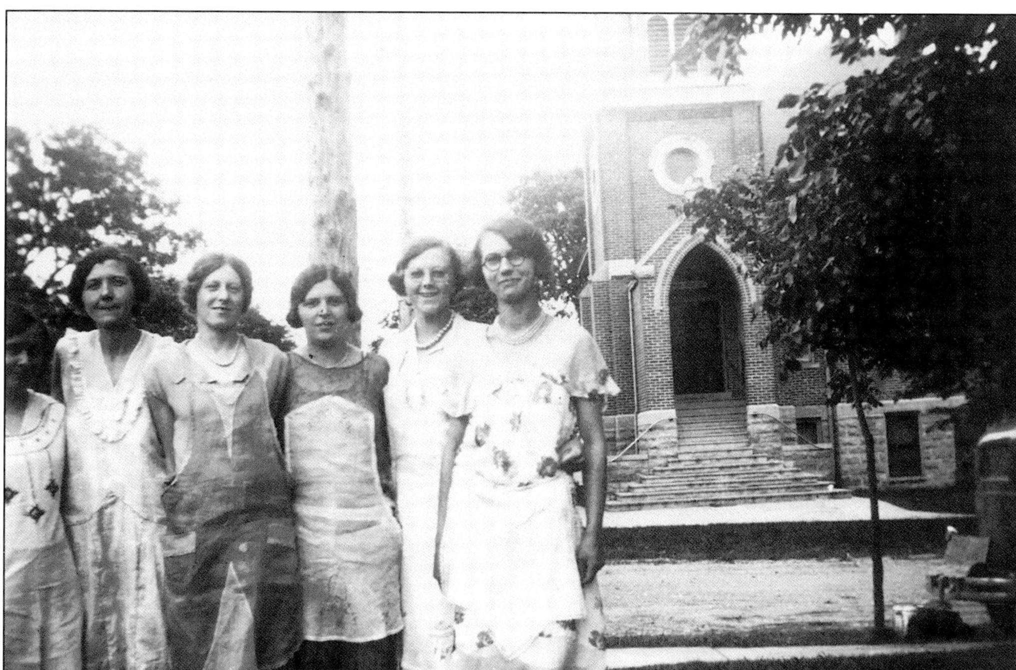

Ladies of Clermont. From left to right are ?, ?, Bess Peters, Elizabeth Priest, Grace Miller, and Elizabeth Rounds, *c.* 1930. The Lutheran church is in the background. This photo was taken in the front yard of the Bigler home.

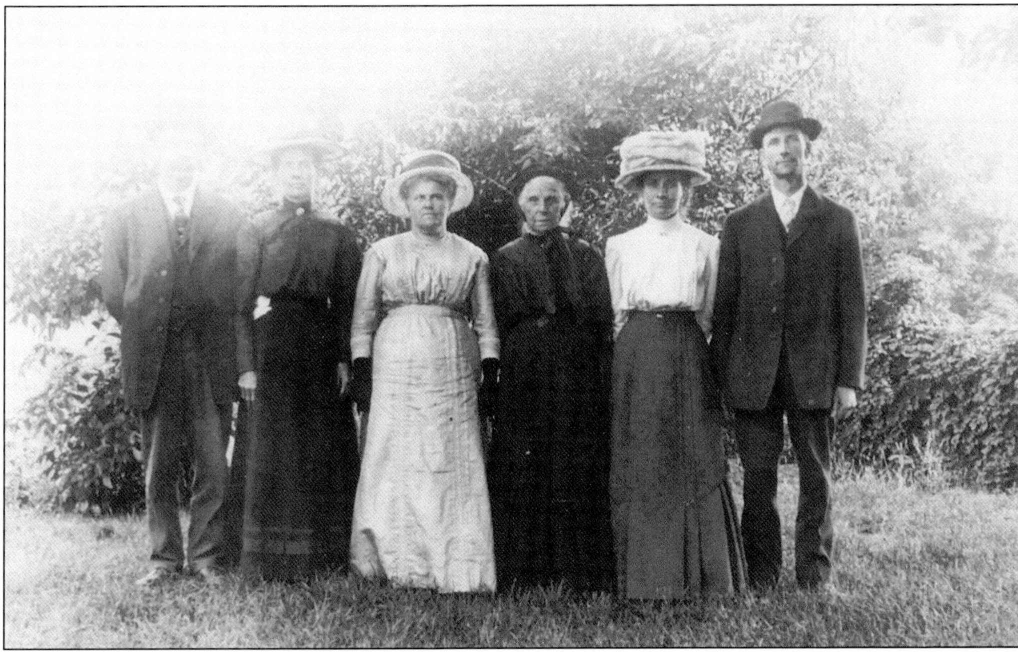

MOTHER AND CHILDREN. Pictured from left to right are Fred Bigler, Lena Bigler, Alice Ford Becker, Susan Wenger Bigler (mother), Lana Bigler Aeschliman, and Louis Sullivan.

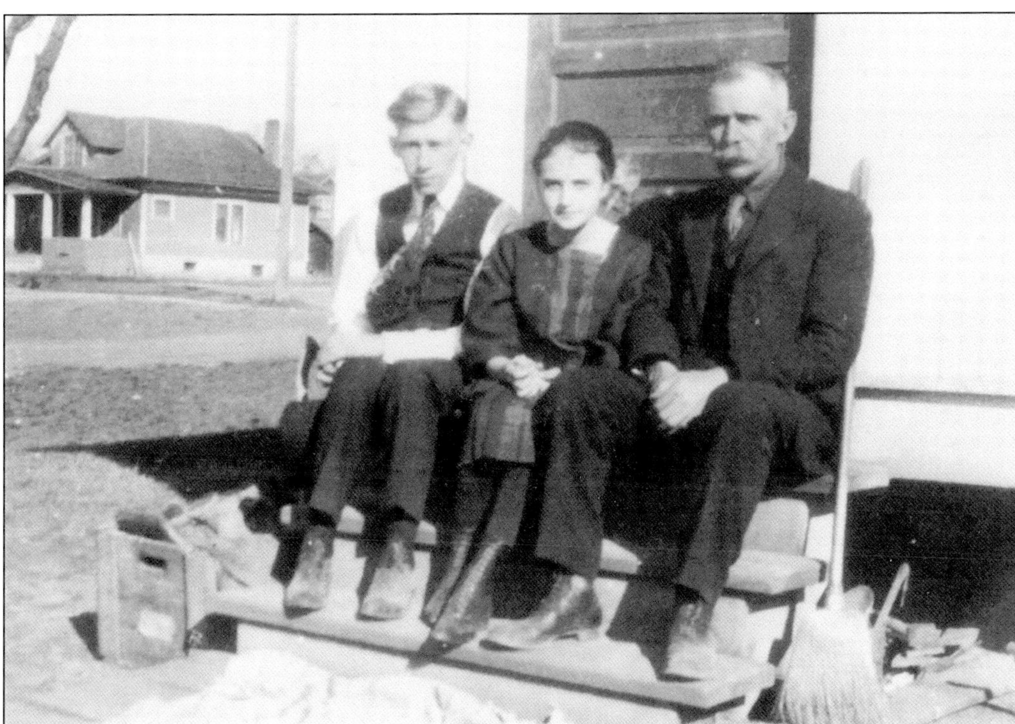

RELAXING AT HOME. Floyd Bigler, Anna Bigler, and Fred Bigler are seated on the back porch of their home, across from the Lutheran church.

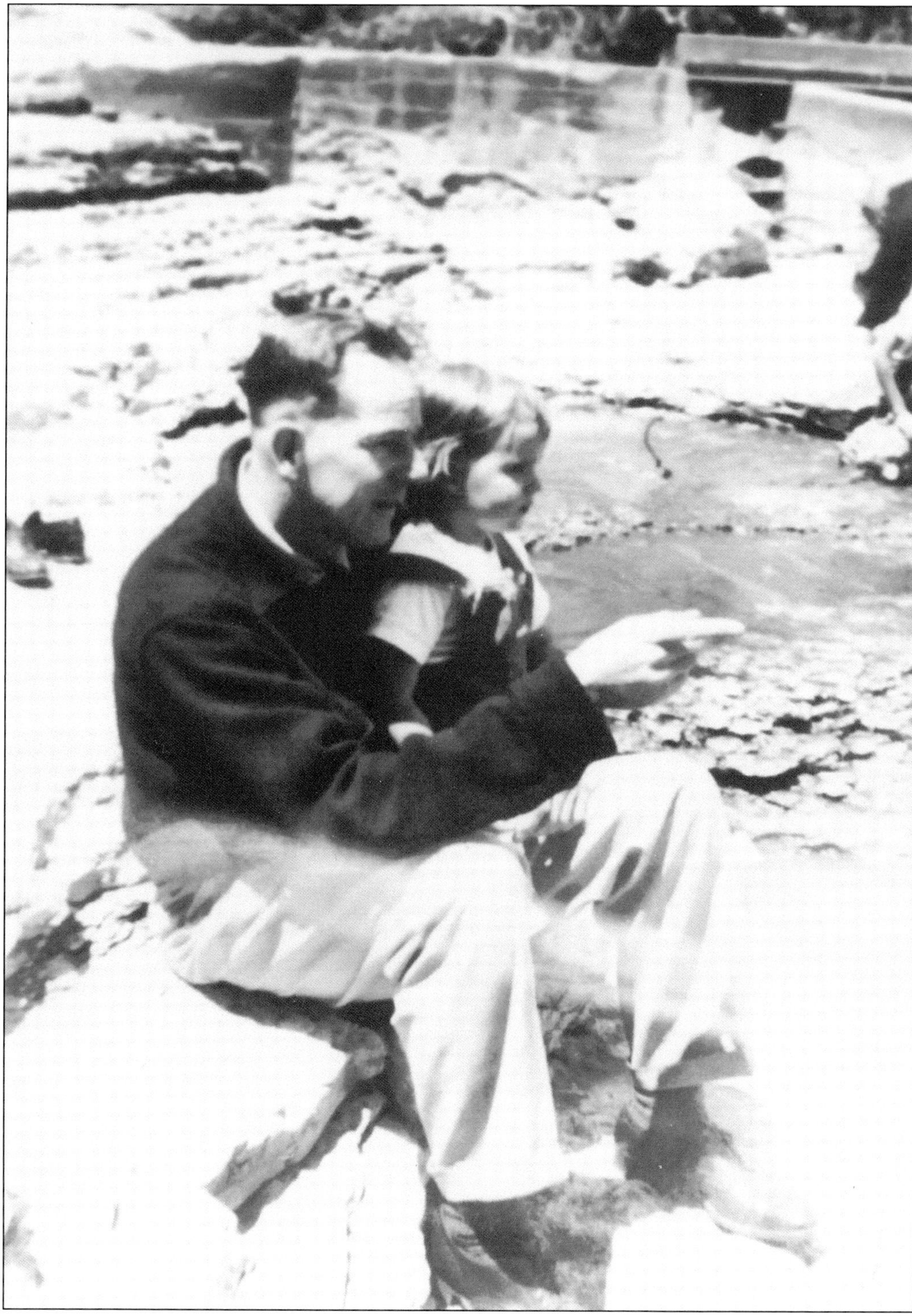

The Author with her Father. Jane and Nicolay Jurgens are pictured here together along the Turkey River, Summer, 1952.